Is Quebec Nationalis
Perspectives from Angloph

Is Quebec Nationalism Just?
Perspectives from Anglophone Canada

Edited by
Joseph H. Carens

McGill-Queen's University Press
Montreal & Kingston • London • Buffalo

© McGill-Queen's University Press 1995
ISBN 0-7735-1341-8 (cloth)
ISBN 0-7735-1342-6 (paper)

Legal deposit second quarter 1995
Bibliothèque nationale du Québec

Printed in Canada on acid-free paper

McGill-Queen's University Press
is grateful to the
Canada Council for support of
its publishing program.

Canadian Cataloguing in Publication Data

Main entry under title:
Is Quebec nationalism just? : perspectives from
Anglophone Canada
Includes bibliographical references and index.
ISBN 0-7735-1341-8 (bound) –
ISBN 0-7735-1342-6 (pbk.)
1. Nationalism – Quebec (Province). 2. Quebec
(Province) – History – Autonomy and independence
movements. 3. Federal government – Canada.
1. Carens, Joseph H.
FC2926.9.N318 1995   971.4'04   C95-900176-X
F1053.2.18 1995

For Michael and Daniel

Contents

Acknowledgments

Except for the contribution by Wayne Norman, all of the chapters in this volume were originally presented in an inter-university faculty seminar on ethics and membership that took place in Toronto from 1990 to 1993. The authors wish to acknowledge the support provided by a Strategic Research Grant from the Social Sciences and Humanities Research Council which made the seminar possible. In addition, we wish to express our appreciation for the intellectual contributions of the other members of the seminar: Leah Bradshaw, Rhoda Howard, Linda Lange, Peter Penz, Cran Pratt, and Brian Slattery. We would like to thank John Parry and Gwen Peroni for the lightning speed with which they have transformed this work from rough manuscript to camera-ready copy.

Parts of three chapters have been published previously. Part of chapter 2, by Joseph H. Carens, appeared in a slightly different form as "Cultural Adaptation and Immigration: Is Quebec a Model for Europe?" in *From Aliens to Citizens: Redefining the Status of Immigrants in Europe*, ed. Rainer Bauböck (Aldershot, England: Avebury, 1994), 149–86. Part of chapter 6, by Wayne Norman, was pubished in French as one section of "Unité, identité, et nationalisme libérale," in *Lekton*, 3 no. 2 (Autumn 1993), 35–64. And part of chapter 8, by Reg Whitaker, appeared in a somewhat different version in *Inroads*, 4 (1995). We express appreciation to the publishers for permission to adapt and reprint these works here.

I came to Canada in 1985 at the age of forty and felt I had finally found the place where I wanted to live the rest of my life.

My children, Michael and Daniel, were born here. Whatever the outcome of the current (and possibly future) debates over Quebec, my deepest hope is that Canada will continue to be a wonderful home for Michael and Daniel throughout their lives. I dedicate this book to them in that hope.

Is Quebec Nationalism Just?
Perspectives from Anglophone Canada

Liberalism, Justice, and Political Community: Theoretical Perspectives on Quebec's Liberal Nationalism

Joseph H. Carens

This book aims at two overlapping audiences. The first is composed of people interested in Quebec's relation to Canada; the second, of people interested in contemporary political philosophy. The distinctive contribution of the book is that it brings the concerns of both groups together. It is a book about Quebec written by philosophers and political theorists who are trained to think systematically from a normative perspective. Overall, the book aims to deepen the character of the debate over Quebec by linking that debate to broader philosophical concerns about liberalism, justice, and political community and to contribute to philosophical discussions within liberal theory by confronting abstract, theoretical concerns with the concrete problems and issues of the case of Quebec.

What makes Quebec so interesting, both politically and philosophically, is that it brings the puzzle of liberal nationalism squarely into view. For some, liberal nationalism is not a puzzle but an oxymoron. Nationalism, they assume, is inherently illiberal and regressive. Yet if there is one point on which all the chapters in this volume agree, it is that the aspiration of Quebecers to control their own political destiny is not fuelled fundamentally by hostility to liberalism. On the contrary, as the chapters confirm, Quebecers are at least as deeply committed to liberal values, institutions, and practices as people in the rest of Canada. But these shared commitments do not resolve the most fundamental and contentious issues in the debate over Quebec. Indeed, as a number of the writers here observe, the demands for more power for Quebec, whether through changes in Confederation or through sovereignty for Quebec, were gathering strength precisely during and after the period when Quebec's values were becoming more liberal and more like the rest of Canada's. In contemporary Quebec, liberalism and nationalism have developed together and have been, in many ways, mutually reinforcing. One of the goals of this book is to explain and evaluate this phenomenon, which appears so puzzling from a conventional liberal perspective.

Yet the mutual compatibility of liberalism and nationalism within Quebec is not the whole story. There are many versions of liberalism, and some of them are incompatible with almost any version of Quebec nationalism. (Pierre Trudeau's liberalism is an obvious example.) There are also many versions of Quebec nationalism, and some of them are incompatible with almost any account of liberalism. (Identifying the Quebec nation with Québécois pure laine is an obvious case.) Even those understandings of liberalism and nationalism that fit together most comfortably will find points of tension and perhaps conflict. So another of the goals of the book is to explore and evaluate different ways of thinking about Quebec as a nation and Quebec as a liberal democratic political community and about the interrelations between the two.

Liberal political communities take many different forms in the modern world. They mark their boundaries, divide their powers, and arrange their constitutional and other legal institutions in many different ways. Liberal principles set some constraints on these matters but leave open many alternative arrangements, with little theoretical guidance about why people should choose one rather than another. So emphasizing shared liberal commitments does not make the challenge of Quebec nationalism disappear, and accusing Quebec nationalists of illiberalism for demanding an independent state is simply wrong.

However, some nationalists assume that people who identify Quebec as their primary political community should necessarily want it to be independent. But that does not follow empirically (as public opinion polls show) or logically. As several of our contributors show, the meaning of national identity in Quebec is subject to a range of interpretations, and the implications of that identity for institutional and political arrangements are complex and contested.

The authors in this volume do not claim to be neutral or detached. All of us are anglophone Canadians. All of us would prefer that Quebec remain part of Canada. But we aspire here to a kind of analysis that goes deeper than a defence of particular political positions. We are interested in the fundamental moral issues at stake, and we try to evaluate Quebec's demands in relation to such concerns as fairness, democracy, individual rights, and self-determination. We focus on how Quebec's demands fit into normative political theory and, in particular, how nationalist aspirations in Quebec relate to liberal principles of freedom, equality, and democracy.

In this book, then, questions about Quebec's distinct society and its possible independence from the rest of Canada are linked to philosophical concerns. For example, all of the chapters are concerned in some way with how we should think about the nature of political community in the modern world and, more specifically, what forms of community are compatible with, or required by, a commitment to liberal democratic principles. Some chapters explore the relationship between membership in a liberal democratic political community and other forms of collective membership or social identity (chapters 2, 3, and 6). Another considers what sort of moral standing, if any, the units of a federal system have (chapter 4). Others ask under what circumstances secession is morally legitimate and how the states created by such a process should relate to one another (chapters 7 and 8). Still another contends that the ideal of liberal democracy presupposes the possibility of a constitution providing a fair and neutral procedural framework within which competing interests and visions of the good may struggle for democratic hegemony (chapter 5).

If connecting the discussion of Quebec to such philosophical questions is intended to deepen the character of the political debate, confronting theoretical concerns with the case of Quebec is intended to add concreteness and specificity to contemporary philosophical discussions. In recent years, much philosophical energy has been spent on the debate between liberals and communitarians. The authors here do not explicitly take up that theoretical debate, but our analyses reveal much about its limitations. Instead of presenting abstract, ideal-typical discussions of liberalism and communitarianism, the book explores tensions between liberal commitments and communitarian aspirations in a concrete political context.

Consider the following questions, all of which are addressed below. Why does Quebec regard control over immigration as an essential tool for its distinct society, and are its immigration policies compatible with liberal democratic principles (chapter 2)? What does Quebec's attitude toward refugees reveal about its communitarian project (chapter 3)? How do the liberal ideals of autonomy and equality shape the debate over the constitutional status of Quebec vis-à-vis the other provinces (chapter 4)? What accounts for the current level of support for secession within Quebec, and what does this reveal about the prerequisites of liberal constitutionalism (chapter 5)? How does the fact that Quebecers share with other Canadians a deep commitment to liberal democratic values affect the question of whether or not Quebec should be independent (chapter 6)? What community is morally entitled to determine whether or not Quebec remains a part of Canada, and how is membership in that community established (chapter 7)? How should negotiations with Quebec be affected by its relation to Canada as a political community – i.e., by whether Quebec is a province or an independent state (chapter 8)?

The answers offered below draw attention to the richness and complexity of moral discourse, with regard to both liberalism and community, as these concepts come into play in an actual political context. It is harder to think of the tension between liberalism and communitarianism as a dichotomous conflict once one has been exposed to the many different dimensions of liberalism and the many different forms of community at stake in the debate over Quebec.

The same sort of point can be made with respect to the concepts of justice and fairness. By the end of the book, readers will have considered several questions. What does justice require and permit with respect to Quebec's policies for the selection and integration of immigrants and refugees (chapters 2 and 3)? Is it unfair to treat some provinces differently from others (chapter 4)? Do Quebec's experiences with actual and attempted constitutional reform in Canada reveal that pursuit of a substantive vision of justice in the constitutional realm is self-defeating (chapter 5)? Does the fact that Canadians share a basic commitment to liberal democratic principles of justice provide an adequate reason for Quebec to stay in Canada (chapter 6)? What does justice require or permit with respect to any decision about Quebec's independence (chapter 7)? Would a fair resolution of the potentially conflicting claims of Quebecers and Aboriginal peoples to communal self-determination take account of both justice and power (chapter 8)?

Whether or not one accepts the answers offered below, one cannot avoid gaining an appreciation for the complex and contested character of both justice and fairness as these conceptions are actually employed in the debate over Quebec. Thus the book as a whole points to the virtue of using *actual* moral and political discourse as the starting point for political theory.

I turn now to a brief description of the chapters themselves. I try to identify the central concerns of each, while taking note both of common themes and points of tension with regard to the other chapters.

The next two chapters, by Howard Adelman and me, are concerned with how Quebec treats certain outsiders – immigrants in my essay (chapter 2), refugees in Adelman's (chapter 3) – who are trying to join Quebec's political community. Both of us regard Quebec's policies on this issue as a crucial indicator of its character as a distinct society because central features of a community's self-understanding are often revealed by the way it exercises control over membership and by the criteria of inclusion and exclusion that it employs. And both of us argue that Quebec's current policies reveal a deep commitment to liberal values that is unlikely to be altered if Quebec were to become independent.

I begin by identifying the demographic, economic, and political reasons why Quebec officials now regard significant levels of immigration as essential to the project of maintaining and developing a distinct society. I claim that most of these reasons would still be operative if Quebec were to become independent, but also that if Quebec chose, as an independent state, to restrict immigration, there would be nothing morally objectionable in that, at least given conventional moral assumptions about immigration.

I then turn to selection of immigrants. Quebec exercises its own administrative control over the selection process and uses somewhat different criteria of selection from the rest of Canada, in particular through assignment of more weight to knowledge of French and less to English. I argue that there is nothing morally objectionable about Quebec's policies, again assuming conventional moral views on immigration. Some criteria of selection (such as race or religion) would be morally objectionable, but Quebec explicitly commits itself to non-discrimination with regard to such factors. The criteria that it does use – education, skills, linguistic background, and so on – are ones that all political communities screening immigrants employ in one form or another.

The second part of my chapter focuses on integration of immigrants into Quebec society. What can Quebec reasonably expect of immigrants by way of adaptation to their new society? I contend that Quebec's commitment to democracy and pluralism significantly constrains the kind of cultural adaptation that it can demand. In my view, it can reasonably require that immigrants accept French as the language of public life, learn the language over time, and send their children to francophone schools. Thus I defend much of Quebec's controversial language legislation (as it applies to immigrants) as comparable to the practices of other liberal democratic communities and as compatible with liberal democratic principles. But I also contend that Quebec would not be morally entitled to expect much cultural adaptation beyond the acquisition of language, and I show that the Quebec government acknowledges this, at least officially.

I conclude by identifying two competing conceptions of Quebec's distinct society, one that ties it closely to ethnicity, culture, and history, and another that links it almost exclusively to the French language. As I see it, ongoing immigration is likely to reinforce the latter, especially at the level of official policy, because the first version of the distinct society cannot easily incorporate immigrants and their immediate descendants. But if immigrants are to contribute to the building of the distinct society, they must become part of it. Ultimately, I argue, integration of immigrants will help to transform not only the identity of the immigrants themselves but also that of Quebec as a political community.

Like Sherlock Holmes who was interested in why the dog did not bark in the night, Howard Adelman starts with a question about something that has not happened. Given that Quebec has demanded (and obtained) extensive control over the immigration process, why has it not also sought control over the refugee determination process for those claimants who are living in Quebec? Adelman proposes that the answer reveals something fundamental about the character of the distinct society in Quebec.

Adelman notes that domestic refugee claimants constitute a significant and growing proportion of the people accepted as landed immigrants in Canada, so that one cannot dismiss the question as insignificant. Moreover, the refugee determination process and the social services needed to enable refugees to adapt to their new society are costly. If Quebec's distinct society project were motivated primarily by economic self-interest, Adelman says, one might expect resistance to such expensive provisions for people who are outsiders. Finally, the refugee determination process is based on a conception of the individual rights of the claimant (who is entitled to stay if she meets the criteria of the Geneva Convention), and the particular form that the process takes in Canada has been significantly shaped by the Charter of Rights and Freedoms. This commitment to individual rights greatly limits the capacity of the political community to admit or exclude on the basis of its own criteria or its own assessment of the good of the community. If Quebec's distinct society project were based, as some suggest, on a communitarian ideology that insists on the need for the public good to trump individual rights and that is deeply hostile to the Charter, one would expect, Adelman argues, that Quebec would want to take over and reshape the refugee determination process.

Quebec's willingness to leave control over refugee determination in federal hands may turn out to be a matter of tactical political restraint, but Adelman doubts that. The more plausible explanation, he says, is that Quebec is as deeply committed to humanitarian values, justice, and individual rights as the rest of Canada and does not regard refugee determination as something properly subject to political or administrative (as opposed to judicial) control. Indeed, he suggests that Quebec might not regard control of the judicial process in this area as essential to its sovereignty, even after independence. What Quebec's inaction with respect to the refugee determination process shows then is that the communitarian character of Quebec's distinct society is shaped and constrained by a deep commitment to liberal values.

If chapters 2 and 3 draw attention to the liberal character of Quebec's distinct society, chapters 4 and 5 explore the contested character of liberalism as this emerges in the debate over Quebec's place in the constitution.

Robert Vipond, in chapter 4, identifies two competing conceptions of federalism that he says shape this debate. One uses the rhetoric of provincial autonomy, the other the rhetoric of provincial equality, and both appeal to liberal values for support. From the time of Confederation, Vipond says, one influential tradition of discourse has defended an ideal of provincial autonomy in the language of liberal rights, drawing both an analogy and a causal connection between the protection of individual rights and the protection of provincial rights. On this view, the greatest danger to individual rights came from the federal government, which might be tempted, among other things, to impose uniform national standards that failed to take account of relevant cultural, religious, and linguistic differences among citizens. (Vipond cites a dispute over national legislation on Sunday closing as an illustration.) The autonomists assumed that the provinces were more homogeneous than the country as a whole and claimed that provincial governments were more representative and more responsible than Ottawa. Hence they saw provinces as vehicles for collective freedom and ones less likely than the federal state to trample the rights of individuals. Vipond argues that this traditional conception of provincial autonomy underlies most of Quebec's constitutional demands and constitutional rhetoric today.

In recent constitutional debates, according to Vipond, one of the main obstacles to a settlement meeting Quebec's demands was a conception of federalism expressed in the rhetoric of provincial equality. Provincial equality meant different things to different people, but one of the most influential formulations, by Newfoundland Premier Clyde Wells, emphasized the connection between equality and fairness, so that anything in conflict with provincial equality was ipso facto unfair. According to Vipond, Wells initially interpreted provincial equality as requiring uniformity with regard to both individual rights (so that people had the same basic rights, no matter where they lived in Canada) and provincial powers (so that no province had special jurisdictional authority).

Vipond draws attention to the ambiguities of equality in the liberal tradition. Equal treatment may not be identical treatment. He notes that a commitment to equality may be interpreted as requiring us to build wheelchair ramps (equal access) or to provide transfer payments to poorer provinces (regional equalization). This approach would seem to open space for meeting Quebec's demands under the rubric of equality, a possibility that Wells himself seemed to envisage, at least to some degree. But Vipond observes that the ideal of equality also provides a powerful basis for criticizing anything that smacks of special treatment. Thus affirmative action (or employment equity) programs evoke deeply conflicting responses, depending on whether people see them as unfair special privileges for certain groups or as mechanisms to ensure that potential victims of unfair discrimination receive equal treatment. Attempts to meet Quebec's concerns have been caught in the same sort of cross-fire. Ultimately, Vipond suggests, the new conception of provincial equality has provided a less satisfactory discourse for Canadian constitutionalism than the older conception of provincial autonomy.

Like Vipond, Janet Ajzenstat, in chapter 5, appeals to an earlier constitutional tradition to criticize recent efforts at constitutional reform in the name of equality and fairness, though the focus of her analysis is somewhat different. She begins with a puzzle. Given the increasing cultural convergence between Quebec and the rest of Canada with respect to liberal values and Quebec's success in protecting and promoting the French language, why has the debate over constitutional change been so conflictual and why have the pressures for independence grown so strong? Her answer, and the sympathy for Quebec's position that it displays, may surprise some: "What is heightening contestation in constitutional negotiations ... is not tension between the procedural constitution and Quebec's pursuit of collective goals, but erosion of confidence in procedural institutions. The breakdown of the procedural constitution is provoking immoderate opposition to Quebec's aspirations and creating the conviction in Quebec that only secession will remedy grievances."

In Ajzenstat's view, Canada's regime was traditionally characterized by a commitment to procedural liberalism. In other words, the constitution was widely regarded as establishing a fair and neutral set of rules for democratic politics. Because these rules were thought not to favour any particular party, ideology, interest, or value, they made politics possible – that is, they established a forum in which parties, ideologies, interests, and values could compete peacefully for electoral support and compromise on particular issues.

Ajzenstat says that Quebec's successful efforts to achieve new powers through negotiations with the federal government in the 1960s and 1970s made other actors aware that political gains could be achieved in the constitutional arena. But, in her view, the Constitution Act of 1982 marked the turning point. It entrenched Pierre Trudeau's pan-Canadian ideology in the constitution, elevating it above the level of ordinary politics where it had previously competed with other visions of Canada, especially with a vision that made a strong provincial state in Quebec the key to the position of French Canada. Thus the act that many view as marking the triumph of procedural liberalism in Canada, because of its emphasis on individual rights and equality, is seen by Ajzenstat as the key moment in the decline of procedural liberalism because of the way in which it undermined confidence in the idea of a neutral constitution.

Now, Ajzenstat says, everyone sees the constitution as just one more context for political struggle, but with the difference that it is an especially important one, in which contestants are apt to employ the rhetoric of justice in advancing their interests, so that compromise and reconciliation become especially difficult. Quebecers are understandably concerned, she says, about whether their vital interests will be respected under such a constitutional regime. She offers no solution to our predicament, only a Humean hope that "the habits of more than 125 years of settled political life under the procedural constitution" will ultimately outweigh the forces undermining it.

Taken together, the chapters by Vipond and Ajzenstat suggest that direct pursuit of justice in constitutional politics may not always be the best way to achieve it. Once the "genie of fairness" (Vipond's phrase) has been let out of the bottle, it may prove mischievous and difficult to contain.

Given the obstacles to a constitutional settlement that would satisfy Quebec, it seems appropriate to consider the morality and politics of secession. That is what chapters 6–8 do. Wayne Norman (chapter 6) provides a critical examination of what he calls the ideology of shared values – the notion that Canada should remain united because most of its citizens share the same basic values. Norman shows that this ideology is widespread in official discussions, but he argues that it is badly flawed.

For one thing, Norman argues, the idea that shared values are a good thing stands in some tension with the liberal commitment to pluralism and individual autonomy, a tension that I also explore in chapter 2, in my discussion of the cultural adaptation expected of immigrants to Quebec. Norman suggests that liberals ought to aspire to no more than a general consensus on principles of justice. Moreover, different kinds of principles exist. Norman suggests that the ones most relevant to national unity are those of federalism – the ones governing the status of provinces in relation to one another and to the federal government. But like Vipond, Norman sees this as an area of disagreement rather than agreement among Canadians.

Like others in this volume, Norman notes that support for independence in Quebec has increased over the past few decades at the very time that cultural differences between Quebec and the rest of Canada have decreased. According to Norman, we should not find this puzzling. As he sees it, the fact that people share a commitment to liberal democratic principles and even other cultural attributes does not provide them with any reason to share the same political community. It is a shared identity, not a shared set of values, that is the key to political unity, and it depends on the experience of a common history, the interpretation and evaluation of which are widely shared.

Can one create a shared identity out of shared liberal democratic values? Norman argues that this is precisely what Pierre Trudeau tried to do. According to Norman, Trudeau saw the need for some strong form of national identity to counteract the separatist pressures emanating from regional identities, especially in Quebec. He tried to build that shared national identity around the project of transforming a conservative society into a liberal one and thus creating a just society. To some extent, Trudeau succeeded. But, Norman says, his project was ultimately vulnerable to an alternative, Quebec nationalist interpretation that stressed the role of the Quiet Revolution and its aftermath in the liberal transformation of Quebec society, thus portraying con-

struction of a just society there as something that Quebecers
achieved for themselves as much in spite of, as in concert with,
the rest of Canada.

If Norman insists that shared values do not provide a strong
reason for keeping Canada together, Howard Adelman (in chapter 7) explores the positive case for secession. He regards Quebec
as an ideal context in which to explore the moral legitimacy of
secession precisely because most Quebecers do share the same
fundamental values as other Canadians, because questions of
past or present injustice are not central to the case for secession,
and even because, in his view, Quebec already has sufficient
powers to preserve its distinct society. In Adelman's view, the
case for secession by Quebec can be made almost entirely in
terms of the legitimacy of collective self-realization, of establishing a fit between the collective identity of the majority of people
living within a jurisdiction and the primary political community
to which they belong.

In exploring that case, Adelman brings to centre stage two
complexities that permeate the debate over Quebec. The first
concerns membership and collective identity in Quebec; the
second, the meaning of sovereignty in the modern world. The
first raises the question of who belongs to Quebec as a community, an issue also explored in chapter 2. Adelman's answer both
complements and conflicts with the one that I offer in chapter 2.
Adelman draws a distinction between Quebecers and Québécois.
The former are members of Quebec as a political community;
the latter, members of Quebec as a national community. Being a
Quebecer is a matter of legal status; being a Québécois, of
subjective identity. Both forms of membership are normally
acquired through birth but may be obtained later through other
means and may also be renounced.

Seeking to respect the complexity of our moral experience,
Adelman ascribes normative significance to both forms of membership with respect to secession. On the one hand, he says, any
formal separation from Canada would have to be approved by a
majority of Quebecers – i.e., a majority of those voting in a
referendum in Quebec. On the other hand, he argues, what is
most important is not legal but affective unity. If a majority of
Québécois feel that it is the political jurisdiction of Quebec that

primarily represents and speaks for their nation, and if they also identify themselves politically primarily as Québécois and only secondarily, if at all, as Canadians, then spiritual secession has already occurred. What remains are just questions about the legal and administrative arrangements between Quebec and Canada, conceived as two different sovereign states, even if Quebec remains within Confederation.

In developing this argument, Adelman draws attention to the complexity of sovereignty in the modern world, where, for example, states routinely acknowledge the jurisdictional authority of both supranational governmental units, as in the European Union, and subnational governmental units, as in federal systems. Political authority, in the sense of roles and responsibilities, can be divided and subdivided in many different ways. Given this complexity, Adelman argues, the real question of sovereignty is what governmental unit a people recognizes as its authentic representative, authorized to act on its behalf in negotiating the best possible arrangements with other governmental units. The Québécois have assigned this task to the government of Quebec. It is a familiar observation that during the 1960s most francophones in Quebec stopped thinking of themselves as French Canadians, a minority in Canada, and started thinking of themselves as Québécois, the majority in Quebec. In effect, Adelman is suggesting that this change in mentality also marked a change in sovereignty.

Finally, Adelman discusses the implications of his analysis for minorities in Quebec: Anglo-Canadians, immigrants, and Aboriginal peoples. He claims that Anglo-Canadians and immigrants have three options: emigration from Quebec, staying in Quebec as a minority, or staying and becoming Québécois. If they stay, they will be entitled to participate in any referendum on separation, and they can support or oppose separation from the perspective of either identity (i.e., as minorities or as Quebec nationals). What they may not legitimately do, according to Adelman, is to demand separation from Quebec, not even in those areas where they constitute a clear majority of the population. For Aboriginal peoples, the case is quite different. "As a people, they may be sovereign," Adelman says, but they lack an established political unit where they are a majority and one with enough powers over a territorial base to act as their sovereign state. They may, however, obtain such a political unit, and then separation from Quebec would become morally possible.

Reg Whitaker's chapter (no. 8) focuses on Quebec's assertion of a right to national self-determination and on the tension between this claim and the assertion by Aboriginal peoples of an inherent right to self-government. While pursuing his own agenda, Whitaker implicitly extends and challenges the analysis offered by Adelman with respect to two crucial questions: What stance should the rest of Canada take toward Quebec? How do Aboriginal claims affect Quebec's moral position?

Whitaker begins with an analysis of the way in which claims to national self-determination by Quebec were asserted in connection with the 1980 referendum on sovereignty-association. Two key points emerge. First, like several of the other authors in this volume, Whitaker sees Quebec society since the 1960s as deeply committed to liberalism. Because the Parti québécois pursued self-determination within a liberal democratic framework that included an explicit commitment to respect for minority rights, Whitaker says, it was not plausible to oppose independence for Quebec in the name of protecting potentially oppressed minorities against an illiberal regime. In this context, political elites, and perhaps ordinary Canadians as well, came to accept the principle that Quebec would be entitled to leave the federation if a majority of voters supported this course in a referendum.

Second, the idea of sovereignty-association promised a type of connection between a sovereign Quebec and Canada that was not within the power of a Quebec government to create, thus obscuring the way in which a vote for sovereignty would change the context of negotiations between Canada and Quebec. Whitaker argues that there is and ought to be a fundamental difference between negotiations among members (including collective members) of the same political community and those between independent, legally sovereign states. Negotiations within a political community are properly shaped not only by self-interest but also by historical commitments, constitutional law, and the network of mutual rights and obligations embedded in community policies and practices. By contrast, he says, negotiations between independent states are properly conducted on the basis of "relative bargaining power and political expediency." It is not that morality is altogether irrelevant in the second case, but rather that fairness does not mean the same thing in the two contexts. In short, an independent Quebec would not be able to make the same sorts of moral claims upon Canada as a Quebec that remained within the federation.

The contrast here between Whitaker's argument and Adelman's is provocative. Whereas Adelman claims that legal separation is and ought to be regarded as subordinate to the question of national identity, Whitaker suggests that our sense of national identity is and ought to be shaped by whether or not a legal separation has been established.

Since 1980, Whitaker says, independence for Quebec has become more feasible politically and economically, but less meaningful because of the way in which supranational economic arrangements, especially the Canada–United States Free Trade Agreement, have reduced the scope for any distinctive national economic policy. The most important obstacle to Quebec's national self-determination now, he says, comes from the potentially conflicting claim to self-government put forward by Aboriginal peoples. Thus he brings to centre stage the issue with which Adelman concludes his essay.

In Whitaker's view, Aboriginal peoples have an even stronger moral claim to self-determination than Quebec because their ability to preserve and promote their distinct national identity within the existing political framework is in much greater jeopardy. But while their position is stronger than Quebec's in terms of justice, it is politically weaker because they lack both the administrative infrastructure needed to carry out the tasks of self-government and the power and resources required to enable them to negotiate effectively. These differences between the positions of Quebec and the Aboriginal peoples matter, Whitaker says, because the demands of the two could potentially come into conflict. In the worst case, with each side asserting the legitimacy of its own claims and ignoring the other's and with the Aboriginal peoples appealing to Ottawa for support, one could imagine a downward spiral of conflict, violence, and bloodshed comparable to developments in the former Yugoslavia.

Though Whitaker insists that Aboriginal people have a superior claim to self-determination in terms of justice, he does not say

that their position ought simply to triumph if it conflicts with
that of Quebec. His argument here complements Adelman's point
about the institutional requirements of sovereignty. Whitaker
suggests both that justice is ineffective if detached from power
and that justice is not the only relevant moral consideration.
With respect to the former, he observes that Aboriginal people
have had justice on their side for a long time but have begun to
gain attention for their just claims only as they have found ways
to exercise power in the political process. With respect to the
latter, he notes that Quebec's claim to self-determination is
firmly rooted in the democratic principle of majority rule and
cannot be dismissed as a mere artifact of Quebec's power. In
short, both sides have power and morality on their side, though
in different proportions.

Though he does not characterize it in quite this way, Whitaker
is implicitly arguing that a conception of fairness that takes
account of the political context of a conflict provides a better
moral guide to action than a conception of justice based
exclusively on principle. He urges a spirit of mutual accommodation so that a solution can be achieved that takes into consideration legitimate moral claims on both sides but also resources,
capacities, and interests.

Anyone familiar with the writings of Janet Ajzenstat and Reg
Whitaker might think of them as unlikely allies, but in this
volume they share at least some of the same concerns about the
relation of politics and morality. Both seek some middle ground
between realpolitik and abstract moralizing. Both worry about the
ways in which the rhetoric of rights erodes the possibility of
achieving reasonable compromises. And both argue that good
political arrangements have to take into account the realities of
power and interest as well as the claims of justice. This is just
one more illustration of the ways in which reflection on the case
of Quebec reveals the complexity of our public moral life and
contributes to political theory.

The debate over Quebec is often passionate and partisan. With
the election of the Parti québécois to power in 1994, its intensity
has begun to increase once again. Yet whatever the outcome of
the referendum on sovereignty in 1995, the deeper questions that

we address in this book will remain. If the referendum passes, subsequent negotiations and relations with the rest of Canada are bound to be affected by what Canadians outside Quebec think about the moral legitimacy of Quebec's national project. If it fails, Quebec nationalism will not disappear. Moreover, the question of the relationship between liberalism and nationalism is of vital and growing importance in many areas of the world. Our hope therefore is that this volume will simultaneously deepen our understanding of the specific case of Quebec and help to map out a theoretical territory that is vitally important in the modern world, yet largely unexplored.

NOTE

I wish to thank Will Kymlicka for illuminating and perceptive comments that greatly improved this chapter.

CHAPTER TWO

Immigration, Political Community, and the Transformation of Identity: Quebec's Immigration Policies in Critical Perspective

Joseph H. Carens

Control over immigration, it is often said, is a crucial feature of sovereignty, a prerequisite for the self-determination and autonomy of a political community. This is a claim that can easily be overstated. The elimination of border controls within the European Union is a significant step, but it is not the most important action that the member states have taken to transfer power to the larger community, nor does it mark the end of their existence as independent political units. Within Canada, the existence of virtually unconstrained mobility among the provinces seems not to have had a major effect on Quebec's capacity (or incapacity) to develop its distinct society as its people desire. Indeed, even those arguing for independence generally put forward a model of the future that includes not only free trade but also free mobility of labour between Quebec and Canada (and often dual citizenship as well).

Quebec has, however, sought and obtained an important role in the selection and integration of immigrants to Canada who settle in Quebec, precisely on the grounds that control over these matters is crucial to Quebec's self-determination, to its ability to maintain and develop its society in accord with its own goals. Moreover, a society's response to immigration can be a key to grasping its self-understanding. The degree of openness to immigrants, the criteria of selection and exclusion, the kinds of adaptation, and the degree of conformity to the dominant population expected of new arrivals and their descendants – all these factors indicate something about who belongs, what is valued, and what membership and citizenship mean. So a study of Quebec's policies toward immigrants may reveal important features of its vision of itself as a political community.

Prior to the Quiet Revolution, the Quebec government showed little interest in attracting immigrants from outside Canada, seeing them primarily as a potential threat to traditional French culture and institutions. Beginning in the mid-1960s, however, the government began to think of immigration as a means of strengthening the provincial economy and counteracting the decline in the birth rate. But it wanted to achieve these goals without undermining – indeed, while enhancing – the francophone nature of Quebec society. The key to that goal was to gain control over the selection and integration of immigrants. To that end, the government negotiated a series of agreements with the federal government, culminating in the recent Canada-Quebec Accord on Immigration which grants Quebec almost all the powers that it had been seeking.[1]

In this chapter I discuss the latest agreement, and especially the Quebec government's policies on immigration, in the context of the debate over Quebec's demand for recognition as a distinct society and in light of the possibility that it may seek independence. I want to pursue two related tasks. The first is empirical and analytical. It involves identifying the conceptions of membership and community that inform Quebec's policies with regard to immigration. To this end I address such questions as the following. Why has Quebec sought these powers with regard to immigration? How, if at all, do its criteria of selection for immigrants differ from those of the federal government? To what extent and in what ways does Quebec expect immigrants to adapt to their new society, and how, if at all, is membership or citizenship made contingent on this adaptation? To what extent and in what ways does Quebec acknowledge an obligation to respect immigrants' pre-existing identities and forms of difference (e.g., linguistic, cultural, and religious commitments)? How do such limits affect its conception of its own distinctiveness and its aspiration to maintain that? How might its policies be different if it were to become independent?

The second task is normative. It involves evaluating Quebec's policies and the conceptions of membership and community that inform them. Let me distinguish between two kinds of moral inquiry and the discourses associated with them. The first kind focuses on what minimum moral standards require or what is morally permissible; the second, on what is good for a particular political community or what goals that community should pursue. Both kinds of inquiry are concerned with normative questions, but they tend to involve different types of moral language. The first is apt to employ words such as "justice" and "rights"; the second is more likely to use such words as "wisdom," "pride," and "tradition" and to intertwine arguments about ideals, interests, and identity. In making a claim about minimum moral standards, one is saying in effect that there is a right answer and a right way to behave, so that, in a significant sense, the community has no moral choice in the matter, no legitimate discretion about how to behave, even if it has the power to violate the minimum standards. By contrast, in making a claim about what is good for the community, one is normally recommending one course of action among alternatives, all of which are presupposed to be within the legitimate discretion of the community – i.e., within the range of the morally permissible.

With respect to immigration, the first kind of inquiry generates questions such as these. Is this policy morally permissible? Does it violate basic individual rights that every society, or at least every liberal democratic society, ought to respect? The second produces different types of questions. Is this a wise policy, in the sense of helping Quebec achieve its stated goals? Or, from a different perspective, does it pay adequate attention to the requirements of Canadian unity? I am concerned below primarily with the first sort of inquiry.

QUEBEC'S GOALS IN IMMIGRATION

I begin my analysis with a review of Quebec's goals in the area of immigration. In describing Quebec's positions, I draw heavily on *Let's Build Québec Together: Vision: A Policy Statement on Immigration and Integration*, published by the government of Quebec (in French and English) in 1990 (hereafter cited as *Vision*; page numbers in the text refer to this document).[2] For a government publication it is truly remarkable. Instead of offering the bureaucratic banalities that such documents usually contain, this one offers a sophisticated, self-conscious articulation of the goals of Quebec's policies and of some of the normative presuppositions underlying them – assumptions about rights, duties, membership, community, democracy, pluralism, history, culture, and individual identity.

Of course, any government document has its limits. As policy, it could be changed by the new Parti québécois government or some later one.[3] As an account of Quebec's understanding of immigration and political community, it cannot claim to be a reflection of the views of the population as a whole or even of all current government practices. As the title itself indicates, the policy statement is about a vision, a goal, rather than an accomplished fact. Nevertheless, the statement puts forward a set of standards, principles, and ideals that it says should guide the development of policy. It thus invites comparison with alternative policies and rationales, from a moral and theoretical perspective as well as a political and practical one.

Vision says that Quebec needs "to increase immigration to meet the major demographic, economic, linguistic and cultural challenges of our society" (p. 8). The primary consideration appears to be demographic: a concern for the negative direct and indirect effects of a reduction in population (both in absolute terms and in relation to the rest of Canada) and of a change in age structure. Quebec's birth rate is currently about 1.5 per woman, well below the replacement level of 2.1. The demographic decline that would result from this rate, if nothing else intervened, would lead to a drop in the overall volume of economic activity. Moreover, a decrease in Quebec's relative share of the Canadian population would lead to a reduction of both its political weight and its share of federal funding. Finally, an ageing population would create labour shortages in some areas and heavy financial burdens on those in the work-force who have to support social programs for the elderly.

According to *Vision*, increased immigration can help to cope with these problems, provided that the immigrants stay in Quebec. Immigration helps to delay a decline in population. (It does not solve the problem in the long run, because immigrants adopt the demographic patterns of natives.) Immigration can improve the age structure of the population by adding young adults. Moreover, if Canada takes in immigrants and Quebec stays in Canada, Quebec has to receive and keep its proportional share to avoid a relative decline in population due to the effects of immigration. In the past, even the recent past, Quebec has received far less than its proportional share – 16.8 percent of immigrants over the past 20 years, compared with its 26 percent share of the population. (It also faces a decline in its relative share of the Canadian population because it has the lowest birth rate of any province and has had a deficit in interprovincial migration apart from the movement of immigrants.) Finally, the government argues that immigration can contribute to economic growth if the selection process is sufficiently sensitive to the requirements of the labour market.

While these demographic and economic considerations provide Quebec with reasons for wanting more immigration, in both absolute and relative terms, one might think that a substantial flow of immigrants would conflict with the goal of maintaining and developing a distinct society. After all, the immigrants will inevitably come from different cultures and ways of life. Many, and probably most, will not speak French as their mother tongue. There are certainly people in Quebec who think that these considerations provide reasons for limiting immigration. The government policy statement explicitly rejects this view, however: "If it [Quebec] advocates a short-term withdrawal and a fragile linguistic security, it will find itself sliding into a demographic decline in the medium term. It will thus be jeopardizing its economic and cultural vitality, which are precisely two of the essential ingredients for a distinct society in North America" (p. 13).

According to the government, the way to cope with any potential tension between immigration and the building of the distinct society is through better selection and integration of immigrants. Quebec should increase the proportion of French speakers among the immigrants, should improve French-language training for others, should strengthen the position of French as a common language and the language of public life, and should ensure that the francophone community is open to "the full participation of people of different origins" (p. 13). Perhaps more surprising, it also says that immigration can help to strengthen the French Fact (i.e., the fact that Quebec society has the only French-speaking majority in North America). Finally, the government says that acceptance of immigrants reflects Quebec's values of "being open to the world," adding that the selection process is non-discriminatory and that Quebec is committed to "taking in people in distressing situations, within the limits of our capacity" (p. 14).

In sum, the Quebec government sees increased immigration as in Quebec's interest, indeed part of the project of building a distinct society, provided that Quebec can control selection and integration of the immigrants. The recent Canada-Quebec Accord helps it to pursue its goals with regard to the volume, selection, and integration of immigrants.[4] I turn now to an analysis and evaluation of Quebec's powers and policies. To simplify the exposition, I consider issues raised by numbers and selection first and then turn to issues raised by integration.

SELECTION OF IMMIGRANTS

The Canada-Quebec Accord Relating to Immigration and Temporary Admission of Aliens, 1991, says that both Canada and Quebec will pursue policies that will provide Quebec a share of the total number of immigrants to Canada at least equal to its share of the Canadian population, with the right to exceed its share by up to 5 percent of the total.[5] Quebec also agrees to accept at least the same proportion of refugees as of immigrants.

In terms of selection among potential immigrants, Quebec gains a great deal of power from the accord. The federal government retains control over "admission," through a limited veto power – the right to exclude people on grounds of health or national security. Quebec acquires complete control over the criteria used to select immigrants other than those in the family class and in the assisted-relative class, and even in those cases it gets to determine how Canada's criteria are to be applied to individual cases. It can also expand the assisted-relative group if it chooses, by developing its own (complementary) selection criteria for that class. If one qualifies under either set of criteria, one gets in. Canada decides who is a refugee, but Quebec gets to establish selection criteria – to decide which refugees it will take and which it will not take of those applying from abroad. The federal government retains full control over refugees already in Canada, such as those who arrive and apply for asylum, including those in Quebec.

What this means is that Quebec has considerable room to pursue the objectives identified above in deciding which immigrants to take in. For example, the government wishes to increase the proportion of French-speaking immigrants among those who come to Quebec. It is free to give extra weight to knowledge of French in its selection criteria, and indeed it does. Canada uses a point system in selecting immigrants, assigning points for factors such as age, education, and knowledge of French or English. Quebec currently gives 15 points for knowledge of French and only two for English (whereas for immigration into the rest of Canada, knowledge of either language is weighted equally). If Quebec wished to double the weight given to French (as some in Quebec have suggested), it would be free to do so. It is unwilling to admit only francophones because that would conflict too much with its other priorities, such as its concern to recruit people with economically valuable skills or resources and its commitment to the principles of family reunification and refugee resettlement (pp. 24–5). But it does have plans to increase the proportion of French-speakers among immigrants through an increase in the weight assigned to French and a more aggressive recruitment effort among francophone populations (pp. 29–30).

Quebec has had its own immigration officials abroad for some time, and the accord confirms this practice and strengthens their authority. It is Quebec officials who review files of applicants, interview them, and ultimately approve (or not) their selection as immigrants to Canada destined for Quebec. I have heard English Canadians express irritation about this arrangement, often on the (putative) grounds that it involves wasteful duplication, since Canadian immigration officials also have to deal with some aspects of these cases. So long as Quebec sets the criteria, they say, why not let federal immigration officials apply them.

I think that there are two reasons why this element of control over immigration has seemed particularly important to Quebec. First, the fact that applicants meet Quebec officials abroad sends them an important message that it is Quebec, not merely (perhaps not even primarily) Canada, to which they are applying for admission. Second, Quebec wants immigrants who are committed to staying in Quebec, learning French, and helping to build the distinct society. Its selection criteria are intended to reflect these goals, but there is inevitably a great deal of discretion for individual officers in interpreting and applying some of the criteria. For example, up to 15 points may be awarded for "adaptability" or "likelihood of successful settlement." This criterion is common to all applicants for immigration to Canada, but Quebec wants its officials to judge applicants' adaptability to, or likelihood of successful settlement in, Quebec. It is particularly important then to have immigration officials who are committed to Quebec's policies and goals, and Quebec reasonably judges that this is more likely to happen if the officials are members of a predominantly francophone civil service directly responsible to the Quebec government than if they are members of a predominantly anglophone bureaucracy responsible to the government of Canada.

Let us now consider, from a normative perspective, what we have learned so far about Quebec's immigration policies. Do they violate the minimum moral standards that we would expect any liberal democratic society to meet? What sort of political and moral ideals do they reflect?

Perhaps what is most striking is how similar Quebec's goals and policies are to those of Canada. Let me say immediately that I do not mean to suppose that Canada is a moral paradigm, so that Quebec's policies should be judged in light of whether they match Canada's. My point is rather an analytical one – that the similarity in policies and underlying goals suggests prima facie that the same sort of moral appraisal will apply to both, whether positive or negative, though one could imagine differences in circumstances between two countries with similar policies and goals that might lead one to judge their policies differently.

The general assumption underlying Quebec's immigration policies is that openness to immigration is motivated primarily by collective self-interest, supplemented by humanitarian considerations in the case of refugees (though even there the selection of particular refugees for resettlement seems informed by self-interest). Quebec's official statements are direct in addressing first the question "What's in it for us?" when dealing with immigration. But in this attitude Quebec does not differ significantly from Canada or any of the other Western countries that are open to immigration. They, too, want immigrants primarily for demographic and economic reasons, though they all accept as well the principles of responsibility for refugees and family reunification.

It would be possible to criticize this sort of orientation, and indeed I have done so elsewhere, arguing that the conventional assumption (i.e., that states are largely free to admit or exclude immigrants other than refugees as their interests and inclinations dictate) pays too little attention to the moral claims of the outsiders trying to get in and assumes too readily that we are morally entitled to protect the privileges and wealth that we enjoy.[6] But here I want to prescind from that sort of argument, because it applies with virtually equal force to all of the industrial nations. I want to ask instead whether there is anything distinctively objectionable about Quebec's policies and goals or about the arrangements made with the federal government to facilitate them.

To that question I think the answer is no. Take the issue of numbers first. Quebec wants to increase, not reduce, the number of immigrants it takes in. It is hard to see what is objectionable about that. Consider the political and moral ideals implicit in such a policy. It suggests that the political community is open, at least in some important respects, and that the character of the community cannot be defined in terms of ethnicity or linked too closely to heredity.[7] In this respect at least, Canada and Quebec have similar conceptions and ideals of political community.

These constraints on closure also work as constraints on morally legitimate criteria of selection for political communities that do accept immigrants. So consider now Quebec's policies with regard to selection. Are those morally objectionable? Again, I think the answer is no. It is not that Quebec's policies are unobjectionable because political communities are morally entitled to exercise complete discretion in selection. Discretion in selection is morally constrained. For example, selection policies based on racist criteria are morally objectionable. The "White Australia" policy was objectionable in this sense, as were comparable (if sometimes less overt) racist policies in Canada and the United States.[8] But Quebec has explicitly committed itself to a principle of non-discrimination.

If Quebec were to refuse to accept any refugees or were to refuse admittance to immediate family members (e.g., spouse, minor children) of people already settled there, one could, I think, reasonably criticize such a society as failing to meet its minimum moral obligations. But again Quebec clearly goes beyond what any conventional notion of the minimum requires in terms of its commitment to family reunification and to refugee resettlement.

The specific selection criteria that Quebec does use, such as knowledge of French, are not objectionable. Competence in French is not a covert way of reintroducing racist criteria, for example, because most of the potential immigrants who speak French come from former French colonies in Africa or Asia, and such competence surely does affect one's chances of successful settlement in Quebec. This is, to some extent, a contingent judgment. The major countries with an announced openness to immigration are ones in which English is the dominant language. If all of them decided to make knowledge of English a major criterion for admission, one might object on the grounds that it would effectively exclude non-anglophones from any chance of movement. But Quebec's preference for French speakers will not significantly reduce opportunities of non-francophones. As I noted above, Canada's criteria give weight to both French and English, though less to either than Quebec gives to French. It is not clear why that would be less objectionable than Quebec's policy. Again, the point is not to establish Canada as the paradigm but to ensure that the same moral principles (and criticisms, if appropriate) are applied to both governments.

The relative value given to knowledge of the French language in Quebec's selection criteria (15 points, as against 2 for English) does say something crucial (if obvious) about Quebec's self-understanding as a political community and how it differs in that understanding from Canada, which grants equal weight to knowledge of French or English and less to either than Quebec does to French. The French language is at the heart of Quebec's understanding of itself as a distinct society, whether that society remains within Canada or establishes itself as an independent state. And I argue below that Quebec's very openness to immigration makes it impossible for it to promulgate a public identity or a conception of membership with much distinctive content beyond that of language.

Some people worry that selection criteria such as adaptability and likelihood of successful settlement are too subjective and likely to be interpreted in ways that introduce discrimination, through the back door, consciously or unconsciously. That is a legitimate concern. As I argued above, the Quebec government insisted on controlling the personnel who make the selections as well as on defining the criteria of selection, precisely because it understood the importance of interpretation in such matters. So it is appropriate to ask whether immigration officials see whites as more likely to adapt than people of colour, Christians as more likely to settle successfully than Muslims. In one sense, of course, they might be correct in making such a judgment. In any society in which antagonism toward racial and religious minorities exists, newcomers who share the racial and religious characteristics of the majority are more likely to fit in smoothly, to arouse less hostility on the part of the existing (prejudiced) population. But that was the supposed justification of the "White Australia" policy, and the moral bankruptcy of that policy is now clear. Indeed, it is a telling indication of the moral status of this sort of differentiation that it could not be publicly acknowledged.

Do Quebec's officials exercise this sort of covert (sometimes unconscious) discrimination in selecting new immigrants? I have seen no studies of this question, but based on anecdotal evidence and my own conversations with people in the immigration area my guess would be that there is considerable room for improvement. Again, though, a comparative perspective is important, because part of the task of this chapter is to ask whether Quebec's powers over immigration into Canada are intrinsically objectionable or lead to morally worse outcomes than would emerge from exclusive federal control over immigration. I have no reason to believe that Quebec officials are more racist or discriminatory than Canadian officials in applying such criteria. (Recall that these criteria are common to both point systems.) I am suggesting not that racism is acceptable in some if it is also practised by others but rather that the effort required to eliminate it may not depend much on whether Canada or Quebec controls the selection of those who get in. The Quebec government has made a formal commitment to non-discrimination. There is no reason to suppose that the commitment is not seriously intended.

Some might argue that the mere possibility of abuse makes it wrong to allow Quebec to exercise so much power over immigration. As a sovereign state, they might say, Canada has ultimate responsibility for what happens in immigration. It is irresponsible, if not irrational, for it to yield its authority to another, subordinate unit. This sort of argument draws, at least implicitly, on a formalistic, legal notion of the state, which is then invested with normative force. It is not clear to me why such a model should be respected. It does not fit the present or past political reality of Canada, with its emphasis on decentralization, federalism, autonomy for the provinces, concurrent jurisdictions, and so on. Indeed, the idea that responsibility for immigration should be shared between the federal and provincial governments can be traced back to Confederation.[9] More generally, this seems like just the sort of issue that is properly the subject of each individual state's own resolution in accordance with its own traditions, its view of federalism, and so on. In my view, the current arrangement clearly falls within the realm of the morally permissible, though that claim leaves open the question whether the arrangement is good for Canada or desirable for other reasons.

A more interesting line of inquiry might be to ask why none of the other provinces has sought to gain control of immigration policy to anything like the degree that Quebec has. Ottawa has made it clear that they have the option of negotiating an agreement in this area, as Quebec has done. They are often jealous of their prerogatives and eager to assert their power in other areas of joint jurisdiction. Why not in this one? The answer is obvious but revealing: Quebec is different. The other provinces do not think that they have anything vital at stake in this area. Quebec does. The other provinces do not worry that immigrants to their provinces will choose to learn French rather than English and thereby contribute to doubts about the status of English as the language of common life in their territories. They can assume without thinking about it much that the immigrants will send their children to English schools. By contrast, until recently, when this option was taken away, most immigrants to Quebec sent their children not to French schools but to English ones. But this leads us on to the question of the integration of new immigrants, and before turning to that I want to pause to consider whether the issues we have been considering would look different if Quebec were an independent state rather than a province of Canada.

Would an independent Quebec still want to take in so many immigrants, and, if not, how should we think about that? As I noted above, the Parti québécois has given no indication that it would seek a fundamental change in immigration policy after independence. Quebec would no longer have to worry about maintaining its population size in relation to the rest of Canada for reasons relating to political representation or transfer payments, but the other arguments for immigration – the ageing of the population, the negative economic effects of a decline in population, and the dangers of isolation and reduced size to the viability of French – would remain as relevant as before.

Suppose that a different government came to power and assessed the risks and benefits of immigration differently, opting for closure to protect the French Fact. Would that be wrong? Not necessarily. Some people might see such a course as a betrayal of a traditional openness to immigration. That would be a very powerful argument in the United States or in Canada, where immigration has been central to the country's self-understanding. It might be less powerful in Quebec, where immigration has been much less central, though by no means absent, in Quebec's sense of its collective history. In any event, if we accept here for the sake of argument that other states may legitimately be closed to immigration, it is not clear why an independent Quebec could not adopt the same course. The arguments against such a course relate to the society's goals, aspirations, and self-conception – precisely the sorts of issues that the democratic majority gets to decide. Even if a policy represents a major change in previous values and commitments, it is not clear why that necessarily renders it illegitimate. After all, Quebec's Quiet Revolution represented just such a radical transformation, and I have not heard of any significant questioning of the legitimacy of that change.

That is not to say that there would be no moral constraints on such a decision. The government would still be obliged to respect the principle of family reunification, so that people who were already residents of Quebec could bring immediate relatives to join them. (This turned out to be a major source of immigrants to West Germany after 1974, when that country stopped recruiting guest workers.) Moreover, Quebec would still be obliged to accept some refugees, though perhaps not as many as it does now. As with respecting the claims of family reunification, taking in refugees is a question of meeting minimum moral obligations. Finally, to be morally legitimate, the move to closure would have to be motivated by a positive desire to protect the French Fact rather than by a racist desire to keep out people of colour. How could one tell? By studying the situation. There are no litmus tests for such issues, but that does not make informed judgment impossible. It is more difficult to conceal the motivations for public actions than for private ones, particularly if the actions are influenced by public opinion. Of course, motives are often mixed, but any policy inspired by racism to any significant degree cannot be morally legitimate.

THE LEGAL STATUS OF IMMIGRANTS

I turn now to the legal status of immigrants, including access to citizenship. Because I have explored these issues in detail elsewhere (though not specifically in relation to Quebec), I limit myself to a few comments.[10]

Under the recent Canada-Quebec Accord, most of the major categories affecting the legal status of immigrants remain under the jurisdiction of the federal government. Most immigrants become permanent residents of Canada at the moment that they arrive in this country. This status gives them virtually all the rights of citizens, except for the right to vote in elections and hold public office. Formal citizenship is relatively easy to obtain, requiring only three years' residence, modest competence in English or French, and limited knowledge of Canadian society. One's legal status for such provincial matters as taxes, social services, and elections depends on one's place of residence. While the provinces have some limited discretion in establishing rules about residency requirements, they have no discretion beyond this with regard to the legal status of provincial membership and Canadian citizenship.

Some Quebecers have argued that immigration policies should be more restrictive with regard to mobility rights, access to social services, and admission to citizenship.[11] Sometimes these changes are advocated as proposals for reform within Canada, sometimes as the sorts of changes that are vital to Quebec's future but cannot be achieved without independence, and sometimes the context is unclear. So far as I know, the government of

Quebec has not endorsed any of these proposals, though it regards the movement of immigrants from Quebec to other provinces as a serious problem. There would certainly be major legal
and political obstacles to these sorts of changes within the
current Canadian context, but it may be worthwhile anyway to
describe the proposals briefly and to assess them from a normative perspective.

Like all permanent residents, new immigrants have the right
to leave the province where they first arrive and settle elsewhere
in Canada – a right guaranteed by the provisions regarding freedom of mobility in Canada's Charter of Rights and Freedoms. In
the past, almost half of the immigrants who arrived in Quebec
soon left for one of the English-speaking provinces, most often
Ontario. While the rate of departures has been reduced, it is still
a matter of serious concern within Quebec. Thus some Quebecers have advocated restrictions on the mobility of immigrants, at
least for a few years after their arrival, on the grounds that such
movement to other provinces conflicts with the original reasons
that Quebec had for admitting them. They should be admitted
provisionally, it is suggested, and granted full status as permanent residents only after they have lived in Quebec for a few
years so that they have a powerful incentive to settle in Quebec
and learn French.

With respect to social services, concern seems based less on
an actual problem of serious proportions and more on popular
perceptions that immigrants draw heavily on social services and
perhaps also on the principle that new immigrants should not
benefit from a system to which they have not contributed. Thus
the suggestion is that new immigrants and their families not be
eligible for unemployment insurance or for various forms of
social assistance for a few years.

Finally, with respect to citizenship, the suggestion is that
Quebec should require a higher standard of social integration
than the current one, insisting on somewhat longer residence, a
greater knowledge of French, and also perhaps deeper understanding of Quebec's history, culture, and institutions.

So long as Quebec remains part of Canada, implementation of
most of the proposed changes would require federal legislation
and, in some cases, constitutional changes or use of the override clause. Nevertheless, I want to leave aside legal and political

considerations here and focus on moral ones. How should we evaluate these proposals from a normative perspective? My primary concern again is with whether the proposals are morally permissible. All the proposals move in the direction of a less generous and less open policy toward immigrants. I find the interests that motivate them not compelling, or at least not as compelling as the reasons for extending a generous and unconstrained welcome to immigrants. For that reason, I would personally oppose these changes. But as I noted at the beginning of the chapter, the question that I want primarily to address is not whether such changes would be wise or admirable but whether they would be unjust or incompatible with liberal democratic principles.

To this question my answer is tentative and qualified and varies somewhat with each topic. Take the issue of formal citizenship first. We can distinguish between two models of naturalization – one that treats it as, in principle, a discretionary decision for the state to make on the basis of its own interests, and one that treats it as a right to which immigrants are entitled after the passage of time and the satisfaction of modest formalities.[12] I have argued elsewhere that only the latter – the entitlement model is morally legitimate – and I do not repeat the details of that argument here.[13] My central contention is that the longer one resides in a society, the stronger one's moral claim to citizenship (if one wants it). If the argument is correct, then the crucial question is whether the changes proposed are intended to move Quebec in the direction of a discretionary model – in which case they would be illegitimate – or whether they are simply moving it from one end of the spectrum to the other within the confines of the entitlement model – in which case they would be morally permissible. The particular proposals that I have seen – changing the residence requirement from three to five years, strengthening the language requirement a bit, and asking for somewhat more knowledge of Quebec culture and history – could all plausibly be defended as still compatible with entitlement, but ones that went much further could not.

What about restricting immigrants' access to social services? Such a policy would move in the opposite direction of the general trend in all Western countries over the past few decades to reduce, indeed virtually eliminate, distinctions between citizens and permanent residents with regard to social and economic rights.[14] Now a trend is not an argument, and some have deplored this development as a devaluation of citizenship. But if one asks why the change has occurred and if one pays attention to the arguments put forward in some of the judicial decisions that have helped bring about the change in some states, it is clear that extension of full social and economic rights to non-citizen residents is closely connected to widely accepted liberal principles regarding equal treatment and fairness, which apply to human beings as such, not just to citizens.[15]

No one would suppose that it would be fair to provide citizens involved in legal proceedings a right to counsel while denying the same right to non-citizens. The case for equal access to social services is less compelling, but still powerful. Take something like unemployment insurance, which is, in North America at least, a self-financing insurance scheme based in large part on mandatory contributions by employers and employees. Would it be fair to require people to contribute to such a scheme without being eligible for its benefits? Even citizens have to work for a certain period of time before they are eligible to collect benefits, so it would obviously be fair to make immigrants wait just as long. But why should they have to wait longer?

Health care is a bit different from unemployment insurance. The costs of the public health care system in Canada are not paid for by payroll deductions or specifically targeted individual contributions. This reflects the judgment that health care is a basic right for those living in Canada and that access to it should not depend on economic resources. Immigrants, like others, do share the general financial burden of paying for health care through taxes. As well, Canada's immigration laws include a medical inadmissability clause, permitting exclusion of potential immigrants with medical conditions likely to impose an excessive burden on the health care system. Having passed that barrier, if an immigrant gets sick after arriving in Canada, why should she be less entitled to health care than a citizen?

Perhaps the strongest case for restricting access concerns general social assistance programs (which are, as it happens, primarily within the jurisdiction of the provinces). This issue evokes the image of "foreigners" taking advantage of "us," though citizens who rely on such assistance are also often subject to similar resentments and immigrants who are not refugees use such programs less than do citizens and again are paying taxes to support such programs. Western governments that have had formal policies denying immigrants access to social assistance have usually not been willing to enforce these provisions, apparently because it would seem inhuman to do so.

In sum, restricting immigrants' access to social services would be not only mean spirited but also unjust, at least in most instances. When you admit people to your society, you ought to take on the human contingencies that come with them.

Finally, what about the proposal to restrict mobility? This is indeed a serious problem from Quebec's perspective. Admitting immigrants does not help Quebec achieve its goals if the newcomers leave for other provinces. Such movement, however, is not unique to Quebec. During the period when half of the immigrants who arrived in Quebec left within a few years, 30 percent of those arriving in other provinces left for some other part of Canada. People move for many reasons. Moreover, most people who leave Quebec are citizens or longer-term permanent residents, not recent immigrants. Their departures create exactly the same sorts of problems for Quebec's economic and demographic goals. Would it be morally permissible to make them stay? I assume that no one would claim that.

The right to move freely is not a trivial concern. It is enshrined in both the UN Charter of Human Rights and in Canada's Charter of Rights and Freedoms. To restrict free movement within the borders of a country is to deprive people of something that is widely regarded as a fundamental freedom. So restrictions on the mobility of new immigrants seem morally problematic for the same sorts of reasons that denying these people any of the other fundamental rights and liberties that they enjoy would be morally problematic. Recognition of the morally problematic character of restrictions on mobility reinforces the importance, for Quebec's goals, of selecting people who genuinely want to settle there and perhaps also points to the significance of Quebec's integration policies as vehicles for inducing people to remain.

Of course, if Quebec were independent and had the sorts of relations with Canada that most states have with one another, new immigrants would not be able to move freely to Canada. But neither would Quebec's citizens. The restrictions would then be a product of the state system as a whole, not of a policy distinguishing between citizens and new immigrants. But those in favour of independence generally advocate free mobility between Quebec and Canada after independence, which points again to the importance of this freedom and thus to the reasons for not denying it to new immigrants as well.

There is one final point to consider. Those who defend the sorts of proposals that I have just criticized usually emphasize that potential immigrants would be informed about the restrictions on their rights before deciding to move to Quebec. Thus, it is argued, if they come they have agreed to the terms of entry and have no grounds for complaint.[16] This moral appeal to a contractual agreement in order to legitimate differential treatment is seductive but specious. It is no doubt true, given the conditions in the world today, that most immigrants would readily agree to these restrictions. But many would undoubtedly agree to much harsher terms, including terms of indentured servitude with no hope of permanent residence. But no one today would defend that sort of contract. Consent alone cannot legitimate any sort of agreement, regardless of circumstances. There are standards of fairness and justice beyond actual consent for assessing the ways in which states treat their own citizens and others.

What we have seen so far is that, in terms of legal status and social rights, immigrants become Quebecers in most respects when they arrive and can become full citizens relatively easily. The Quebec government does not advocate any major departures from these policies, nor would such departures be morally justified.

CULTURAL ADAPTATION AND SOCIAL MEMBERSHIP

I turn now to questions about the social integration of immigrants. How do immigrants become Quebecers, not legally but morally, in the sense that Quebec regards them as full members? The immigrants must become Quebecers in this fuller, social sense because otherwise their presence would be a threat, not a contribution, to the project of building a distinct society. Indeed, this is precisely how immigrants were viewed prior to the Quiet Revolution, when francophones in Quebec generally shared an understanding of their community that linked it not only to language but also to Catholicism, to a traditional rural way of life (except for a small elite), and, for the most part, to descent from the original French settlers. This constituted a powerfully cohesive and also closed communal identity, which immigrants could not easily share and were not invited to join. Hence the arrival of immigrants (who then integrated with the English-speaking community in Quebec) was seen as a threat to the survival of the French community, which was already endangered by the presence (and economic dominance) of the English.

Now, however, Quebec wants the immigrants to become full members of the distinct society. How does it seek to achieve this goal and how should we evaluate its efforts? The Canada-Quebec Accord on Immigration granted Quebec complete authority over the integration of immigrants, subject only to the broad provisos that the services provided must be open to all permanent residents without discrimination and must, in their totality, correspond to those provided by the federal government in the rest of the country. In return, Quebec receives financial compensation from Ottawa for the services that it would otherwise have provided, with an amount added because the lower proportion of francophones than anglophones in the immigrant population makes the demands of integration and adaptation greater in Quebec than in provinces where English is the dominant language. Thus Quebec has considerable powers and resources to use in pursuit of the integration of immigrants.

More important than particular policies on integration are the underlying assumptions that guide Quebec's approach. What are its assumptions about adaptation, identity, belonging, and membership? In other words, what are its social expectations of immigrants? I refer here not to sociological expectations but to normative ones. My question is not how Quebec thinks immigrants will adapt in the course of living there but how it thinks they *ought* to adapt. In what ways (according to Quebec) ought immigrants to change their behaviour, their beliefs, their cultural practices, or their identities? What does Quebec think that they ought to do in order to become Quebecers, not just legally but in some deeper, social sense? When, in its view, are they morally entitled to feel that they belong, that they are full members of society? And how does it think that it ought to adapt to the immigrants? In what ways does it feel obliged to respect the immigrant's existing behaviour, beliefs, cultural practices, and identities? What sorts of acceptance and welcome does it think that it ought to extend? In short, what, in Quebec's view, do the immigrants owe Quebec and what does Quebec owe the immigrants?

Let me repeat that I am not concerned here primarily with legal status and legal rights, which are discussed above. My focus now is on the normative conceptions of membership and community that govern the process of integrating immigrants and that inform particular policies. My primary task is to identify and evaluate these normative conceptions.

The social integration of immigrants poses new complications. Above, I hypostatized Quebec; when speaking of Quebec's demands or goals, I have been referring implicitly or explicitly to the government of Quebec. I continue to employ this approach, but I want to mention ambiguities in the hypostatized concept "Quebec" that can affect a discussion of social integration. When the issue at hand is the criteria of selection for immigrants or the legal status of immigrants, then construing Quebec as its government is a reasonable simplification. It may be important in some contexts to take into account not only formal laws and policies but also the actions of those interpreting and carrying out the laws and policies (as in my discussion above of how immigration officials apply criteria regarding adaptability), but actual practice still involves what the government does, and on this sort of issue what the government does is what Quebec does.

Things are not so simple for social expectations, membership, belonging, and identity. On these issues, the attitudes and behaviour of the whole population matter. An immigrant is not likely to feel as though she belongs, regardless of what government officials say, if most people see her as an outsider. To say that Quebec expects this or that of immigrants or that Quebec feels that it owes this or that to immigrants thus may pose a certain ambiguity. It is reasonable to ask whether the population as a whole shares the government's attitudes and assumptions. That sort of question need not be asked – or at least it does not have the same urgency – when one considers the criteria of admission or the legal status of new entrants.

Despite this complication, I focus here on the government's view of these issues, because I am trying to identify and evaluate the normative presuppositions of public policies. Moreover, while the government cannot entirely control the process of social integration, its policies and pronouncements play a major role in constructing norms of discourse about immigrants, membership, and community.

The second complication concerns the relevance of a formal policy statement such as *Vision*. Why focus on what Quebec *says* about its principles with respect to the integration of immigrants? We have seen vis-à-vis application of selection criteria, how actual practice may differ from announced intent. Here the problem seems even more acute. Doubts about the relevance of formal policy statements go well beyond the kinds of concerns that can be generated about the application of formal criteria to particular cases. Formal policy pronouncements are notoriously unreliable as a guide to actual practice. What is said in one document may be contradicted in another, or officials may speak in codes, using language that formally respects certain conventions while expressing the opposite in a way that is understood by all who care to listen. Moreover, actual policies often differ greatly from formal policies, and outcomes often do not correspond to intentions.

In studying social policy, social scientists tend to follow the advice of H.R. Haldeman (an aide to US President Richard Nixon subsequently sent to jail for his role in the Watergate scandal), who said, "Don't watch what we say; watch what we do." (To his chagrin, some reporters heeded his recommendation.) So social scientists want to learn about what is actually done; if they do study what is said, they pay particular attention to the contradictions and codes rather than the formal pronouncements. They justify this approach on the grounds that real commitments, values, and principles are manifested in practice. Indeed, this sort of approach is entirely appropriate, in my view, when the task at hand is to explain what the government is doing and why.

But if the question concerns what people think is morally right (and what they should think), then a formal statement of principles becomes much more important. For purposes of critical reflection on legitimation, public discourse matters. Even the use of codes reveals something significant about public criteria of legitimation. Hypocrisy is the tribute that vice pays to virtue, as the old saying goes, and what public officials say they are doing can be a useful indicator of what they think is generally regarded

as the boundaries of the morally permissible, especially when
they intend to do something else. Moreover, there are often
genuine disagreements about what is and is not morally permissible. To criticize actual practices or even codes – except perhaps
on grounds of ineffectiveness or inconsistency – one has to
speak from a normative perspective. My task is to elucidate that
perspective and to subject it to critical reflection.

Quebec's Moral Contract with Immigrants

The policy document *Vision* is particularly revealing about the
government's normative presuppositions. It proposes a moral
contract between immigrants and Quebec as a society, and it
outlines the rights and responsibilities of each party in the
integration process. By explicitly invoking the language of morality to describe the principles undergirding Quebec's policies, it
sets out a clear claim to moral legitimacy that invites scrutiny –
and, in my view, can largely sustain that scrutiny.

According to *Vision*, three principles guide the integration process, principles based on the "social choices that characterize
modern Quebec" (p. 15). On this account, Quebec is: "[a] society
in which French is the common language of public life[; a]
democratic society where everyone is expected and encouraged
both to participate and contribute[; and a] pluralist society that is
open to multiple influences within the limits imposed by the
respect for fundamental values and the need for intergroup ex-
changes" (p. 15). Immigrants are expected to accept these characteristics of Quebec society. That is their primary moral responsibility with regard to integration. These characteristics also entail
certain rights for the immigrants, not only legal rights but also
moral rights – legitimate expectations about the way they will be
treated and accepted. For its part, Quebec as a society has a
moral right to expect immigrants to accept these three characteristics but also a moral duty to meet the legitimate expectations of
the immigrants and to make possible the integration that it
expects.

What should we say about this moral framework? Obviously,
we need to "unpack" it a good deal before we can evaluate it
adequately. Still, one feature of the general picture is striking.
Given the emphasis that Quebec has placed on building a *distinct*

society and the importance that it has attached to gaining control over all aspects of immigration and social integration, one might expect its policies on integration to be strongly assimilationist. What is surprising from this perspective is how little adaptation Quebec expects of immigrants and how little of that seems "distinct." I spell this out in detail in the rest of this subsection and explore why Quebec would be led to such a policy.

French as the Language of Public Life
Let us examine each of the three characteristics of Quebec society in more detail and what each entails for the integration of immigrants. First, consider the context of the assertion that French must be accepted as the common language of public life. The fact that a substantial majority of Quebecers (over 80 percent) are francophones is at the heart of Quebec's self-understanding as a political community, as is the potential vulnerability of that fact, given Quebec's history and the overwhelming dominance of the English language in the rest of North America.

Quebecers are acutely aware of the rapid and substantial diminution of the use of French among francophone emigrants from Quebec to parts of Canada where anglophones constitute a majority. In many cases in the past, the French language was deliberately and forcefully suppressed. But even if one sets aside such overt suppression and indeed takes the cases today where the francophone population outside Quebec receives the strongest public support, with bilingual institutions ostensibly in place and systems of public education in French, assimilation to English is rapid and widespread, except where a particular francophone population is relatively isolated and self-contained geographically. In the North American context, the English language has an overwhelming presence. That is why Quebecers have concluded that bilingualism in Quebec would lead to the erosion and eventual demise of French.

Compared with the position of French in the rest of Canada, not to mention the United States, English enjoyed a privileged position in Quebec until quite recently, and, in some major respects, it still does. There was never any suppression of English in Quebec. On the contrary, Quebec established a system of anglophone public institutions – not only schools but also hospitals, major universities, and legal and social service institutions – that has no parallel in terms of francophone public institutions outside Quebec. The creation of these institutions may have been the result of anglophone political and economic hegemony, but they remain largely in place even now after anglophone hegemony in Quebec has disappeared. Even though English speakers have always been a minority in Quebec, they dominated commercial life, including most managerial posts down to the shop floor. Until quite recently – the last fifteen years or so – it was more advantageous in terms of economic opportunity to be a unilingual anglophone than to be a bilingual francophone, and many francophones could not use French in the ordinary course of their work. These are the sorts of facts that francophone Quebecers remember and resent when Quebec is criticized for its efforts to ensure that French will be the central language of public life.

Prior to the 1970s, immigrants to Quebec tended overwhelmingly to learn English rather than French (if they were not themselves already francophones) and, most important, to send their children to public schools in which English rather than French was the language of instruction – an option that was normally completely open to them. They chose this course because knowledge of English offered social and economic advantages even within Quebec and was overwhelmingly advantageous in the rest of North America and because the francophone community was largely closed and insular.

Beginning with the Quiet Revolution of the 1960s, successive governments in Quebec have taken various actions to establish and secure the position of French. French is to be "the language of Government and the Law, as well as the normal and everyday language of work, instruction, communications, commerce and business" (p. 15). But its centrality is politically significant for more than instrumental reasons. "It is also a symbol of Quebec identity" (p. 16). The Liberal government that issued *Vision* thus took preservation of the French Fact and promotion of the French language as a crucial political goal. The current Parti québécois government obviously does as well, and any foreseeable future government, whether Quebec remains part of Canada or becomes independent, seems certain to share this commitment.

What does this mean for immigrants to Quebec? In general terms, the following: "[T]he Government and the vast majority of

Quebeckers view the learning of French and its adoption as the common language of public life as the necessary conditions for integration ... The host-community therefore naturally expects immigrants and their descendants to be open to the French Fact, to make the necessary effort to learn the official language of Quebec and to gradually acquire a sense of commitment to its development" (p. 16).

The message seems clear. If you want to belong in Quebec, both to feel that you belong and to have the rest of the population feel that you belong, you have to learn French and accept its dominance in Quebec society. There is nothing wrong, the government seems to be saying, in making full social membership contingent upon this sort of adaptation. It is a reasonable expectation that immigrants are morally obliged to meet. The document speaks about "the need to send immigrants and Quebeckers from the cultural communities a message about the importance of French. This should be correctly perceived as a message about belonging to Quebec society" (p. 47). It is hard to be more explicit than that.

Linguistic adaptation is the strongest demand that the moral contract makes on immigrants. Moreover, this is one moral demand that the government is prepared to enforce with legal regulations in certain respects. For immigrants, the most important of these stipulations is in the law that says that the language of instruction in the public schools to which immigrants send their children will be French, thus removing the option previously available to them, and still available to anglophones, of sending their children to schools in which the language of instruction is English.[17] This requirement ensures that most children of immigrants will learn French, whether their parents do or not.

What are the limits on the demand for linguistic adaptation? First, the government asserts that the expectation that immigrants learn French and accept its place as the language of public life is not a demand for "linguistic assimilation" (p. 16). Individuals have the right to use the language of their choice in "private communication" (p. 16). Moreover, "heritage languages" are viewed as "an economic, social and cultural asset for the whole population of Quebec" (p. 16). Thus Quebec actually promotes retention of heritage languages among the children of immigrants through various publicly funded school programs. Finally, the government recognizes that linguistic adaptation is something that occurs over time and that the length of time required depends on people's circumstances.

What may immigrants expect of Quebec with regard to linguistic adaptation? First, the government acknowledges that expecting immigrants to adapt linguistically entails an obligation for the government to provide services that make it possible and attractive for them to learn French. Second, it says that the existing francophone community has an obligation to be open to immigrants, as it was not prior to the Quiet Revolution, and that the desired linguistic adaptation will not occur without that openness. The goal is to make it possible for "the French language [to] become part of the shared heritage of all Quebeckers, whatever their origin" (p. 16).

Learning the official language of the society to which they are moving might seem like the prototypical example of the sort of adaptation that a society can reasonably expect of its immigrants. And so it is – or so I argue below. But the preceding paragraph shows that even with respect to linguistic adaptation, the expectations for change are not all on one side. Before examining the merits of Quebec's claims to be making legitimate demands of immigrants in asking them to learn French, however, I want to consider more briefly the two other elements of Quebec's moral contract with immigrants: democracy and pluralism. Commitment to these principles may entail some kinds of adaptation by immigrants, but it also sets strong limits to the kinds of changes that can be demanded and imposes obligations on the receiving society as well.

Democracy and Pluralism

The principle that Quebec is "a democratic society in which everyone is expected and encouraged to participate and contribute" seems to demand more of the society itself than of immigrants. On the one hand, immigrants must exert themselves. Quebec "is entitled to expect newcomers to make the necessary effort to engage gradually in the economic, social, cultural and political life of Quebec" (p. 17). On the other hand, Quebec must make this participation possible and encourage it.

Quebec's commitment to the democratic ideal means that it "assigns the highest importance to the values of equal opportunity and social justice" (p. 16). Thus Quebec has promulgated various human rights documents committing it to principles of non-discrimination on various, familiar liberal grounds, including language and ethnic or national origin, categories of special significance for immigrants. But the government goes further than a promise of formal equality: "[I]mmigrants can expect the host-society to provide them socio-economic support during the initial period and to back them up whenever they or their descendants confront institutional or social barriers that deny them equal access to employment, housing or various public and private services. Furthermore, immigrants can also expect the host-community to allow them, like all Quebeckers, to help define the major orientations of our society" (p. 17). Thus Quebec acknowledges a duty to promote the full participation of immigrants in economic and political life.

With respect to pluralism, the government draws a sharp contrast between traditional Quebec society, which it says "advocated a uniform cultural and ideological model to be shared by all Quebeckers," and modern Quebec, which it says "has for more than 30 years resolutely styled itself as a pluralist society" (p. 17). People are free to "choose their own lifestyles, opinions, values and allegiances to interest groups within the limits defined by the legal framework" (p. 17). Ethnic minorities, including recent immigrants, have "a right to maintain and develop their own cultural interests with the other members of their group" (p. 17). All this clearly is incompatible with the notion that immigrants have an obligation to repudiate their cultures of origin and to adopt the culture of Quebec or that this sort of cultural transformation is a prerequisite for becoming a full Quebecer. The principle of pluralism seems to rule out any strong version of cultural assimilation.

What does Quebec demand of immigrants with respect to the principle of pluralism? Does it expect any cultural adaptation beyond the learning of French? It does expect immigrants, like all Quebecers, to respect the democratic values in which the commitment to pluralism is embedded. The government emphasizes three concerns in this context: "equality of the sexes, the status of children and the censure of all discrimination based on race or ethnic origin" (p. 18). Beyond this, the language is much more tentative. The main emphasis is on openness between groups. The government certainly suggests that immigrants will integrate more effectively if they learn about the history and culture of Quebec, but it is also at pains to acknowledge that immigrants and "the cultural communities" have contributed to Quebec's history and culture in the past and continue to do so in the present and that Quebec has an obligation to be open to these contributions. It talks about the history of Quebec as a "common heritage," while insisting that "Quebeckers from the cultural communities must be recognized as full-fledged Quebeckers with their similarities and differences" (p. 75). Moreover, these differences may sometimes oblige Quebec to adapt, to modify its practices out of respect for these differences. Thus, for example, it acknowledges that in matters of "dress, dietary prescriptions, work schedules and the observance of religious holidays," the practices of religious minorities may differ from those of the Christian majority and should be respected wherever feasible (p. 72).

In all this, the contrast with the much stronger demand for linguistic adaptation is striking. There the message is: "Learn French and adopt it as the language of public communication if you want to be accepted." Here the message is not: "Learn about Quebec culture and adopt it as your own public culture if you want to be accepted." There the message is: "The immigrants' responsibility is to learn French, and the government's responsibility is to make that possible and attractive." Here the message is not (as it could conceivably be) "The immigrants' responsibility is to internalize Quebec's culture, at least with respect to public interactions, and the government's job is to facilitate that adaptation for them." On the contrary, the message is that all Quebecers, whatever their cultural origins and commitments, have an obligation to be open to one another.

Evaluating the Moral Contract

How should we evaluate this moral contract? Is it morally permissible for a liberal democratic society to impose these sorts of expectations on newcomers? Would the proposal look any different from a normative perspective if Quebec were independent?

And what does this tell us about Quebec's self-understanding as a political community?

Let me first repeat here a point that I made above in another connection. Talk of a "moral contract" may seem to suggest that the expectations are legitimate because immigrants were informed about them in advance and came anyway, thus accepting the terms of the contract. *Vision* evokes this normative view when it says: "Applicants will be able to make an informed choice between Quebec and other host-societies" (p. 18). But, as I argue above vis-à-vis restrictions on mobility and other rights, the mere fact that Quebec informed immigrants in advance about its expectations would not make the expectations legitimate, not even if the immigrants explicitly said that they understood and accepted them. Quebec does have an obligation to let the immigrants know what it expects, even if the expectations are morally permissible. To that extent the idea that informed choice matters is correct. But we can invoke independent moral standards for evaluating the legitimacy of the expectations themselves. We can insist, at a minimum, that they must be compatible with liberal democratic principles and respect for human rights to be morally defensible.

Do Quebec's expectations meet these standards? I think so. Let me reverse the order of exposition by starting with an assessment of the way Quebec invokes the principles of democracy and pluralism before I turn to its demands with respect to French.

The Demands of Democracy and Pluralism

Quebec says that immigrants ought to recognize and respect Quebec's fundamental commitment to democracy and pluralism. Is that a morally permissible demand? Some immigrants may come from cultures in which democracy and pluralism are not esteemed.[18] That is clearly the presupposition of the government's document at many points. But it is not entirely clear what recognition of and respect for Quebec's commitment to democracy and pluralism requires of immigrants. Is Quebec asking them to abandon or at least transform the values of their cultures of origin to the extent that their original cultural values conflict with Quebec's understanding of what democracy and pluralism require? If so, is that morally defensible? If not, what is being demanded?

As I see it, immigrants to Quebec ought to recognize and respect the values of democracy and pluralism, not (as *Vision* seems at times to suggest) because these are Quebec's "social choices" but rather because respect for these values is the precondition for maintenance of a morally legitimate political order. Speaking more generally, we ought to distinguish between those aspects of the public culture of a particular liberal democratic society that are required by liberal democratic principles (however they may have emerged historically) and those aspects of a society's culture that reflect its particular history, traditions, and forms of life but cannot be construed as ways of instantiating the requirements of liberal democracy. It is morally legitimate to require immigrants to recognize and respect the former but not the latter. Indeed the respect for pluralism that is essential in a liberal democracy significantly limits the degree to which a society may demand cultural adaptation by immigrants apart from acceptance of the principles of liberal democracy itself. Habermas puts the general point this way: "The identity of a political community, which may not be touched by immigration, depends primarily upon the constitutional principles rooted in a political culture and not upon an ethical-cultural form of life as a whole. That is why it must be expected that the new citizens will readily engage in the political culture of their new home, without necessarily giving up the cultural life specific to their country of origin. The *political acculturation* demanded of them does not include the entirety of their socialization. With immigration, new forms of life are imported which expand and multiply the perspective of all, and on the basis of which the common political constitution is always interpreted."[19]

Why is it morally permissible to expect immigrants to accept the values of democracy and pluralism, especially since this may not fit with the political values of their culture of origin? One answer, sufficient in itself, is that everyone in the society is expected to accept these norms because they are the preconditions for a just political order. To repudiate these values, at least with respect to the public culture, is to advocate injustice. This answer obviously presupposes a defence of liberal democracy as the only just political order, at least under modern political conditions, but elaboration of such a defence goes beyond the scope of this chapter.

A second answer might be connected more specifically to the immigrants' position vis-à-vis the receiving society. Immigrants should accept pluralism and democracy on the grounds that they provide the very values that provide immigrants with a moral basis for challenging certain kinds of demands for cultural adaptation or cultural conformity. Why are Quebecers morally obliged to respect the pre-existing social identities of immigrants at all? What would be morally objectionable about coercive forms of assimilation or about the social and political subordination of those who refuse to assimilate or are incapable of doing so? If the answers to these questions depend on appeals to liberal democratic conceptions of people as free and equal moral agents, then they presuppose a commitment to the values of pluralism and democracy as outlined in *Vision*. Hence it would not be possible for immigrants to reject pluralism and democracy without rejecting the very principles that they need to employ in order to claim moral standing in the first place.[20]

These general arguments conceal some deep perplexities, however. In what sense are immigrants morally obliged to accept the values of pluralism and democracy? Is "acceptance" a question of behaviour or of belief, of external conformity or of internal integration?

All that is required, in my view, is that people accept these values as political values – as the principles that regulate the public life of the society. Liberal democratic principles establish norms about actions and even about discourse that people are morally obliged to respect in the public sphere. But this does not mean that every person must be a liberal democrat in her heart of hearts. It is not morally forbidden in liberal democracies to believe, say, that Plato's views on justice and the relative ranking of regimes are correct.[21]

Liberal democracies have a very deep commitment to freedom of religion, of conscience, of thought, and of opinion. One might expect sociologically that most people's beliefs will eventually tend to conform to their actions and that they will find ways to reinterpret their values so as to make them compatible with the ways in which they are expected to behave, so that people living in liberal democratic regimes will tend to adopt liberal democratic values, at least over the long run. But that is very different from saying that people have a moral obligation to abandon their

philosophical judgments, moral convictions, or religious beliefs
in so far as these conflict with democracy and pluralism. On the
contrary, liberal democratic societies characteristically are (or
ought to be) open even to views that challenge the basic presuppositions of the regime.[22]

The distinction between public and private has been much
criticized in recent years, and often for good reason, given the
uses to which it has been put historically. But a commitment to
pluralism obliges us to limit in one way or another the sphere of
public life and the activities that the state may regulate.

Cultural difference and gender equality. Take the norm of "equality
of the sexes," which Quebec cites as a fundamental democratic
value. *Vision* seems to suggest at several points that immigrants
who come from cultures that do not accept this concept must
learn to do so. In what ways can Quebec legitimately expect
immigrants to accept equality of the sexes, and in what ways
must it tolerate cultural commitments of immigrants that conflict
with the principle?[23]

We should begin by distinguishing between two cultural contexts: a group culture, like that of a religious or ethnic group, and
the public political culture of a liberal democratic society such as
Quebec. A commitment to pluralism will require us to respect, in
certain ways, the internal culture of a group, even when its culture is patriarchal or otherwise incompatible with gender equality. But this does not require us to endorse gender differences in
the public political culture. Pluralism is not relativism, and respect for diversity does not entail indifference to the way the
public culture treats gender.

Consider the issue of gender construction within groups.
Different traditions have different views of the proper roles of
men and women and the proper relations between the sexes. For
example, some religious and moral traditions sharply differenti-
ate the roles of men and those of women, assigning women to
the domestic sphere and limiting their public activities, and emphasizing the authority of the husband within the family. Other
traditions, particularly as they have evolved in recent years, seek
to minimize the differences between the sexes, encouraging both
females and males to develop their talents and capacities whatever they might be and teaching that men and women have similar responsibilities in the public and domestic spheres.[24]

Within broad limits, a liberal democracy ought to tolerate these sorts of cultural differences among groups. This follows from a general commitment to pluralism. These differences may affect the life chances of group members. For example, other things being equal, women raised in the former sort of tradition seem less likely to pursue professional careers than women raised in the latter. But some consequences of group differences are unavoidable if one is to respect group cultures at all.

There are limits to toleration, however. A liberal democratic state will properly prohibit the genital mutilation of young girls, whatever the importance of that practice within a group's culture.[25] It will set its own rules regarding the legal rights and duties of spouses (e.g., with regard to divorce and property rights), regardless of the group's norms. Apart from prohibiting violence, however, it will probably not try (or be entitled to try) to regulate directly the character of relationships between spouses or between parents and children, even where a group's culture establishes patterns of authority and deference quite at odds with gender equality.[26] Some traditions might oppose formal education for women on principle, but a liberal democratic state will override that position and insist on certain kinds of education for all children, girls as well as boys, up to a certain age. But would it be entitled to try to regulate their dress, for example, by prohibiting Muslim girls in school from wearing veils on the grounds that this was a symbol of women's subordination within Islam? I think not, though some would dispute the point. Certainly a liberal democratic state would not be entitled to prohibit an adult woman from wearing such a veil, even in public.

A liberal democratic state may also try to limit the ability of people to act on the basis of their group culture in their relations with those who do not share their views, at least in certain contexts. For example, laws that prohibit discrimination on the basis of sex are supposed to prevent men whose group culture teaches that women belong in the home from acting on those beliefs in the public sphere.

Even where it does not impose formal limits on group cultures, the public culture is not neutral. For example, a liberal democratic regime will tolerate a patriarchal religion as part of its commitment to pluralism. But if it grants equal legal rights to women, it communicates a message about the status of women that is subversive of traditional patriarchal values and creates a resource that makes it easier for a woman to leave a social context ordered by that patriarchal religion.[27] A young girl raised as an Islamic fundamentalist in Quebec will receive one image of what it is to be a woman from her family and another, quite different one from the larger society. Her socialization and her objective situation are very different from those of a girl raised in Iran, where the public institutions support the values of Islamic fundamentalism. A liberal democracy ought to respect diversity, but it cannot be equally congruent with all values and ways of life and should not try to be. It will quite properly support some and undermine others simply by being true to itself.

Pluralism and traditional Catholicism in Quebec. I have been talking about what sorts of cultural transformations a liberal democracy may legitimately expect of immigrants. The same principles apply, however, to non-immigrant members of the society. Let me place this issue in a more concrete context with regard to Quebec. The traditional Catholicism that was such a deep part of Quebec's culture prior to the Quiet Revolution was deeply patriarchal. Indeed, it seems fair to say that it was hostile to the principles of democracy and pluralism, at least as they are generally interpreted in Quebec today.[28] But like every revolution, the Quiet Revolution met some resistance. It did not elicit unanimous support. Presumably there are people in Quebec today who still hold to this traditional Catholicism, perhaps even young people who have acquired traditional beliefs and values from their parents.[29] What does Quebec expect of them? Presumably it does not expect them to abandon their religious convictions. Certainly it does expect them to obey the laws, which include laws against discrimination on the basis of sex and also laws requiring them to send their children to schools where they may be exposed in various ways to the values of gender equality, and more broadly of pluralism and democracy.[30] Quebec can reasonably demand the same of immigrants. But no more.

Democracy, pluralism, and the distinct society. I have been exploring whether Quebec is morally entitled to expect immigrants to accept the principles of pluralism and democracy – two of the three elements in Quebec's proposed moral contract with immigrants. My answer has been "yes," with the qualifications and clarifications discussed. But Quebec is entitled to expect this adaptation of immigrants, at least according to my analysis, only because these norms are not unique to Quebec but are characteristic of all liberal democratic societies.

Not only are Quebec's demands regarding democracy and pluralism not unique, but the very liberal democratic commitments that Quebec wants immigrants to respect severely limit the kinds of cultural adaptation or personal transformation that it can demand. The fact of becoming a newcomer cannot mean that one has given oneself up to the receiving society to be made over according to its will, at least not in a liberal democracy. The government's document obviously reflects awareness of this and develops the point in talking about free choice of "lifestyles, opinions, [and] values" as well as in its affirmation of the rights of minorities to pursue their own cultural interests. Given such principles, on what basis could Quebec claim that immigrants have an obligation to accept some specific aspect of Quebec's culture? It will never be a sufficient reason to expect conformity to say that the values and norms in question are shared by most of the non-immigrant population. In their dress and diet, in their reading and recreations, in their interests and inclinations, in their relationships, and, generally, in how they live, immigrants should be left free to choose their own course, including retaining as much of their culture of origin as they wish, without suffering any moral disapprobation or social pressures to the contrary from the government or the people of Quebec.

I do not mean to overstate the likelihood that immigrants will not adapt to the dominant culture. On the contrary, as a matter of sociological fact, most immigrants do undergo profound cultural transformations if they move to a country in which most people share a very different culture. Even trying to retain one's original culture in that sort of environment requires adaptation and change. Moreover, market forces alone have a powerful socializing and homogenizing effect in modern mass-consumption, capitalist societies. Furthermore, one should not assume that adaptation always goes against the grain for immigrants. Many newcomers have a strong desire to integrate culturally, at least to some extent. In addition, their children face even more powerful and basic socializing experiences in the public schools, even if the institutions are committed to pluralism and are open to influences from sources outside the dominant culture. For all these reasons and more, immigrants are likely to become much more like the rest of the population after they have lived there for a while than they were before they arrived.

But would Quebec be satisfied with such empirical expectations, coupled with and constrained by the public recognition that Quebec as a society is not entitled to expect or demand any specific cultural adaptation from immigrants? I think not. What would this leave of the vision that immigration can help Quebec to build a distinct society? The phrase "distinct society" certainly evokes the image of a society with a distinctive culture. Immigrants can contribute to building a distinct society then, only to the extent that they contribute to and share in that culture. Is that to be left as a purely contingent, empirical development? Is there no sense in which Quebec can say that it expects immigrants to join in the project? Clearly the thrust of the document is exactly the opposite. The whole point of the moral contract is to provide a normative foundation for the claim that immigrants will help to build the distinct society, to say that Quebec can legitimately expect them to assist in the task (as well as to identify Quebec's obligations to them in return). But what we have just seen is that the principles of democracy and pluralism are in no way distinctive to Quebec and that commitment to them limits severely any normative demand for adaptation to a distinctive, local culture. So what kind of obligation might the immigrants have that would be specific to Quebec's distinct society, not common to any liberal democracy?

The Moral Status of Quebec's Commitment to French

The answer, of course, is the third element of the moral contract – the principle that immigrants should accept French as the language of public life. As we saw above, there are specific and strong normative expectations of immigrants put forward in connection with this principle, such as that newcomers should try to learn French and should accept the fact that their children will be educated in French in the public schools. Are these expectations justifiable? I argue that they are, but also that the corresponding obligations that they impose on Quebec require a public, official understanding of the distinct society that is at odds with, and may eventually lead to a transformation of, the popular understanding of the concept.

Is it legitimate for Quebec to make the French Fact such a central political goal and to establish French as the official language? If not, then it obviously would not be legitimate for it to insist that immigrants and their children should learn French.

This issue is much contested, and I cannot provide a full account here. It may be useful to recall the distinction I drew at the beginning of the chapter between arguments about minimum moral standards and those about the goals of a community. Most (though not all) of the objections to Quebec's policies are inspired by the latter sort of concern. Many people have a different vision of Canada as a bilingual state from the one that is reflected in Quebec's policies. They want a Canada that has two official languages throughout its territory, so that (ideally) citizens could use French or English as they wished wherever they were in Canada. At the very least, they would be able to receive public services in French or English, including public education, anywhere in the country.[31] This approach has been called "personal bilingualism." Quebec's view, by contrast, has been referred to as "territorial bilingualism." It also is based on a vision of Canada as a bilingual country, with two official languages for its national institutions. But most social institutions are under provincial jurisdiction, and Quebec's view is that each province should be free to establish itself as bilingual or to adopt one of the two official languages. Quebec, of course, has followed the latter policy, declaring French its official language.

I am not trying to assess the merits of these competing visions of Canada. Rather I wish only to argue that Quebec's vision is morally permissible – that it does not violate the minimum moral standards that a liberal democratic society ought to meet.

We might start by asking why there is a need for an official language at all. In fact many societies do not formally establish an official language as such, but only because everyone knows what it is. It is the language that the vast majority of people speak as their native tongue. It is the language that will be spoken by legislators and judges, by police officers and fire fighters, by bureaucrats and civil servants, by teachers and telephone operators, by postal workers and physicians – in short, by most people in most walks of life. If you do not speak this language, you are simply at a disadvantage that people will feel no obligation to rectify, except perhaps in a few, highly special-ized situations, such as a legal trial. If you are lucky, in other situations you may find someone who can interpret for you.

If you are an immigrant in such a society, and there are enough others like you, you may find an enclave where it is possible to conduct most of your affairs in your native tongue. No one will forbid you to use your language either in the enclave or outside it, but outside, few people will understand it. If you hope to act effectively outside the enclave, you have to learn the dominant language. If you send your children to public schools, they will be taught in the dominant language – if not immediately, then eventually.

Is there anything morally objectionable in this? I do not see why. Assuming, for the purposes of this argument, that there is no compelling reason for preferring one language over another in principle, there seems no obvious reason for people to be obliged to learn or speak any language other than the one they learned in childhood. So the language that most people speak will become the language of social and public life, even if it is not designated as such.

But what if there is a substantial minority that speaks a language different from that of the majority? The principle of majority rule suggests that it would be wrong to establish a minority language as the only official language of a society, at least if that went against the wishes of the majority. So the majority is entitled on simple democratic grounds to have its language as an official language. But is the principle of majority rule sufficient to establish the language of the majority as the only official language of a society, or does that violate the moral rights of minorities?

This is a troubling question for which I have no theoretically satisfying answer. In general, I would say that the choice among alternative ways of recognizing the claims of different linguistic groups seems to me to be just the sort of issue that political communities may legitimately decide for themselves within broad limits.

What are those broad limits? The most important perhaps is that a political community must not try to suppress a language or a linguistic community regardless of its size. It would be wrong to prohibit people from speaking a language, or teaching it, or publishing books or newspapers in it, or using it generally as a vehicle of cultural or political communication, though all these policies have been pursued at one time or another.

When is the language of a minority entitled to recognition as an official language, and what would such recognition entail? How large must a linguistic minority be in order to be entitled to recognition? Is it a question of relative numbers in the population as a whole, or of relative numbers in a given area, or both? Is it just a question of numbers, or does history matter as well – and if so, how? Do recent immigrant groups have less claim to recognition as linguistic communities than long-settled groups – and if so, why?

Again, I can offer no theoretically satisfying answers. There are many examples in the modern world where these are real and relevant questions to which the answers are not obvious – at least not to me. Consider, for example, the concentrations of Spanish-speaking people in certain areas of the United States. Are they entitled to some sort of status as a linguistic minority or perhaps as a linguistic majority in these areas? Or is that simply a matter for political deliberation, with any outcome that does not involve suppression being morally permissible? What about the Russian-speaking minorities in the Baltic states and in other states newly independent from the former Soviet Union? Do they have any moral claims?

I am sure that there would be circumstances under which refusal to recognize a linguistic minority would constitute an unjustifiable form of oppression. For example, imagine a state divided both linguistically and geographically, in which a long-established minority of 40 percent of the population constituted an overwhelming majority in a particular section of the country. Surely we would say in such a case that imposition of the majority's language as the only official language throughout the country was unjust. But it seems difficult to specify the conditions fully in advance.

In practice – though it is not the only practice – some linguistically divided societies follow the principle of majority rule within subnational territorial boundaries to determine a single official language within these units, while establishing more than one at the national level. In some cases this means that individual members of a group whose language is recognized officially at the national level may nevertheless be unable to receive public services in their own language in the place where they live. Belgium and Switzerland offer familiar examples. Is there anything wrong with this sort of approach? I think not, at least in principle. There are other ways of coping with linguistic divisions, of course, but I do not see why this one should be considered wrong.

The Belgian and Swiss cases resemble Quebec's vision in some respects, but Quebec provides extensive public services to its anglophone minority. With respect to public schooling, this situation largely reflects the requirements of the Canadian constitution, but in other ways the services go well beyond what is required by federal law. Is Quebec morally obliged to continue this level of support for anglophones? I do not see why. It may be prudent policy to do so in the current political context, but that is another matter.

If Quebec were independent, would it be obliged to continue any of the services, including the system of public education? In terms of the standard of moral permissibility, I do not see why continuation of such support would be mandatory. In Canada today, the recognition of both English and French as official languages (but not any others) is normally justified almost exclusively on historical grounds, connected to the founding of Canada as a state. If Quebec were to become independent, this historical argument would carry much less weight both within the new Canada and within Quebec. Again, it might be wise or prudent to continue the support for English in Quebec, and the Parti québécois has announced its intention to do so, but wisdom and prudence are different moral virtues from justice.

I have been arguing that modern societies necessarily establish one or more official languages (whether they designate them as such or not) and that this necessity carries with it a moral justification. In other words, because it is unavoidable for a modern society to declare a limited number of languages to be the ones used for official institutions such as schools, courts, and legislatures, it is morally permissible to do so, provided that there is no attempt to suppress linguistic minorities. From this perspective, there is nothing morally problematic about Quebec's decision to make French its official language. But what about the somewhat stronger claim that French should be the language of public life?

As I noted above, I am focusing on the distinctive challenges that immigrants might pose to Quebec's language policies rather than on those that might be posed from the perspective of long-standing cultural minorities such as anglophones and Aboriginal peoples. I can imagine two moral objections that might be launched specifically from the perspective of immigrants against Quebec's policies naming French as the language of public life. First, it is not justifiable to treat the acquisition of French as a precondition for full acceptance into Quebec society and to impose a moral duty to learn it and to accept it as the language of public life. Second, the policy of requiring immigrants to send their children to French-language public schools (if they send them to public schools) is unfair when native-born anglophone Canadians have the right to send their children to English-language public schools.

How should we evaluate these objections? First, the policies to which the objections refer must be understood in the context of the potential vulnerability of the French language for the historical and demographic reasons described above. The policies are defensive. In other words, they are not aimed at establishing the hegemony of French over the disparate languages of origin of the immigrants. If that were the only linguistic contest, Quebec could simply rely on the normal social advantages of the majority language in a society to create sufficient incentives for immigrants and their children to learn French. Indeed, as I observed above, Quebec actually spends money to support heritage language programs for immigrants. Quebec's primary worry, obviously, is that immigrants will choose to learn English rather than French, because of the dominance of English on the North American continent. Quebec rightly fears that such a pattern of linguistic adaptation would render French vulnerable over the long run, if Quebec continued to take in substantial numbers of immigrants.

The first objection is informed partly by the sense that expecting people to learn French, or at least treating its acquisition as a moral duty, asks too much of people. The overall approach of *Vision* is to present a version of liberal democracy that links rights with duties both for the immigrants and for Quebec. In that respect, it differs from some versions of liberalism that focus almost exclusively on the rights of individuals against society, and I think that it is generally on the right track. The duty to learn French is intimately linked to the duty to contribute to and participate in society, which is connected, on this account, to fundamental democratic principles. Learning French is, among other things, a necessary means to participation in society, so that if one can defend the duty to participate – and I think one can – one can defend the duty to learn French. Moreover, the goal of this discourse about duty is not the legitimation of moral condemnations of, say, isolated immigrant women for failing to learn French. On the contrary, *Vision* makes clear that Quebec must reach out to immigrants, especially to those who are socially isolated, to make it possible and attractive for them to learn French. Furthermore, the document recognizes that language acquisition is something that occurs over a long period. Undoubtedly, there might be particular circumstances in which it would be unreasonable to expect an immigrant to learn French, but on the whole it seems to me that *Vision* is setting up a reasonable expectation that immigrants to Quebec ought to meet.

Despite this general defence, it may be useful to consider more closely what is being demanded to see whether it asks too much of immigrants. What does it mean from the immigrants' perspective to have to learn French as a condition of integration? What sort of personal transformation does this entail? How significant a demand is it in terms of the immigrants' pre-existing or future cultural commitments?

In addressing these questions, let me distinguish between two conflicting ideal types of what language acquisition entails with respect to one's own cultural commitments. The first sees language in purely instrumental terms, as a means of communication and no more. On this account, learning a language has no necessary or even likely impact on one's other cultural commitments. Call this the "thin" theory of language. The second view sees a shared language as central to the cultural structure of a community. Learning a language thus shapes our cultural options in profound ways. Call this the "thick" theory of language. My own view is somewhere in between the two, though I have no convenient category for this position.

Overall, I suspect that the cultural significance of language acquisition varies considerably, depending on the conditions under which it takes place. An immigrant who learns French as an adult may already have deep cultural commitments. Learning French does not require her to abandon any of them, though it is likely to open her to new influences and to make her less tied to, because less dependent on, her culture of origin. For adults then, learning French is, at least potentially, a liberating experience that opens new possibilities without foreclosing old ones (though not everyone experiences liberation as something positive).

An immigrant to Quebec who learns French as a child is likely to be much more profoundly affected by the experience than one who learns it as an adult. To learn a language as a child is normally to acquire a culture, at least to some extent, in part because one learns the language primarily in the course of learning other things. In school, children hear stories and acquire models for behaviour, both formally, through the things that they read and experience in the curriculum, and informally, through interaction with other people, especially with their peers. Thus it seems plausible to argue that a language acquired when one is a child is normally much more likely to have the intimate connection to one's cultural structure that the thick theory ascribes to it than a language acquired as an adult. Still, one ought not to overstate the cultural significance of language or to posit a necessary connection between language and cultural orientation. In a society committed to pluralism, as Quebec is, the same language may be a vehicle for widely different and conflicting cultural values and perspectives. And the cultural messages that a child receives from her family and local community may or may not be congruent with the ones that she gets at school from authorities and peers.

On the account I have just given, the norms about learning French are much more significant for the cultural commitments of children than of adults. That makes the second objection, which focuses on the exclusion of immigrants' children from the English-language public school system in Quebec, particularly important.

Primary education is compulsory in Quebec (as in every Western society), and in restricting immigrants to French-language schools, Quebec has deprived recent immigrants of a right that previous immigrants had enjoyed. Nevertheless, I think that this policy is entirely justifiable. The previous right was never a fundamental moral entitlement. No one is entitled to an education at public expense in the language of his or her choice. And the previous system did not provide that option. It offered education in only two languages. In removing the English-language option for immigrants (and for francophone Quebecers, too), Quebec was making the sort of choice among alternative educational policies that democratic governments are fully entitled to make – judging what allocation of educational resources and options will best meet the needs of the community as a whole over the long run as well as the needs of particular students in the short run. No action has done more to integrate immigrants with the francophone community, and none is more likely to have such lasting, long-term effects with respect to linguistic integration.[32] These are important and legitimate social goals. The change reduced the options for immigrants, but it did not deprive them of anything to which they had a fundamental right.

If Quebec were an independent state without any system of public education in English, no one would suppose that immigrants had a moral right to expect that their children should be educated in a language other than that used by the vast majority of the population. What could ground such a right? It is only because Quebec is part of Canada and has a system of public education in English in place that this view seems at all plausible.

One argument against Quebec's policy focuses on the principle of equal treatment. It goes something like this. Perhaps Quebec has no moral obligation to provide a system of public education in English, but if it does have such a system it must provide it as an option to all, not just to some. By restricting the English-language system to the children of people educated in English in Canada, Quebec is discriminating against the children of immigrants.

If the option of attending English language public schools were open to the children of francophone Quebecers, but not to the offspring of immigrants, this argument would be more plausible. As it is, the argument depends on the claim that the children of anglophone Canadians are unduly privileged in Quebec in relation to everyone else. It is a claim that seems implausible on its face. An independent Quebec could respond to such a criticism by abolishing the English-language system of education altogether, thus treating everyone the same. Quebec as a province of Canada is bound by constitutional requirements to provide just those services to the children of anglophone Canadians that it is then criticized for not providing to others, about whom the constitution is silent on this point. Thus the question becomes whether the Canadian constitution is morally justified in providing special guarantees regarding education in the language of one's parents to the two major language groups in Canada. I think that that is a morally permissible policy, but I do not try to prove that here, since my focus is on Quebec.[33]

Integration and Identity

Having argued for the moral permissibility of Quebec's policies on integration, I want to turn once again to the question of how those policies affect Quebec's self-understanding as a political community, or, to hypostatize less, how Quebecers who support these policies are likely to think of Quebec as a distinct society.

We have seen that Quebec's commitment to pluralism means that the only distinctive cultural commitment (i.e., the only commitment not common to every liberal democracy) that it requires of immigrants for full social membership is knowledge of French. Immigrants do not have to prove their loyalty to Quebec by proclaiming an attachment to its symbols or an identification with its history, though Quebec seeks to promote both of these attitudes, as we see below. They can be full members of Quebec's distinct society even if they look and act differently from the substantial segment of the population whose ancestors inhabited Quebec and even if they do not in any way alter their own customs and cultural patterns with respect to work and play, diet and dress, sleep and sex, celebration and mourning, so long as they act within the confines of the law.

On this account, given the commitment to pluralism, Quebec's distinct society becomes identified, almost exclusively, with the French Fact. That is, its distinctiveness consists essentially in the fact that it is a society situated in North America in which the vast majority of the population speak French (whether as a first or second language is irrelevant) and in which French is the language of public life. There may be other facts about Quebec that would mark it off to an outside observer as different from other societies or other cultural commitments that are widely shared by Quebecers and not by members of other societies, but such facts and commitments are not and cannot be normatively central to Quebec's project of building a distinct society.

Some see Quebec's claim to cultural distinctiveness as superficial, if not false. They argue that its embrace of liberal capitalism since the 1960s has in effect destroyed the distinctive culture that it once enjoyed and rendered it virtually indistinguishable from other North American societies, despite the linguistic differences. Can one build a distinct society on the basis of language alone? Is a shared language sufficient for a claim of cultural distinctiveness? I do not have any particular views on this question. It seems to me to be just the sort of issue that ought to be left to the people of Quebec to decide. How much do they value this form of distinctiveness? Do they regard it as significant, as something relevant to their identities as individuals and as citizens?

These questions point to an ambiguity in the principle that French is to be accepted as the language of public life, because immigrants must be included in the group to whom these questions are addressed. Unlike the commitment to democracy and pluralism, which can be defended on independent moral grounds, the commitment to French as the language of public life clearly is something that derives its normative status entirely from the fact that it is Quebec's "social choice" – i.e., from the fact that the majority of Quebecers are deeply committed to this principle. But that commitment could change. In saying that immigrants are morally obliged to accept French as the language of public life, then, the government must appeal to respect for the democratic process. But once immigrants are members of Quebec's society, and certainly once they have become citizens, they have a right to participate in that process, or, as the document itself says, "to help define the major orientations of our society" (p. 17). But language policy cannot be excluded from the democratic process in which the immigrants participate. If immigrants or their adult children choose to try to reshape Quebec's linguistic orientation – say, by supporting a more bilingual public policy – they cannot legitimately be criticized for violating the moral contract.

The importance of this issue will increase as the proportion of immigrants in the population grows, which it will if the policies outlined in the document are followed. Moreover, immigrants would not have to constitute a majority of the population in order to have significant, perhaps even decisive weight if the Quebec-born francophone population were divided. In the long run then, the viability of Quebec's distinct society and maintenance of the French Fact may depend in major respects on the extent to which immigrants and their children identify with, and are committed to, that project. To be sure, if the children have been educated in French, if they have become francophones, they may feel that their interests would be served most by preserving the position of French in Quebec. But the project of maintaining the distinct society may well depend on their having a deeper, less instrumental commitment than that.

How can that commitment be created? By making sure that the project of the distinct society is genuinely open to them, that it is not too closely identified with a particular group – namely, those descended from the early francophone settlers. What appeared above as a moral imperative arising out of a belief in pluralism – a conception of Quebec society with no specific cultural commitments beyond democracy, pluralism, and the French language – reappears here as a political imperative arising from the need to enlist the support of immigrants and their children in the effort to preserve the French language in Quebec. In integrating immigrants, Quebec is transforming not only their identity but its own as well.

In Quebec the word "multiculturalism" has pejorative connotations, in part because a federal royal commission created in 1967 to develop policies for Canada based on its bicultural and bilingual character recommended, after consultation with immigrant groups among others, that Canada think of itself as a multicultural and bilingual country. Francophone Quebecers were outraged by this decision, seeing it as a policy that placed their culture on a par with that of minority ethnic groups and that betrayed the conception of Canada as a country built upon two "founding nations." The alternative term in vogue in Quebec seems to be "intercultural," and it is often used in a way that suggests it stands in sharp contrast to "multicultural." These sorts of terms can be interpreted in many different ways, and I do not doubt that there are some interpretations that would put them radically at odds. Nevertheless, I do not think either that the fundamental problem that Quebec faces is profoundly different from that faced by the rest of Canada or that the range of morally acceptable solutions is different.

If the collective identity of Quebec is too closely tied with the "founding nation" and with its particular history and culture, then immigrants and their children will find it hard to feel as though they belong to that collectivity and will be disinclined to support its projects. But if the collectivity is defined in the open way that I have been suggesting, with an almost exclusive emphasis on the French language as the shared cultural commitment and without any claim of privilege or priority for the more particular features of the history and culture of the descendants of the settlers, then Quebec is committed to its own internal version of multiculturalism, whatever the term it chooses to use.[34]

One might object here that the policy document on which I have been relying so heavily in my analysis is not representative of the views of the government as a whole, not to mention of the population at large. After all, it was produced by a ministry that is responsible not only for immigration but also for "the cultural communities" of Quebec. It would not be surprising if this institutional location led to an official line from this ministry that was more open and more pluralistic than that of others, even though the document was published in the name of the government of Quebec after consultation with and approval by the other ministries.

There is certainly something to this concern. Indeed the document itself is titled *Vision*, which may suggest that there is some gap between the principles that it professes and the social and political realities of immigration in Quebec. Surveys of the population on attitudes towards immigrant and membership in Quebec indicate that the positions proposed by the document are not universally accepted. Moreover, the document itself expresses a degree of frustration over the fact that other parts of the government do not seem to feel it necessary to think about the implications of their policies for immigrants and the cultural communities, treating that concern as the preserve of a single ministry.

While there are reasons for caution therefore in viewing Quebec through the lens provided by *Vision*, I think that the document nevertheless captures something fundamental about the normative logic of immigration in Quebec, and perhaps in any modern liberal democracy. I illustrate the working of this normative logic by discussing briefly a couple of examples of the ways in which the presence of immigrants has affected discourse about Quebec's identity and policies in apparently unrelated areas.[35]

The first illustration concerns a report drawn up for Montreal's School Council, called *Les francophones québécois*.[36] The council had already commissioned a series of reports on Montreal's ethnic communities and their cultures and thought that it would be useful to ask for a report on that huge part of the population that had French as a mother tongue and that was not composed of or descended from recent immigrants. I use this awkward phrase to describe the population to be discussed because, as the report indicated, there was no convenient label. The report rejected the terms *Canadiens* and *Canadiens français*, which had formerly been employed to refer to this population but which fell into disfavour with the rise of a nationalist sentiment closely tied to the territory and government of Quebec. What about *Québécois français*? Too narrow, it said, because settlers from Ireland, Scotland, and elsewhere integrated with this group culturally and linguistically centuries ago. And, I suspect, that phrase might have sounded a bit too much like the description of an ethnic group, and the authors did not want this population to be thought of as just another ethnic group, no matter how large. Finally, it settled on *francophones québécois* while acknowledging that this label, too, was unsatisfactory because it placed primary emphasis on language and the point was to identify and describe a shared historical culture. Besides, did the term include recent francophone immigrants from places such as Haiti and Belgium? To exclude them would seem insulting. What are they if not francophones québécois? But to include them would distract the project from its central focus.

This long discussion of labels reveals an ambiguity about identity and legitimacy that runs throughout the report. The authors are clearly committed to linking Quebec's distinct society and its nationalist project to a specific history and culture, but they want to do that without repudiating pluralism and democracy. They want to affirm a Quebec in which everyone is a full member, regardless of origin, and simultaneously one in which a particular culture holds a privileged place. This leads to a tortuous discussion at many points.

In general, the report faces the following dilemma. The more closely it identifies Quebec with the francophone community and culture, the more open that community and culture have to be to people who speak French but are not descended from French settlers and thus open to diverse cultural influences. The more it ties the identity of the francophone community to a specific history, to specific cultural practices, and especially to specific lines of descent – the more particularistic it is – the stronger the claim for the distinctiveness of this community but the weaker the claim for identifying this particular group, even though numerically very large, with Quebec as a state. Others can then say, "We are citizens too, and we clearly do not belong to your group and can't join it because it's an ascriptive group, so it is not fair to identify the state with a group that comprehends only part of the population, even if it is the largest part. In particular, it is not fair to use the state to impose the norms and values of your group on people whom the group is not willing to accept."

The report dances around these issues in various ways, at times emphasizing the historical particularity of the francophonie québécoise and at times emphasizing its openness to others on pluralist, not assimilationist, terms. Despite the authors' commitment to making the historical francophone community central, on the question of the integration of immigrants it comes up with a list of expectations remarkably similar to the one provided in *Vision*: learning French; sharing fundamental values of democracy, liberty, toleration, citizenship, and equality of the sexes; and participation in economic, cultural, and political life. To this it adds learning about the territory, institutions, and history of the francophonie québécoise and respecting and appropriating the symbols at the heart of public life in Quebec, such as the flag and the national holiday (St-Jean-Baptiste day, 24 June). The last addition brought a sharp retort from a representative of ethnic groups in Quebec about their preferring the Canadian flag – illustrating again the ways in which Quebec's status as a province creates dilemmas for its nationalist project, since Canada provides alternative symbols of political legitimacy to which those who are disaffected with Quebec's course or who feel excluded from its project can appeal.

In the minds of most people, both inside and outside Quebec, the phrase "distinct society" is intimately connected to the preservation and development of the (evolving) historical culture shared by people most of whom are primarily descended from the original French settlers. But in a society that takes in substantial numbers of immigrants and tries to integrate them with francophone institutions and public life without requiring cultural assimilation, that connection is harder to maintain. It does not entirely disappear, of course, but it loses much of its normative force. Such historical links can no longer serve as a criterion of authenticity for what is or is not part of the culture of Quebec's distinct society. With the opening of francophone institutions and public life to immigrants, it becomes necessary to think of the culture of Quebec's distinct society as including whatever is part of the culture of the inhabitants of Quebec.[37] Indeed, the very concept of francophone culture in Quebec takes on a systematic ambiguity.

Let me reinforce this point with another story that illustrates the dynamics at work here and the ways in which immigration transforms the identity of Quebec as a community even while immigrants are being transformed into Quebecers. The Quebec government set up a program in Ontario (and a few other provinces) to support francophone culture outside Quebec. This effort was motivated largely by a desire to respond in some way to the complaints of francophones outside Quebec that they had been thrown to the anglophone wolves by Quebec's focus on provincial autonomy rather than on linguistic solidarity. Those complaints aroused some sympathy in Quebec because of the sense that these francophones outside Quebec shared the same cultural and ethnic roots as Quebec's francophones.

One day representatives of a group of francophone Afro-Canadians applied for a grant under this program to support a cultural newspaper for francophone Afro-Canadians in Ontario. How were Quebec officials to respond? This was clearly not the sort of thing that they had had in mind in setting up the program. If they gave the grant, people in Quebec might ask why the Quebec government was spending its money on multicultural activities for recent immigrants to Ontario. Wasn't that the job of Ontario or of the federal government? What did these people have to do with Quebec? But if they denied the grant, what grounds could they use? The applicants were francophones after all. Could they say that they had intended the program for those with ethnic ties to Quebecers? Not really. Besides some of these people probably did have ethnic ties to Quebecers – to the new Quebecers from francophone Africa. And if francophone culture within Quebec is now genuinely open to Asian and African francophones, as the public rhetoric declares, how could the francophone culture outside Quebec worthy of support be narrowly defined, in terms of ethnic or historical links to Quebecers of European descent? In the end, the officials could not say no (though they did not just say yes either).[38]

The case shows, I think, how the integration of immigrants within the francophone community of Quebec has begun to and will continue to change the identity of that community. Where once "francophone Quebecer" implied a specific culture, ethos, history, and way of life, all of which helped define Quebec as a political community, now a logic of multiculturalism (both sociological and moral) has been introduced that will lead Quebec to look more and more like a French-speaking version of English-speaking, multicultural Canada or at least will make it hard to defend in public an alternative vision of Quebec.[39]

CONCLUSION

In a widely discussed article, Charles Taylor has posited a fundamental difference between liberalism in Quebec and liberalism in the rest of Canada.[40] I want to use that article to highlight some of the central themes of this chapter.

English Canada, Taylor says, is committed to a version of liberalism based on individual rights and neutral procedures that precludes the pursuit of collective national goals. By contrast, he says, Quebec has a deep commitment to a particular collective good: "the survival and flourishing of French culture in Quebec."[41] Quebec is a liberal society, however, because it is also committed to respect for minority rights.

There may well be something to Taylor's distinction between the political cultures of English Canada and Quebec, though I argue below that he overstates the differences. Whatever its validity, the distinction marks a political, not a moral, divide, at least if the fundamental principles of liberal democracy are rightly understood. On this point I believe that Taylor and I are in accord.

It is unquestionably true that some people in English Canada, especially academics, but perhaps not only they, have the individualistic, procedural view of liberalism that Taylor describes. However, I do not think that a strong view of liberal neutrality accurately characterizes anglophone-Canadian institutions and practices, nor would I regard it as intellectually coherent at a theoretical level for reasons discussed above in connection with Quebec's language policies.[42] Nevertheless, I would not claim that the pursuit of such a vision of liberalism is morally impermissible. However, I think that it would be a fundamental mistake to suppose that this particular view of liberalism is the only one ultimately compatible with liberal democratic principles.

I think that Taylor overstates the contrast between Quebec and English Canada by emphasizing the importance of the Charter in English Canada and linking that to the procedural liberalism that he regards as incompatible with Quebec's collective project. After all, Quebecers often point with pride to the fact that Quebec was the first jurisdiction within Canada to adopt a charter of rights and freedoms. Even the Canadian Charter is relatively popular with Quebecers in terms of its content; their principal objection has to do with its political and symbolic role in entrenching Trudeau's vision of Canada and Quebec in the constitution, and that without Quebec's consent.[43] So, Quebecers, too, are deeply attached to individual rights.

The collective goal of survivance in Quebec that Taylor identifies is open to many readings. In my view, those versions of it requiring a collective commitment to the preservation of a highly specific, thick, particularist culture would be in tension not only with procedural liberalism as Taylor has described it but also with any defensible view of liberalism. No doubt there are some people in Quebec who would insist on this sort of interpretation. Taylor himself evokes such an understanding when he says, "Political society is not neutral between those who value remaining true to the culture of our ancestors and those who might want to cut loose in the name of some individual goal of self-development" or when he says that "a society can be organized around a definition of the good life."[44] These formulations do not seem to contain the commitment to pluralism that is so marked in Vision and that seems to me required by any version of liberalism.

Yet I do not believe that a highly particularistic understanding of survivance is true to the social realities of contemporary Quebec or an accurate reflection of Taylor's own views. The rest of Taylor's essay reflects a concern for finding ways to respect diversity in Quebec as well as in the rest of Canada. And I have argued throughout this chapter that *Vision*'s project of reconciling pluralism and democracy with governmental efforts to ensure the ongoing vitality of the French Fact is morally legitimate and fully compatible with liberal democratic principles.

Let me conclude with two points. First, establishing the moral permissibility of Quebec's treatment of immigrants and its related national project, as I have tried to do here, obviously does not resolve all the political conflicts between Quebec and the rest of Canada. Even if people in the rest of Canada recognize Quebec's political project as a legitimate variant of liberalism (which I take to be one of the main points of Taylor's article), there remains the question of whether they are willing to accept this project as a central part of what defines Canada as a political community or whether Quebecers are willing to pursue that project within the confines of Canada. These are the questions of what choices we make within the realm of the morally permissible, and for these, I think, political theory offers relatively little guidance.

Second, my insistence throughout that Quebec's collective self-understanding will and ought to evolve in a more pluralistic direction should not be construed as a critique of the distinct society project. On the contrary, the same argument applies to a great extent to every contemporary liberal democratic society, because virtually every one has received some significant number of immigrants and refugees and can expect more, whether it wants them or not. Quebec's way of coming to terms with this phenomenon as outlined in *Vision* may provide a model for other liberal democratic societies, especially in Europe, of a way to combine a strong sense of national identity with a deep commitment to liberal democratic values.

NOTES

Over the past two years, I have presented versions of this chapter to audiences in Amsterdam, Louvain-la-Neuve, Ottawa, Paris, Toronto, Vienna, and Washington. I wish to thank all the participants for their comments and criticisms. In addition, I want to thank the following people for their detailed responses to previous drafts: Veit Bader, Rainer Bauböck, Frank Cunningham, Dilek Çinar, Steve Dupré, Will Kymlicka, Jenny Mansbridge, Marie McAndrew, Peter Russell, and Don Schwartz. A version of part of this chapter (pp. 38–72) appeared under the title "Cultural Adaptation and Integration: Is Quebec a Model for Europe?" in *From Aliens to Citizens*, ed. Rainer Bauböck (Aldershot, England: Avebury Press, 1994), 149-86.

1   Quebec would like these powers to be entrenched in the constitution, however, and thus given more permanent legal standing than the accord provides. That constitutional status would have been provided by the failed Meech Lake and Charlottetown accords and is one of the prerequisites that Quebec has insisted must be met by any future constitutional proposals that it will consider.

2   *Let's Build Québec Together: Vision: A Policy Statement on Immigration and Integration* (Quebec City: Ministère des Communautés culturelles et de l'Immigration du Québec, 1990).

3   The official policy documents of the Parti québécois that I have seen (the *1994 Programme du Parti Québécois* and the *Programme électorale du Parti Québécois*) do not seem to challenge *Vision*. The documents declare that a sovereign Quebec will continue to be open to immigration. Like *Vision*, they emphasize immigrants' speaking or learning French as the key to integration and speak of socioeconomic integration, participation, and pluralism. They also support efforts against ethnic and racial discrimination toward immigrants. Overall, they do not appear to insist on a more substantive form of cultural adaptation than is called for by *Vision*. Of course, they are much less detailed than *Vision*, and the party's position could change. In the light of the recent disputes about girls wearing the hijab in Montreal schools, the issue of cultural adaptation of immigrants may become more politically salient and more contested. At the moment, however, the party does not seem to have made any attempt to distinguish its position on immigration sharply from that of the previous Liberal government.

4   The accord extends and deepens a previously established pattern whereby Quebec has exercised considerable power over immigration. I will not trace the course of these developments but merely identify the powers that Quebec now enjoys under the accord, including ones that it had previously exercised. In constitutional terms, immigration is defined as an area of concurrent federal and provincial jurisdiction, with federal paramountcy. Hence in the accord Ottawa promises to avoid legislation or administrative regulations that would conflict with provincial legislation in the areas identified by the accord. My thanks to Steve Dupré and Peter Russell for clarifying this point for me.

5 The Meech Lake Accord had guaranteed Quebec a share of immigrants at least equal to its share of the Canadian population, with the right to exceed its share by up to 5 percent of the total. The Canada-Quebec Accord adopts the same goals but drops the word "guarantees" and speaks instead of both parties undertaking to pursue policies to achieve these goals. Some people had objected that Meech Lake would have enabled Quebec to reduce the overall level of immigration into Canada by invoking the word "guarantee" and claiming that it could take in only a relatively low number. That interpretation was certainly disputable, and the new agreement clearly suggests that Canada ought to take Quebec's receptive capacity into account in setting its target levels, so the difference between the two may not amount to much, but the Canada-Quebec Accord also places an obligation on Quebec to pursue a policy that will enable it to receive its appropriate share of immigrants, so there is perhaps more ambiguity here if conflicts should develop between Quebec and Ottawa over immigration levels.

6 See Joseph H. Carens, "Aliens and Citizens: The Case for Open Borders," *Review of Politics*, 49 (Spring 1987), 251–73.

7 I say "too closely" rather than "at all" because I want to reject the claim by some authors that a country such as the United States or Canada that permits both immigration and voluntary expatriation is a political community built on the principle of consent rather than on that of ascription or heredity. In every political community, the dominant way in which citizenship is acquired is through descent, and that would be true even in a world of open borders. For the reasons why this matters, see Joseph H. Carens, "Who Belongs? Theoretical and Legal Questions about Birthright Citizenship in the United States," *University of Toronto Law Journal*, 37 (1987), 413–43.

8 For a discussion of the "White Australia" policy, see Joseph H. Carens, "Nationalism and the Exclusion of Immigrants: Lessons from Australian Immigration Policy," in Mark Gibney, ed., *Open Borders? Closed Societies: The Ethical and Political Issues*, (Westport, Conn.: Greenwood Press, 1989), 41–60.

9 See R.A. Vineberg, "Federal-Provincial Relations in Canadian Immigration," *Canadian Public Administration / Administration publique du Canada*, 30 (Summer/Été 1987), 299–317.

10 See Joseph H. Carens, "Membership and Morality: Admission to Citizenship in Liberal Democratic States," in *Immigration and the Politics of Citizenship in Europe and North America*, ed. William Rogers Brubaker (Lanham, Md.: German Marshall Fund of America and University Press of America, 1989), 31–49.

11 See, for example, Gary Caldwell, "Immigration et émigration: vers un solde migratoire positif," *Action nationale* (March 1988), 9–16.

12   See William Rogers Brubaker, "Citizenship and Naturalization: Policies and Politics," in *Immigration and the Politics of Citizenship in Europe and North America*, ed. William Rogers Brubaker (Lanham, Md.: German Marshall Fund of America and University Press of America, 1989), 108–9.

13   See Carens, "Membership and Morality."

14   See William Rogers Brubaker, "Membership without Citizenship: The Economic and Social Rights of Noncitizens," in *Immigration and the Politics of Citizenship in Europe and North America*, ed. William Rogers Brubaker (Lanham, Md.: German Marshall Fund of America and University Press of America, 1989), 145–62.

15   See, for example, Peter H. Schuck, "The Transformation of Immigration Law," *Columbia Law Review*, 84 (1984), 1–90.

16   See, for example, Caldwell, "Immigration et émigration."

17   This way of describing the requirement oversimplifies things a bit. The actual rule stipulates that only children who have at least one parent who received a primary education in English in Canada are entitled to have access to English-language public schools. Thus, for example, the children of British or American immigrants to Quebec would not be entitled to an education in English. Some have proposed softening this rule to permit immigrants whose native tongue is English – a relatively small proportion of immigrants – to send their children to the English-language schools, but this proposal has not yet been adopted.

    Immigrants are also affected by the other language legislation in Quebec designed to ensure that French is used at work, in commercial transactions, and so on, but this legislation is clearly aimed primarily not at immigrants but rather at anglophone Quebecers. The moral status of this legislation is contested, of course, but it seems to me that that issue does not depend in any way on the position of immigrants and their moral claims to membership. (In other words, if the legislation is defensible vis-à-vis native anglophones in Quebec, it will be so vis-à-vis immigrants, and if not defensible for anglophones, then not so for immigrants either, though the latter claim is not as self-evident as the former.) Because this chapter focuses on moral arguments about immigration, I do not discuss this other language legislation.

18   Of course, the fact that immigrants come from illiberal cultures does not mean that they accept illiberal values. Perhaps they left in part because of their dissatisfactions with the prevailing culture in their country of origin. Moreover, as I discuss below in this section, people born and raised in Quebec may have cultural commitments at odds with democracy and pluralism. Still, it is reasonable to assume that some immigrants will come with views or values in conflict with democracy and pluralism, and it is appropriate to ask how to respond to that fact.

19   Jürgen Habermas, "Citizenship and National Identity: Some Reflections on the Future of Europe," *Praxis International,* 12 no. 1 (April 1992), 17.

20   This argument presupposes that immigrants are seeking to engage in a moral dialogue with Quebécers who themselves accept democracy and pluralism and that the immigrants are appealing to principles that such Quebecers would respect. To develop this argument at a deeper level, one would have to show that there is no alternative (illiberal and anti-democratic) set of principles that is morally superior to democracy and pluralism, or at least one would have to make a positive case for democracy and pluralism. Here I am simply assuming the moral validity of liberal democratic principles and trying to explore what they entail.

21   Of course, Plato himself thought that democracies permitted all sorts of opinions, including opinions about the merits of different regimes. This uncontrolled freedom – of opinion and everything else – was what made democracies such an inferior form of regime, in his view. See Plato's *Republic,* Book VIII.

22   I am not suggesting that this openness is unlimited. This is the familiar problem of the toleration of the intolerant in liberal democratic societies, and it can be argued that there is no obligation to tolerate those who actually threaten the existence of the regime. But the mere fact that some people may hold illiberal or undemocratic views does not in itself constitute such a threat. See John Rawls, *A Theory of Justice* (Cambridge, Mass.: Harvard University Press, 1971), 216–21.

23   I assume without further argument that a commitment to equality of the sexes is entailed by liberal democratic principles, as the Quebec government claims. I think that the claim is correct, though what equality requires is much disputed even among those most committed to the principle.

   The next several paragraphs are adapted from my essay "Difference and Domination: Reflections on the Relation between Pluralism and Equality," in John Chapman and Alan Wertheimer, eds., *Majorities and Minorities: NOMOS XXXII* (New York: New York University Press, 1990), 226–50.

24   In referring to the evolution of moral and religious traditions, I do not mean to suggest that any religion (such as Islam or Christianity) or any moral tradition (such as liberalism) is homogeneous. On the contrary, every major tradition contains different and conflicting elements, some more conservative and others more reform-minded. I also do not mean to suggest that these religious and moral traditions have evolved autonomously or that contemporary concerns with gender equality are primarily a result of their evolution. It seems plausible that the changes in the traditions were largely the result of independent socioeconomic changes and of political struggles by women, but I am not trying here to address

the question of why the changes occurred. My point is simply that there is now a significant range of views on the issue of gender.

25 I use this example with some hesitation. On the one hand, it is a real issue in the sense that genital mutilation is widely practised in some countries and some immigrants do try to continue the practice after arriving in their new country. Thus the example clearly illustrates one limit to toleration about which I expect little dispute. On the other hand, the example risks reinforcing the highly objectionable pattern in some discussions of immigration of making this issue the crucial symbolic representative of all of Islamic culture, thus identifying the West with civilization and Islam with barbarism, and of categorizing all immigrants from predominantly Islamic countries as threats because they are assumed to be bearers of this barbaric culture. This anti-Islamic discourse necessarily makes no mention of the considerable internal opposition to genital mutilation within Islamic countries, opposition based on religious and cultural grounds. For further discussion of this issue, see Joseph H. Carens, "Complex Justice, Cultural Difference, and Political Community," in *Pluralism, Justice, and Equality*, ed. David Miller and Michael Walzer (Oxford: Oxford University Press, 1995), 61–4.

26 Whether such patterns of inequality can in fact be maintained without violence is, of course, a crucial question. Certainly, violence plays a key role in maintaining the subordination of women within existing liberal democratic societies, whatever the formal norms of the regime.

27 I do not mean to suggest that legal equality is enough to overcome patriarchy or that patriarchal domination is not a powerful force in contemporary liberal democracies. But I do think that legal equality is a necessary step in overcoming patriarchy and that it makes a difference.

28 This is evident even in *Vision* (p. 17). It is this earlier, illiberal Quebec that opponents of Quebec often evoke in criticizing the federal government's willingness to have Quebec exercise so much power over immigration and in insisting that final authority on matters relating to individual rights and liberties should rest with Ottawa. They imply and sometimes even explicitly say that the transformation is only skin deep. Quebecers respond with understandable irritation, noting that the record of the rest of Canada, both the central government and the other provinces, is far from unblemished in protecting rights and liberties (not least of francophones) and that Quebecers almost always do as well as or better than non-Quebecers in surveys on toleration and liberal values generally. On the similarity of values between Quebecers and other Canadians, see Stéphane Dion, "Explaining Quebec Nationalism," in *The Collapse of Canada*, ed. R. Kent Weaver (Washington, DC: Brookings Institution, 1992), 99, and the studies cited therein.

29 Of course, the Catholic church went through its own revolution with

Vatican II, but not everyone joined that revolution either, and it has arguably been reversed much more than Quebec's Quiet Revolution. Many traditional Catholic beliefs and values (e.g., on issues of gender equality) continue to play a significant role in the lives of some Catholics and are not easily reconciled with Quebec's current understanding of democracy and pluralism.

30 This is undoubtedly an optimistic reading of what goes on in Quebec's schools (if they are anything like other schools in North America), but it would not be unrealistic to think that the messages that students get from Quebec's schools today are generally more sympathetic to gender equality, pluralism, and democracy than those that they would have received in a traditional Catholic education forty years ago.

   Quebec does permit private schools, but even private religious schools are subject to public regulation to some extent. In fact in Quebec, as in other parts of Canada, much of the public school system has an explicit religious affiliation as either Catholic or Protestant, so that the incentive for the Christian segment of the population to create separate private schools is substantially less than in the United States, where the constitutional requirement of the separation of church and state greatly restricts the connections between religion and public education. Of course, Quebec's denominational public schools are subject to closer scrutiny and greater restraints than private religious schools.

31 Various aspects of this policy have been implemented, at least in theory, including a requirement that commercial packaging contain product information in both French and English. However, in some parts of Canada, one is much more likely to find a cereal box with French on it than a public servant who understands French.

32 For some supporting data see Dion, "Explaining Quebec Nationalism," 91–2.

33 For a defence of this sort of distinction in treatment between immigrants and long-standing national minorities, see Will Kymlicka, *Multicultural Citizenship: A Liberal Theory of Minority Rights* (Oxford: Oxford University Press, 1995), chap. 5.

34 See Raymond Breton, "From Ethnic to Civic Nationalism: English Canada and Quebec," *Ethnic and Racial Studies*, II (Jan. 1988), 85–102.

35 Normative logics do not always triumph in politics, but it is instructive to understand them.

36 Gerard Bouchard, Francois Rocher, and Guy Rocher, *Les francophones québécois* (Montreal: Conseil scolaire de l'île de Montreal, 1991).

37 Perhaps I should say "the culture of those inhabitants who use French (and not simply those for whom it is the mother tongue)." This more qualified phrase leaves open, in particular, the possibility of thinking about anglophone culture in Quebec as a minority culture rather than as

an integral part of the culture of the distinct society. Many people would object, arguing that anglophones must also be counted as full Quebecers and that their culture also contributes to the distinct society. I do not want to enter that debate here.

38 Their solution was to provide only part of what had been requested and to stipulate that the grant was to support the francophone (rather than the African) dimensions of the project – a distinction that I imagine could prove open to contestation in the future.

39 See again Breton, "From Ethnic to Civic Nationalism."

40 Charles Taylor, "Shared and Divergent Values," in *Reconciling the Solitudes: Essays on Canadian Federalism and Nationalism*, ed. Guy Laforest (Montreal: McGill-Queen's University Press, 1993), 155–86, especially 172–84; chapter originally published in Ronald L. Watts and Douglas M. Brown, eds., *Options for a New Canada* (Toronto: University of Toronto Press, 1991), 53–76.

41 Ibid., 175.

42 For a fuller treatment of this point, see Kymlicka, *Multicultural Citizenship*.

43 See chapter 5, by Janet Ajzenstat, in this volume and Alan Cairns, "Reflections on the Political Purposes of the Charter: The First Decade," in *The Charter: Ten Years Later*, ed. Gerald A. Beaudoin (Cowansville, Que.: Les Editions Yvon Blais Inc., 1992), 163–91.

43 Taylor, "Shared and Divergent Values," 175–6.

CHAPTER THREE

Canada, Quebec, and Refugee Claimants

Howard Adelman

What is the character of Quebec separatism? That is, what are its basic values? One way of getting at those values is to analyse the motives of various types of sovereigntists. Is Quebec separatism a political movement motivated by nativist, ethnic-exclusive passions? Is it an ideology promulgated by one elite wanting power in Quebec versus another French-Canadian elite quite content with the power that it has achieved in Ottawa? Or do Québécois sovereigntists believe that their economic self-interest would best be fulfilled in a separate Quebec state? Or are the separatists motivated primarily by a belief that they have been cheated within Confederation, contending that the Canadian system of distributive justice has been unfair to them?

In this chapter I argue that the quest for Quebec sovereignty, whether in its federalist or its separatist guise, does not appear to be narrow and chauvinistic, though undoubtedly there are many chauvinists in both camps. Nor does the quest for sovereignty seem to be motivated primarily by resentment or economic self-interest. I use Quebec's policies on immigration and on refugees as litmus tests of the character of the sovereignty movement and, hence, of its basic motivation. The tests indicate that the sovereigntists have a high regard for human rights. Further, with respect to refugee determination, they seem just as ready as other Canadians to set aside economic self-interest to uphold individual rights, even on an issue where Canada, and therefore Quebec, have surrendered a critical aspect of sovereignty. Further, the intake of these refugees by and large undermines the francophone proportion of Canadians and Quebecers.

In this chapter I attempt to tease out the character of Québécois separatism from what might appear to be an odd angle – the study of Quebec's approach to refugees, in particular, refugee determination. The issue may appear an unlikely source of illumination – after all, refugee claimants are not Canadians. They are not even foreigners whom Canadians choose to allow to become members of the Canadian polity. They arrive spontaneously and claim refugee status. If they succeed, they are allowed to remain in Canada and then can join the Canadian polity. In other words, Canadians do not choose them. Because refugees seem to have little to do with Canadian self-determination and sovereignty, the refugee issue would seem to be remote from any analysis of sovereigntists' motives.

However, this is precisely why the issue proves so useful. Refugee claimants – uninvited guests – challenge the very essence of sovereignty – the right of a people to choose freely who can or cannot join the community. They enter and become members, not because Canadians choose them, but because they can satisfy the government that they are refugees according to a set of standards and procedures that Canadians have agreed accord with international agreements and obligations. Canadians do not choose them, yet choice of new members is central to both the quest for sovereignty and its essential conception. Therefore an examination of Quebec's approach to the issue, in light of its quest for increased and even fundamental sovereign control, provides a unique insight into the motivation behind and the character of Quebec separatism.

First, I provide a brief overview of the history of Canada's post-war immigration and refugee policy. Second, I introduce the refugee determination system and, in relation to that system, analyse various possible motives for separatism. Third, I probe the struggle between Quebec and Ottawa over control of immigration and then try to show that there has been no parallel struggle over refugee determination. Fourth, I consider the absence of any effort by Quebec to take over refugee determination, even though the motivation to do so is strong on other grounds. This absence contrasts markedly with efforts to gain control over immigration. Fifth and finally, I seek to demonstrate through the refugee issue that the sovereigntist movement, though concerned principally with a communitarian ethos, also respects individual rights.

REFUGEE POLICY IN CANADA

Why have Canadians allowed refugees to enter their country in the past? After the Second World War, refugee policy was overwhelmingly concerned with humanitarian refugees – people selected abroad under relaxed immigration criteria. Only in the last twelve years has the focus been on Convention Refugees, who arrive in Canada and claim the right to stay if they can prove that they are refugees in accord with the Geneva Convention, to which Canada is a signatory. But because humanitarian refugees were admitted as a result of government policy and deliberate action, in contrast to spontaneous arrivals, this history provides an excellent opportunity to understand Canadian motivation for admitting refugees.

Though such a historical overview reveals a wide range of motives, differing with each refugee movement, it is helpful to begin by comparing these motives to those behind the rest of the immigration program.[1] Canadian immigration policy in general has sought, first, to protect and develop economic growth by importing skills, expertise, and capital. Second, it has aimed at population growth, particularly to offset the low birth rate, especially in Quebec; Quebec has been anxious about the demographic issue, given its concern with maintaining its proportionate share of the Canadian population, most notably those who would reinforce the Québécois culture. Third, policy has been intended to keep a balance in Canada in the proportions of workers and of the aged. Fourth, it reflects a desire to maintain Canada as a country that stresses law, order, and good government while rewarding industry, diligence, and creativity.

Immigrants who have been admitted, based on skills, labour, or capital contribution, have been accepted because of Canada's needs and self-interest. The other major source of immigrants, those who enter under family reunification, were allowed admission based on a conception of the right of individuals in Canada to be reunited with members of their immediate family, a right that is rooted in the self-interest of those Canadian citizens, as well as the national interest in promoting family life and the happiness of its citizens. Enforced separation of family members would be detrimental to such goals.

In the case of refugees, in addition to self-interest, there has been another motivating factor – maintenance and development of Canada's role as a humanitarian country committed to helping resolve crises in the world. Each movement of refugees into Canada has been driven by a mixture of humanitarianism and self-interest. In some movements, self-interest has been the primary factor; in others, humanitarianism. Quebec has not expressed opposition to any of these movements. On the contrary, it has frequently actively supported admission, even though, in most cases, the majority of the refugees were drawn toward the anglophone culture and increased the proportion of anglophones in Canada. This was true of the Hungarians in 1956, the Czechs in 1968, the American draft dodgers and deserters through the late 1960s and early 1970s, the Ugandan Asians and Chileans in 1973, the Indochinese beginning after 1975, and the Central Americans through the 1980s.

However, these *humanitarian* refugees were allowed entry under relaxed immigration criteria. And, as I indicate below, Quebec did eventually insist on controlling selection of these refugees. The only ones given the right to enter, without any reference to whether their arrival served Canadian self-interest, were those who entered Canada and claimed refugee status. It is to that group that I now turn.

REFUGEE DETERMINATION POLICY

By the mid-1980s, there began an explosive growth in the number of individuals who arrived in Canada and made a refugee claim. Early in the decade, spontaneous arrivals could be counted in the hundreds. Between 1983 and 1986, the numbers grew from 6,000 per year to 18,000. In 1990, there were 36,000 claims. Canada had used an administrative system for determining refugee claims until a constitutional challenge appeared before the Supreme Court of Canada using the Charter of Rights and Freedoms, which had been proclaimed on 17 April 1982. "In *Re Singh and Minister of Employment and Immigration [1985]* 1 SCR 177, [it was] decided that the procedural guarantees of the *Charter of Rights and Freedoms* extended to foreign, non-resident refugee claimants, and that the existing determination system was unconstitutional."[2]

As a result, Canada switched to a quasi-judicial, or adjudicative model for dealing with refugee claims. Canadian law still laid out grounds of entry and criteria for determination of refugee status within the bounds of the Refugee Convention. But Ottawa surrendered administrative control to a 'rights' regime, administered by a system subject to review according to accepted standards of justice.

Introducing such a system has been costly. By the later 1980s, refugee claimants created significant difficulties for the Canadian policy process. They posed a problem of increasing and uncontrollable numbers. There were high costs of processing and greater demand for language and other settlement services. Some people even argued that the same funds could aid many more refugees overseas than those being assisted in Canada.

The government introduced new laws in an attempt to control the intake. Under Bill C-55, for example, arrival of self-selected refugee claimants would, it was hoped, be controlled by use of a safe-third-country provision which permitted the Canadian federal cabinet to designate nations as safe if claimants had sojourned there en route to Canada and if those countries had signed the Geneva Convention and did not *refoule* refugees back to the homelands from which they fled and where they would be in danger. Refugee claimants who sojourned more than 48 hours in such countries, where they could have made a refugee claim but did not, could be sent back there without a hearing. Behind the legislation was an attempt to ensure that any nation that was generous in interpreting the Geneva Convention would not get saddled with a disproportionate number of refugee claims. Meanwhile, whether because of foreign policy considerations or practicality in arranging the return of the claimants, no nation has ever been designated as a safe third country.

Clearly, the right to exclude, the right to establish the basis for such exclusion, the criteria for limitation and selection (in juxtaposition to Canadian obligations to specific groups), and the right to establish the conditions for entry – in other words, the sovereign right to control who could and who could not become members of the Canadian polity – had been seriously qualified by Canada's granting the right to become a Canadian to virtually anyone who arrived in the country and made a successful refugee claim before a quasi-judicial panel. Canada did not choose Convention Refugees. Refugee claimants alone, who arrive and can prove that they qualified as refugees under a set of norms, chose Canada. Canada had qualified its sovereignty in an unprecedented way. So had Quebec.

There was a growing perception that the refugee claims system was attracting and allowing through not only those targeted for persecution or associated with targeted groups but also those fleeing situations of general violence and disastrous economic situations created by war and environmental disasters. A generous interpretation of the norms governing the convention led many Canadians to believe that many others than those who were strictly Convention Refugees were gaining admission.

This meant that the numbers could increase exponentially and, under quasi-independent adjudication could not be controlled by the Immigration Department (though it could somewhat reduce numbers by imposing visa requirements on sending countries and fining airlines for transporting refugee claimants to Canada with false documents).

The large numbers of claimants[3] (36,000 in 1990, and 31,000 in 1991) seemed to threaten to continue growing. Since the figures rose again in 1992 (though they declined in 1993 and are expected to total just over 20,000 in 1994), there was a perception that claimants could make up a significant portion of the immigration intake, especially since their acceptance rate was high – averaging 75 percent of all claimants in 1990. Though the acceptance rate declined to just over 65 percent in 1991, in the first nine months of 1994 it had again risen, to 69 percent. Further, the deportation rate was low. As a result, there was a widespread belief, supported by some data, that the migration stream could increasingly be made up of those who chose Canada rather than of immigrants whom Canada or Quebec chose.

In addition to there being concern over types of refugees being allowed entry and the large numbers making claims, especially given the small numbers deported, the program was very expensive relative to any other form of intake, because of case-by-case adjudication. Even some humanitarians suggested that this program diverted funds that could better help refugees overseas at far less cost per refugee.

Some observers feared that a monster had been unleashed, with all the paraphernalia of legal approaches – including postponed hearings, long delays, lawyers with vested interests in the system, and a legal-aid and welfare-support system paid for by the provinces. It was believed that the fairest and most generous system had ended up attracting a disproportionate number of cases; the greater the generosity of approach, the greater the burden borne.

In this context, there seemed to be more than enough reason for Quebec to become involved in refugee policy, particularly since it made such strenuous efforts to attain control over immigration.

QUEBEC AND IMMIGRATION POLICY

A central element in the tug-of-war between Quebec and Ottawa has been control over immigration. The Constitution Act, 1867, granted the federal government ultimate control over immigration but placed responsibility for implementation with the provinces. It permitted provinces the right to make immigration laws, provided that they were not repugnant to federal legislation.[4] Since many Quebecers view their predominantly Québécois culture as threatened with extinction, partially because of the very low birth rate in the province, as well as immigrants' tendency to assimilate into the English rather than the French culture, they view immigration as a key to cultural survival.[5] The federal Immigration Act, 1976, shifted power to the centre by giving adjudicative authority over immigration issues to the Federal Court, whereas it had previously rested with the provincial courts. However, the act required cooperation between Ottawa and the provinces in the area of adaptation while mandating that the bilingual character of Canada be maintained.[6]

Thus Quebec and Ottawa negotiated the Cullen-Couture agreement of 1978, which, instead of simply letting the province implement federal programs, allowed its Immigration Review Board to determine who could be selected for entry into Quebec from abroad and which residents could sponsor relatives, provided that such selection and sponsorship procedures and practices did not contravene federal policies. Quebec then set up its own Department of Immigration and actively sought out immigrants who would reinforce the French-speaking majority in the province.

Control over immigration was one of the five demands that Quebec made leading up to the Meech Lake Accord.[7] Constitutional transfer of powers and financial resources to Quebec to control immigration was part of that accord.[8] Following the failure of Meech Lake, the federal government, through intergovernmental arrangements, transferred to Quebec the resources and authority needed to implement resettlement programs for immigrants headed for Quebec, since control of selection and intake had already been transferred.

The Canada-Quebec Accord Relating to Immigration and Temporary Admission of Aliens, 1991 (File M.Law, 1991, 0013), set out the terms of cooperation on the selection and settlement of foreign nationals wishing to settle in Quebec "in order to provide Quebec with new means to preserve its demographic importance to Canada, and to ensure the integration of immigrants in Québec in a manner that respects the distinct identity of Québec."[9] Whereas Canada retained sole responsibility for admission of immigrants under the family and assisted-relative classes and for the criteria of selection of the family class, Quebec could establish criteria for selection for assisted relatives and for the actual selection of both classes. Further, Quebec would determine and apply any financial criteria for family members sponsoring relatives. Quebec's consent was also required for admitting foreign students not chosen under government assistance programs for developing countries, foreign temporary workers, and foreign visitors who arrive in Canada for medical treatment.

Quebec also assumed effective control over the intake of humanitarian refugees but yielded exclusive control over Convention Refugees to Ottawa. With respect to selected refugees (chosen overseas on humanitarian grounds), those picked by Ottawa and destined for Quebec are required to meet Quebec's selection criteria. Further, if they meet the latter standards, they must be admitted by Canada unless they are members of a nonadmissible class. However, in the case of Convention Refugees, the federal government alone makes such a determination. If permanent-resident status is granted to such a refugee, Quebec's consent is not required.

CONTROL OF REFUGEE DETERMINATION

The Quebec government, in the accord of 1991, agreed to leave refugee determination in Ottawa's hands, though it assumed effective control over the intake of humanitarian refugees and other immigrants. Further, neither the Liberals nor the Parti québécois, when in power, sought to take over processing of refugee claimants who arrive in Canada and apply to remain as refugees.

This omission appears odd for at least five reasons. First, successful refugee claimants were in the 1980s by far the fastest-growing source of landed immigrants. Whereas in 1980 the numbers were negligible, by 1990 they constituted 15 percent of the total. Why would Quebec not seek control of a significant and growing segment of migration to Quebec when the takeover of the immigrant program is so central to the platforms of both of Quebec's political parties?

Second, it is not difficult to spot refugees who are most likely to settle in Quebec. Immigrants overseas may ask to be processed for entry into Canada by Quebec officials because they believe it easier to get through the Quebec door, assuring these officials that they intend to settle in the province, while planning to move to Toronto or to a western destination after arrival. Refugee claimants do not pose the same problem. They already live in Montreal, and their claims are being processed there. Quebec could ask for control of the refugee adjudicators appointed in Quebec and to administer the Montreal office. Further, assuming that proportionate funds for refugee determination were transferred to Quebec, as they have been in administration of immigration policy, appointments to the Refugee Board would be under the province's control.

Third, part of the debate between Ottawa and Quebec is over waste of financial resources and limiting of expenditures. The refugee determination system is very costly. Total expenditures for 1991 are estimated at $300 million, of which Quebec's proportion is some $75 million.[10] The cost per refugee claimant rejected and deported is estimated at from $40,000 to $100,000.[11] The system touches one of the most sensitive areas of concern to Quebec – immigration. Yet Quebec has made no overtures to take over the part of the program administered in Quebec, and an explicit agreement cedes exclusive control to Ottawa.

Fourth, no area of immigration is as central to sovereignty as the refugee issue. No immigrant has the right to claim status in Canada. An individual who arrives on Canadian shores and makes a successful refugee claim has virtually an automatic right to become a citizen. Sovereignty involves the ability to select who can and who cannot become members of one's own society.[12] To the extent that a state surrenders power over this issue, it has qualified its absolute sovereignty.[13] In fact, the debate over Bill C-55 focused on the unwillingness of mandarins in Canada Employment and Immigration to cede control over numbers and selection of refugee claimants. Yet in this one crucial area, Quebec has never made any claims.

Fifth, central to the debate between federal Liberals and both Quebec's Liberal party and the Parti québécois is Quebec's apparent preference for a communitarian ideology over a human rights one. The universalist thesis on human rights holds that the rights of individuals are prior to and transcend states; the communitarian thesis, that rights are an offshoot of the development of state and interstate law and practice as manifestations of a society's values. Strong communitarians adapt a prescriptive thesis as well: human rights must be made subordinate to the needs of national survival and development. The rights of refugees to claim status in Canada would seem to derive from an internationalist human rights perspective. Why would Quebec's major parties, both with a strong communitarian ideological streak, not seek power over the refugee determination system, which is built on such a different ideology and which allows a large intake of migrants, with Quebec having no say over numbers and selection?

Central to the issue of refugees is the question of justice for those individuals who lack membership in a state that guarantees their protection. Once they are on the territory of "your" state, presumably built on a principle of justice, they claim the protection of "your" state. A litmus test of that state's belief in justice is its protection of refugees. If Quebec had indeed opted out of a fundmental commitment to a just society in preference to use of state power (even in an only moderately oppressive way) to ensure at least minimal cultural homogeneity (if only in language) – that is, if it had retreated from pluralism toward a community "marked by a greater degree of moral, religious, or cultural homogeneity"[14] – its treatment of refugees would be an indicator of such a shift.

SOVEREIGNTY AND THE REFUGEE ISSUE

I now turn to the link between the motivation underpinning the push for Quebec sovereignty and the refugee issue. As I have shown, Convention Refugees are not selected on the basis of what they contribute to the economy; further, the selection process is very expensive. If the motivation for Quebec separatism is economic, one might expect Quebec to raise some objections to the system or insist on some control and input. The fact that it has not done so suggests that economic considerations are not a primary factor in the push for sovereignty.

An alternative thesis is that Quebec separatism is not about economics at all but about values. Some people claim that, in the 1980s, a big divide emerged between Quebecers and other Canadians over the Charter of Rights and Freedoms. The Charter, it is argued, followed the American model of emphasizing the rights of the individual. Anglophone Canada embraced the Charter as the holy grail of its values as a political community. By contrast, Quebec stressed the collective goal of the survival of the French community and the French culture in Quebec and, to this end, was prepared to override the Charter through use of the "notwithstanding clause."[15] Thus, to some, the issue of separation should be construed as a debate over the good versus the right. Do rights trump the public good, or does the interest of advancing the public good, in the form of strengthening the French culture, language, and community in Quebec, override rights?: "Here are two incompatible views of liberal society ... The resistance to the distinct society [of the Meech Lake Accord] which called for precedence to be given to the Charter came in part from a spreading procedural outlook in English Canada ... coq [Canada outside Quebec] saw that the 'distinct society' clause legitimated collective goals. And Quebec saw the move to give the Charter precedence imposed a form of liberal society that was alien and to which Quebec could never accommodate itself without surrendering its identity."[16]

The refugee issue appears to be a critical mode of determining whether Quebec believes that the public good trumps rights and whether the trump occurs in such a form that procedural justice has to be set aside in the interests of sustaining the public good. Elaboration of the laws and protections afforded refugees was given its thrust forward by the Charter, as I indicated above in reference to the Singh case. Quebec's attitude on the issue would seem to indicate that sovereigntists' claims, whether within the Canadian federation or in a separate Quebec, are being pursued while individual rights are being upheld. This would suggest that Quebec's quest for sovereignty is primarily a liberal one; it is not based on nativist sentiment or a power grab. Nor does it seem to be based primarily on a sense of injustice or a different sense of justice.

CONCLUSION

There is no evidence that Quebec has planned a takeover of the Convention Refugee determination system for a later date, and every reason to accept the word of its government that this is a matter properly left to Ottawa while Quebec remains within Confederation. First, intake and selection of immigrants are critical to the province's population policy. The Convention Refugee system completely removes intake and selection from mandarin control and places them under a quasi-judicial system.

Second, there appears to be no significant difference in the humanitarian underpinnings of Quebec and the rest of Canada. Both seem to have the same commitment to humanitarian values.

Third, if the European model is any indication, there is a tendency to relegate rights to tribunals that go beyond the borders of sovereign states as long as assignment of such jurisdiction poses no direct challenge to a communitarian commitment and to preservation of a distinct society. In other words, Quebec might have no interest in taking over the refugee determination system even if it became a sovereign state because the values that gave rise to that system are shared by most Quebecers and because it is a rights issue best adjudicated at a level higher than that of a sovereign state. Precisely because refugee determination is not a matter of sovereign control, it can be left to Ottawa or to a supranational jurisdiction. Defence of nationalism is not incompatible with pursuit of justice and defence of individual rights, even if a higher priority is granted to communitarian self-preservation.

I began this chapter by positing that refugee claimants are a group of people not chosen by Canadians for admission into membership. Because they are not chosen (choosing new members is central to sovereignty), the issue would appear to provide a unique insight into Quebecers' quest for increased or total sovereign control. But neither of the Quebec's political parties has indicated an interest in taking over the refugee claims system. Both have insisted on assuming control over immigration intake into Quebec. Refugees make up a significant percentage of immigrant intake. Further, the determination program is costly. Yet Quebec has not pushed for control over the system in spite of the impression that it seems willing to sacrifice rights to the communitarian goals.

I suggested above that its attitude to refugees could indicate the character of Quebec's sovereignty movement, its conception of justice, and the priority that it gives to rights. Is Quebec willing to sacrifice protection of rights to preserve its communitarian goals? Is the movement for sovereignty motivated by economic self-interest or by resentment against the principles or practices of distributive justice in Canada? Since different groups of refugees have been brought or allowed entry into Canada for both self-interested and humanitarian motives, and there appears to be virtually no economic self-interest in allowing refugee claimants entry into Canada, the refugee issue allows us to gain some insight into Quebec's priorities.

My conclusion is that the sovereignty movement is not motivated primarily by economic self-interest or resentment against a misaligned system of distributive justice. In fact, the refugee test suggests that Quebec shares virtually the same high value given to both rights and the plight of refugees. The thesis that Quebec and the rest of Canada have grown apart in values and on the priority of rights would seem to be incorrect. The issue gives no indication that Quebec is willing to sacrifice protection of individual rights for preservation of the French language and culture and the quest by the separatists to obtain for this unique identity an independent status on the world stage.

NOTES

1 Cf. Howard Adelman, "Canadian Refugee Policy in the Postwar Period: An Analysis," in *Refugee Policy: Canada and the United States*, ed. Howard Adelman (Toronto: York Lanes Press, 1991), 172–223.

2 David Cox and Patrick Glenn, "Illegal Immigration and Refugee Claims," in *Immigration and Refugee Policy: Australia and Canada Compared*, I, ed. Howard Adelman et al. (Toronto: University of Toronto Press, 1994), 296. Harbhajan Singh and six others claimed a right to an oral hearing when making a refugee claim under Canadian rights legislation. In the Supreme Court of Canada's decision of 4 April 1985, all six justices hearing the cases agreed that an oral hearing was required, dividing only on whether the Charter of Rights or the Bill of Rights (1960) justified the decision. Cf. also David Matas with Ilana Simon, *Closing the Doors: The Failure of Refugee Protection* (Toronto: Summerhill Press, 1989), 119–21.

3 All figures are taken from the quarterly statistical reports of the Immigration and Refugee Board.

4 Cf. Julius Gray, *Immigration Law in Canada* (Scarborough: Butterworths, 1984).

5 Cf. Gil Remillard, "L'Accord constitutionnel de 1987 et repatriement du Québec au sein fédéralisme canadien," in *L'adhesion du Québec à l'Accord du Lac Meech: Points de vue juridiques et politiques* (Montreal: Editions Themis, 1988); Clare F. Beckton and A. Wayne Mackey, *Recurring Issues in Canadian Federalism* (Toronto: University of Toronto Press, 1986); and Allan Blakeney, *Current Issues in Canadian Federalism* (Toronto: Osgoode Hall Law School, 1988). See also Alice A. Pellegrino, "Meech Lake and the Canadian Constitutional Crisis: The Problem of Provincial Immigration Control in Federalist Nations," *Georgetown Immigration Law Journal*, 5 no. 1 (Winter 1991), 760.

6 Cf. Immigration Act, 1976, which allows Ottawa to enter into agreements with provinces to "facilitate the formulation, coordination and implementation of immigration policies and programs."

7 Cf. "Reforming the Constitution: The Meech Lake Accord," *Canadian Parliamentary Review*, 10 no. 3 (Autumn 1987), 18–28.

8 Cf. Brian Mulroney, "Canada's Constitution: The Meech Lake Accord," *Parliamentarian*, 69 no. 3 (July 1988), 141–5. Section 95B(1) of the Meech Lake Accord granted to "any agreement concluded between Canada and a province in relation to immigration ... the force of law," thus eliminating the possibility of any constitutional challenge to the Cullen-Couture agreement of 1978.

9 This is an equivocal way of saying that Quebec must preserve its proportionate share of the Canadian population. "For years, the English–French ratio in Canada was about 70–30. Then, in the sixties, immigration began to rise and the birthrate among Canada's francophones began to plummet, causing a dramatic drop in their numbers across Canada. From census to census, the decline has been inexorable. From 1951 to 1991, their numbers dropped from 29 per cent to 24 per cent." *Globe and Mail*, 10 Dec. 1994, D2.

10 Cf. "Refugee Determination Bill C-55 Revisited," *Refuge*, 11 no. 2 (Dec. 1991). The total costs consist of $90 million in direct costs for the Refugee Board, $60 million in costs for legal counsel for the refugee claimants, and another $150 million in welfare costs for claimants while their claims are being processed.

11 The high-end estimate comes from taking a maximum figure of 3,000 people a year deported and dividing this number into the total costs. This estimate does not include those who leave voluntarily or those who withdraw their claims.

12 "[T]he sovereign state must take shape and claim the authority to make its own admission policy, to control and sometimes restrain the flow of immigrants ... The restraint of entry serves to defend the liberty and welfare, the politics and culture of a group of people committed to one another and their common life." Michael Walzer, *Spheres of Justice: A Defence of Pluralism and Equality* (New York: Basic Books, 1983), 39.

13 Howard Adelman, "Refuge or Asylum: A Philosophical Perspective," *Journal of Refugee Studies*, 1 no. 1 (1988), 7–20.

14 William A. Galston, "Pluralism and Social Unity," *Ethics*, 99 (July 1989), 717. The whole point raised in this section was inspired by Galston's paper.

15 "Quebec feels that its distinct culture is threatened by the Charter of Rights which was carved into the Canadian constitution in 1982." Pellegrino, "Meech Lake," 760.

16 Charles Taylor, "Shared and Divergent Values" in *Reconciling the Solitudes: Essays on Canadian Federalism and Nationalism*, ed. Guy Laforest (Montreal and Kingston: McGill-Queen's University Press, 1993), 177; originally published in *Options for a New Canada*, ed. Ronald L. Watts and Douglas M. Brown (Toronto: University of Toronto Press, 1991), 53–76.

CHAPTER FOUR

From Provincial Autonomy to Provincial Equality (Or, Clyde Wells and the Distinct Society)

Robert Vipond

The most recent round of constitutional negotiations was supposed to be different from the Meech Lake round which preceded it – more inclusive, more open, and, as a result, more successful. It did not turn out that way. Like Meech, the Charlottetown Accord did not survive the process that produced it; it was rejected decisively in a national referendum. Despite the referendum and the mini-constitutional conferences that came before it, the process was still criticized for being elitist and anti-democratic. And while the referendum was defeated both in Quebec and in English Canada, the debate unfolded quite differently in the two places and underscored the impression that the constitutional fault lines between English Canada and Quebec run very deep.

The argument of this chapter is that the constitutional stalemate in which we find ourselves follows from a fundamental, but incomplete and contested, shift in the way many Canadians – especially English Canadians – think about federalism. I want to argue that much of the divisiveness of current Canadian politics stems from the pressure of two competing conceptions of federalism. The first, which can be traced to the Confederation settlement itself, is anchored to the venerable but still vital principle of provincial autonomy and is typically expressed in the liberal language of rights. The second, which is of more recent origin and threatens to overwhelm the first, centres on the notion of provincial equality and fairness. What do these rival conceptions entail? And in this land of different constitutional languages, is there some way to make them comprehensible to each other?

INDIVIDUAL AND PROVINCIAL RIGHTS:
THE LIBERAL CONNECTION

The core notion of provincial autonomy has been a powerful element in Canadian constitutional discourse since at least 1867. I have tried elsewhere to show that the concession of provincial autonomy (or independence) was crucial to Confederation in that some solid guarantee for government by local majorities was one – albeit only one – of the impulses that drove the movement for Confederation.[1] While not everyone may accept this archaeology, it is undeniable that, by the end of the nineteenth century, the principle of provincial autonomy had become the foundation of a formidable constitutional doctrine, an almost unassailable cliché of constitutional discourse.

In its mature form the constitutional doctrine of provincial autonomy consisted of three separate but related claims. First, Ottawa has no right to interfere in those subjects placed within the control of the provincial legislatures by the BNA Act, 1867 (now renamed the Constitution Act, 1867). In other words, provincial legislatures are sovereign or supreme within their jurisdiction just as, conversely, the federal government is sovereign within its sphere. By this account legislatures are independent of, not subordinate to, the federal Parliament – a proposition that became especially controversial when Ottawa attempted to use its open-ended veto power of disallowance to strike down provincial laws.

Second, true federalism requires a balanced division of powers between the central and provincial governments, such that neither level is able to overwhelm the other by virtue of clearly superior political resources. Here too there was controversy, for the autonomists' attempt to breathe life into provincial power over "property and civil rights" and "municipal institutions," among others, collided directly with John A. Macdonald's centralism. The ensuing skirmishes over jurisdiction absorbed an enormous amount of energy at the time, and they remain central to the unfolding constitutional story.

Third, provincial autonomy was expressed in terms of contractualism. The autonomists argued that Confederation was a pact or contract, though it has always been unclear whether the parties to the original contract were the various colonies that "had expressed their desire to be federally united" or the country's two founding (European) peoples. Either way, the assertion that Confederation was a contract whose terms could be changed only by the parties to the agreement was meant to legitimate a provincial role in amending the constitution. Though few have been persuaded by the compact theory itself, the myth of an original "Confederation deal" remains a powerful symbol in the ongoing amendment controversy.

Now, the story of provincial autonomy in Canada is usually told from the perspective of "the lawyer's constitution," in which legal cases involving the division of powers have pride of place and in which, therefore, the salience of provincial autonomy has been defined largely in terms of the size of provincial jurisdiction under section 92 of the Constitution Act, 1867. The case-oriented perspective is limiting in two ways, however. First, it underestimates the extent to which the ideology of provincial rights infiltrated political debate and so helped to shape not simply legal but political culture in Canada. Second, the tendency to understand provincial autonomy as a series of self-contained jurisdictional claims obscures the connection that the autonomists posited between federalism and liberalism, between provincial and individual rights.

What was this liberal connection all about? At the level of rhetorical strategy, the autonomists found it extremely useful to feed off the strength and appeal of classical liberalism by enlisting rights-based language to explain and justify the claims of provincial sovereignty. In retrospect, that seems natural enough. Most of the leading provincial autonomists identified themselves as liberals, and it is hardly surprising therefore that they saw an important connection between the struggle for provincial autonomy and the protection of liberty.

What is intellectually distinctive about the autonomists' expression, however, is the rather blunt and direct way in which they analogized individual and provincial rights. This analogy was especially useful in explaining why Ottawa had no right to disallow or veto provincial legislation within provincial jurisdiction. The argument was as powerful as it was simple: just as the state has no right to tell individuals what clothes they should wear or what religious opinions they should hold, so the federal government has no right to tell the provinces how they should act on matters assigned exclusively to them. As individual rights are meant to guarantee autonomy from the (liberal) state, so provincial rights are meant to protect autonomy from the (federal) state.[2] Both protect freedom of choice, and both rest on the assumption that power and responsibility should be conjoined "by leaving him who has the greatest possible motive to discover the right way and to follow it, to decide what shall be done."

The analogy between provincial and individual rights, however, cut both ways. For if individual rights could serve as the model for unconditional and absolute provincial rights, the analogy also served as a reminder that a provincial majority – a "faction," as the framers of the us constitution had put it – could quite easily violate the rights of an individual or minority. If individual rights were as sacrosanct as the autonomists' analogy suggested, then it was by no means clear that the best way to ensure individual liberty was to allow provincial legislatures complete freedom to act as they wanted on every matter constitutionally assigned to them. In that sense, the autonomists' appeal to individual rights was deeply paradoxical, for it introduced a wild card that could be used to limit the very provincial sovereignty that the autonomists were trying so hard to establish.

For people today, who have lived with the Charter of Rights for more than a decade, the deep tension in the autonomists' argument is too obvious to miss. If individual rights are such valuable political goods, they should be protected from all legislative majorities – including, and perhaps especially, provincial majorities. Yet in the heyday of the provincial rights movement, the tension between provincial and individual rights did not seriously weaken the autonomists' resolve. While most thoughtful observers in the early years of Confederation recognized that provincial majorities could act tyrannically, controlling provincial legislatures in the name of individual rights simply did not become the major issue that it easily could have.[3]

Why not? For one thing, John A. Macdonald's government chose for various reasons not to act as the defender of individual rights against intolerant provincial majorities. And in the absence of an American-style Bill of Rights and judicial review, there was really no other body to press for individual rights. Moreover, Canadians did not have a well-established tradition of fundamental- or natural-rights thought on which to draw. Most mainstream liberals in late-nineteenth-century Canada, whether provincial autonomists or not, were quick to concede that an individual's liberty could be limited quite legitimately in the name of some more important community goal. The extent of individual liberty typically came to depend on striking a balance between individual freedom and the public interest. And local legislatures could make the plausible claim that they should be the ones to weigh the various interests, since they best understood local needs, traditions, and traits.

Beyond this, however, the provincial autonomists blunted the rights critique by turning the question of individual rights on its head. They believed deeply that the most dangerous threat to individual liberty came from elements without, not from factions within, the provinces. Educated in the Whig tradition of constitutional or political liberty, they were deeply suspicious of rule by any body other than "the people assembled in parliament." From their perspective, the federal government was a distant "foreign" power, disallowance was a throwback to the days when monarchs exercised arbitrary prerogative, and John A. Macdonald was an unscrupulous and self-serving representative of an aristocratic clique. It required no elaborate argument to convince Canadians schooled in the triumph of responsible and representative self-government that individual rights would be better protected by provincial legislatures, leaving the ultimate check to the electorate.[4] The autonomists were thus able to claim, rather successfully in fact, that provincial liberty and individual liberty are mutually reinforcing, not contradictory.

The synthesis of political with individual liberty was particularly compelling as a response to cultural, linguistic, and religious differences. Here, I think, an example may help. One of the more interesting parliamentary debates of the 1890s centred on the attempt, through the Lord's Day Act, to create a national, uniform regime of Sunday closing. The sponsors argued that a national law was necessary, whether to enforce a "natural law" or to produce well-rested and hence more productive workers.[5]

Most of the significant provincial autonomists, in contrast, opposed the act. Sabbatarian restrictions that regulated behaviour in this way were, in their view, clearly a matter of "civil rights" and so fell properly to the provincial legislatures. Besides, it was clearly a violation of religious liberty to force the country as a whole to live by the religious rules made in Protestant Ontario. If Ontario wanted to prevent rural post offices from remaining open on Sunday as part of a policy of honouring the sabbath, then its legislature should consider such a law. But such a prohibition should not be forced on those individuals – most notably, Catholic Quebecers – who interpreted the fourth commandment less strictly and who wanted to preserve the freedom to retrieve their mail on the way home from church. As one Quebec MP remarked pointedly: "When we joined Confederation, we joined it as a commercial partnership, and not as a salvation army. We do not believe in this Parliament turning itself into a salvation army, and with drums and fifes trying to force us into heaven."[6]

For the autonomists (including many from outside Quebec) this was an easy case: To support provincial control over Sunday closing was to back political and individual liberty, provincial rights and religious freedom. Since "they" were attempting to define "our" rights of conscience, it was easy to conflate individual and collective forms of liberty. Yet even when the autonomists spoke of the rights of those religious minorities outside the Protestant-Catholic mainstream – Jews and Seventh Day Adventists, for example – they still assumed that provincial legislatures were better equipped to deal with religious questions.[7] If the autonomists were worried that different moral and political standards would apply from province to province, or that local majorities would be intolerant of individuals and minorities within the provinces themselves, they rarely admitted it. The leading autonomists seem to have assumed that the various provincial communities were largely homogeneous, or at least tolerant. Either way, the real threat to diversity came from the misguided attempt to impose national, uniform standards on culturally, religiously, and linguistically distinct provinces.

At the time of Confederation, the logic of provincial autonomy was best understood in Quebec, and Québécois politicians and publicists articulated the principle with a clarity and precision that were unmatched. Thereafter, the doctrine's appeal broadened to become a truly national movement, and as it did so leadership shifted to the government of Ontario. Oliver Mowat, premier from 1872 until 1896, spearheaded a broad interprovincial assault on John A. Macdonald's centralism, and by the end of the century courts both in Canada and in Britain had given official recognition to provincial autonomy. Even a coterie of prominent national politicians – most of them Liberal, and many of them anglophone – considered themselves staunch defenders of provincial rights. Still, the logic of provincial autonomy was nowhere more compelling than in Quebec, and it is there, and perhaps only there, that it remains the central, organizing constitutional principle.

Now, it is obviously risky to assert a pattern of historical continuity against a background of massive social, economic, and political change. The development of modern Quebec nationalism has obviously changed the terms of political debate in that province, bringing with it neologisms such as sovereignty-association. Yet for all of the recent discussion about some post-federal political arrangement between Quebec and Canada, the dominant constitutional language in Quebec is anchored to the recognizable categories of provincial autonomy. Again, this should not be completely surprising, since the discourse of provincial autonomy combines the moral authority of history with political versatility. Thus when Marcel Masse, a prominent member of Brian Mulroney's Tory cabinet, broke ranks with his own leadership by criticizing the parliamentary blueprint for constitutional reform produced in September 1991, he stressed the continuity of Quebec's demands and the repeated historical failures to meet them. "I believe that Quebec forms a nation, and it has a will to live together, and it needs legislative powers to fashion itself," Masse is reported to have said. "That is the reality. And it flows from everything that has been sought from [nineteenth-century Quebec Premier Honoré] Mercier to Robert Bourassa."[8]

Even more striking is the official and current position of the Liberal party of Quebec, adopted at its annual convention in March 1991. The party's position, set out in what has come to be known as the Allaire Report, rests a proposal for a "new Quebec-Canada structure" squarely on a classic defence of provincial autonomy.[9] Like the early autonomists, Allaire is sharply critical of Ottawa's "centralizing practices," its "inflexible will to standardize public services to the utmost,"[10] and its attempts to meddle in matters in which it has no business interfering. Like the original provincialists, Allaire defines autonomy in terms of the ability to exercise exclusive constitutional authority in areas that touch on political and cultural distinctiveness.[11] And also like them, Allaire ultimately defends provincial autonomy as a form of collective freedom – a Quebec that has sufficient autonomy is a "A Quebec Free to Choose." This is turbo-charged, nationalist-driven provincial autonomy, but it remains within the boundaries of conventional Canadian discourse – at least for now.

There is still one crucial difference, however, between Allaire and the classic, nineteenth-century stance, and that concerns the relation between provincial autonomy and individual rights. It is not that Allaire ignores the question. On the contrary, he tries to reconcile provincial autonomy with individual rights in the old provincial-rights style. Thus he wants to establish that the most important problem of minority rights in Quebec is to protect Québécois from the majoritarian pressures imposed by the rest of Canada. He argues explicitly that protection of minority rights should not be a major problem in Quebec anyway, because where the rest of Canada "has become diversified through immigration and emerging regionalism," Quebec is "much more homogeneous and remains essentially 'French' in culture."[12] Quebec doesn't have the same problem of watching out for minorities, in other words, because it has a "high degree of social cohesion."[13] And even if protection of minorities were a problem, "throughout its history, Quebec society has demonstrated profound respect for rights and freedoms." In short, "Quebec is a tolerant society," and that tolerance is reinforced by the province's own charter of rights and freedoms.[14]

Whereas in the 1880s and 1890s the provincial autonomists had some success in arguing that provincial rights and individual liberty are mutually reinforcing, the same hypothesis is now greeted with considerably more scepticism. It should be obvious to anyone who has followed Canadian politics over the last several years that individual rights in Quebec – especially concerning language – have become an explosive issue. The autonomists of the late nineteenth century had no Bill 101 to address, no Charter of Rights to reconcile, and no Pierre Trudeau to outflank. These factors in themselves make the situation rather different.

Yet in a certain sense it seems to me that posing the problem this way – as if beatification of individual rights through the Charter were the fundamental impediment to mutually acceptable constitutional renewal – misses the point. The current constitutional crisis is not just about protection of individual rights, any more than the original doctrine of provincial autonomy was just about expanded provincial jurisdiction. Rather, it seems to me that the strong rights-based critique of Quebec's constitutional aspirations is best understood as part of a larger counter-theory of Canadian federalism, anchored to a conception of provincehood governed by equality rather than autonomy. If we hope to find a way beyond the current stalemate, we must find a way to reconcile the contending theories of provincial autonomy and provincial equality.

A NEW DOCTRINE: PROVINCIAL EQUALITY

Provincial autonomy did not go unchallenged in the late nineteenth century; nor, as even a casual observer of recent debates can attest, has Quebec's version of the same principle escaped criticism in the late twentieth century. That challenge issued from various sources and manifested itself in various ways, but one of the most powerful and oft-heard criticisms during the Meech phase (1987–90) was that Quebec's constitutional demands could not be reconciled with the constitutional equality of the provinces. How provincial equality came to achieve such rhetorical power so quickly is an intriguing question, but not the appropriate one to ask here. The point is simply that the notion is now widely accepted, at least in English Canada, as a fundamental precept of Canadian nationhood. Thus the Charlottetown Accord declared provincial equality to be one of the foundational principles on which the Canadian nation is built. And while many people found the so-called Canada clause wanting in many respects, few commentators seem to have found the commitment to provincial equality at all out of place.

My goal here is to explain what provincial equality means and how it collides with, or presents an obstacle to, provincial autonomy. In so doing, I want to pay particular attention to the defence of provincial equality developed by Clyde Wells, premier of Newfoundland. I have chosen to concentrate on him for several reasons. First, his name has become associated more closely with the idea than any other major participant in recent constitutional discussions, and he has gone out of his way to elaborate and operationalize it. Second, his attitude arguably provides some insight into the public constitutional mind; his defence of provincial equality captured the public's imagination at the time of the Meech debate, and he is one of the few national or provincial leaders who continues to enjoy public confidence and support.[15] Third, his relentless support for provincial equality illustrates the potential, but also the perils, of attempting to realize an ideal of federal community that is derived from contemporary liberalism.

The idea of provincial equality may have three separate, though related, meanings and applications. First, it could refer to the part played by the provinces in the amending process – a basic part of the constitutional deal of 1981–82 and a matter of some continuing controversy since. If provincial equality underlies the amending formula, one might argue that every province ought to have a veto over amendments – or, put the other way round, that all amendments should require the consent of all of the units affected by it.[16] Egalitarian principles could just as easily be used, however, to support a more majoritarian understanding in which each province is granted an equal voice and the majority (or a substantial majority) carries the day.

Both approaches seem in fact to lurk in the Constitution Act's complex amending rules – which may be why Wells has shied away from committing himself to a principled position on the matter. While he has said repeatedly that he opposes an amending formula that would require provincial unanimity, he has been careful to base his argument on a pragmatic consideration – namely, that a requirement of unanimity would almost certainly paralyse the amending process.[17] He has said explicitly, indeed, that from his perspective the principle of provincial equality does not govern the amending formula one way or the other.[18] For the purposes of this chapter at least, that is sufficient reason to lay the amending formula aside, important though it may be.

Second, provincial equality may refer to provincial representation in national institutions, most notably the Senate. This clearly is much closer to Wells's concerns. The premier's much-publicized support for a "Triple-E" Senate has been a central element in post-Meech constitutional discussions. Quebec's opposition to a Senate with equal representation for each province put the two sides on a direct collision course. And one can easily argue that the ingenious but wildly unpopular Charlottetown compromise – equal provincial representation in the Senate combined with firm guarantees for Quebec's representation in the House of Commons – would not have been necessary but for the perceived need to recognize the principle of provincial equality at all costs.

Wells himself, however, has never believed that a Senate based on equal provincial representation would threaten Quebec's constitutional interests and aspirations. He has always argued that a Triple-E Senate, if properly constructed, could actually be made to protect Quebec's distinctive interests at the national level.[19] And though it is a peculiar argument, it is not, I think, a disingenuous one. Wells really does believe that reform of national institutions on egalitarian principles will respond to regional discontent – including Quebec's.[20]

Third, provincial equality may take the form of what Wells typically calls legislative equality. The place to begin here is with the premier's explicit and much-publicized objections to the distinct society clause in the Meech Lake Accord. At the time, Wells insisted on analysing the provisions of the accord in light of the "fundamental principle" that "every province in any true federation is in its status and rights as a province ... equal to every other."[21] Wells claimed that he did not oppose some innocent constitutional recognition of the "fact" of Quebec's distinctness – in a constitutional preamble, for instance. But if, as he feared, the clause found in Meech would allow Quebec to claim "special" legislative powers or rights not available to other provinces, then the constitution would sanction a form of inequality and preference that he simply could not bring himself to support. Wells insisted that the constitution must not "create a special legislative status for one province different from that of the other nine provinces,"[22] and this argument from provincial equality quickly became a touchstone for public opposition to Meech.

Legislative equality is a catchy slogan, but what does it mean exactly? It will help us "unpack" Mr. Wells's opposition to Meech to understand that in articulating his misgivings he used the term *legislative equality* to refer to two different, but related, phenomena. On the one hand, he worried that the Meech version of the distinct society clause would permit Quebec's national assembly to infringe individual rights within Quebec, in a way that would be unacceptable elsewhere, on the pretext of cultural survival. The Meech version "undermines the integrity of the

Charter of Rights and Freedoms" because it "clearly allows the Quebec legislature to override Charter rights with laws designed to preserve and promote the distinct society."[23] Though Wells typically eschewed the giving of examples, his audiences would have filled in the blank here with any number of real or imagined possibilities – beginning with the threat to individual language rights posed by Bill 101.

On the other hand, Wells feared that Quebec would use the distinct society clause to claim greater and special jurisdictional authority over matters that were otherwise within federal jurisdiction, thus creating a form of "asymmetrical" federalism in which one of the "supposedly equal provinces [would have] a legislative jurisdiction in excess of that of the other provinces." In short, Wells was concerned with both possible contraction of individual rights and expansion of jurisdictional powers, thus combining the old with the new critique of provincial autonomy.

During the Meech debate, Wells was careful not to commit himself to a particular understanding of what basic rights must be protected or what the best division of powers might look like. Instead, by emphasizing equality, he made universality or uniformity the test of constitutional propriety. The premier's basic premise thus was that "all Canadians have common rights and freedoms regardless of where we live."[24] And the Meech Lake Accord was defective because, if it were allowed to pass, "the nature of our basic rights would henceforth vary depending on the province in which we live, and the linguistic group to which we belonged."[25] From the Wellsian perspective, the accord would not simply permit an assault on the Charter and individual rights. The real problem was broader – namely, that Meech would have introduced difference and unevenness, both as to rights and to powers, where equality was meant to prevail. In his case at least, the conflict at the heart of Meech therefore was not between the Charter and federalism, or between individual and collective rights, much less between those who respect rights and those who don't. The conflict rather was exactly what he and the Quebec government said it was: a collision between two understandings of community, one tied to the universal implications of equality, the other more sensitive to the diversity that follows from autonomy.

INDIVIDUAL V. PROVINCIAL EQUALITY

The question I want to pose is simply this. Is there any way to reduce the tension between Quebec's claims of provincial autonomy and Clyde Wells's interpretation of the principle of provincial equality?

Let me explore one line of reasoning to see if it will help loosen the Gordian knot. Recall, first of all, that the power of the doctrine of provincial autonomy derived in part from the deep analogy between federalism and liberalism. Provinces in a federal system are like individuals in the liberal state – they ought to be given the greatest freedom to act that is consistent with the public/national good. One may object that this identification between provinces and individuals commits a "category" error in that it anthropomorphizes the federal system and conflates the individual and the governmental. However that may be, the analogy is deeply entrenched in Canadian constitutional discourse, and I want to pursue the rhetorical possibilities of intermixing different forms of equality.

Now, in almost every major speech devoted to constitutional issues, Clyde Wells has said that provincial equality is only one of several species of a more general principle of equality that must guide constitutional reform. He sees three equalities as fundamental "precepts" of the Canadian nation. Thus just as "every province in any true federation is in its status as a province ... equal to every other," so "every citizen is, in his or her status and rights as a citizen, equal to every other." And just as citizens have equal rights, so "the two founding linguistic cultures" are equal.[26]

But what does equality mean in this (triple) context? Consider individuals' or citizens' equality. At a minimum, it means that seats in the House of Commons must be apportioned according to population so as not to exaggerate the influence of one class of persons.[27] Beyond this, "it is important" that citizens have "equal opportunities" to promote their well-being.[28] The difficulty in creating such equality, however, is that citizens find themselves differently situated and, through no fault of their own, require different material conditions in order to attain "equal well-being."[29] It is a respectable liberal argument, therefore, to say that equality of opportunity properly understood need not, and perhaps cannot, always entail equal or identical treatment. Ronald Dworkin has summarized this position neatly by noting the difference between equal treatment and treatment as an equal, and he believes that liberals can support both without contradiction.[30]

Few liberals, for instance, question the fairness of making special efforts to ensure that physically disabled citizens have access to public buildings – even though provision of wheelchair ramps, wide doors, and special elevators will increase construction and maintenance costs. Most liberals can support affirmative-action programs for women or racial minorities to the extent that they attempt to overcome a legacy of systematic exclusion, marginalization, and unequal treatment. Such programs do not treat women or racial minorities identically and universally; indeed, their purpose is precisely to provide some (usually) modest advantages as a way of overcoming explicit and implicit barriers to career choice and advancement.

Moreover, this liberal argument has been extended in Canada in a way that blurs the boundary between individual and province. Since at least the days of Pierre Trudeau's governments, for instance, regional development policies have been premised on the observation that some provinces and regions require extra resources to ensure that their citizens enjoy services reasonably comparable to those provided in more affluent regions. Such grants are paid directly to provincial governments, we call them equalization payments, they enjoy constitutional status, and Clyde Wells himself defends them explicitly as an example of, rather than an exception to, the equality principle.[31] Or consider section 6(4) of the Constitution Act, 1982, which permits provinces with higher-than-average unemployment (and only those provinces) to give preference in hiring to their own residents over people who have migrated from other provinces. This is affirmative action, for that is what the Constitution Act explicitly calls it.[32] Yet it makes sense to label it thus only if one believes that provinces, not just individuals, suffer disadvantages that can and should be ameliorated.

If the principle of equality of opportunity is robust enough to support legislative initiatives on behalf of some individuals and "have-not" provinces, then why may it not be used to support the claim that Quebec's cultural vulnerability may require it to act differently from other provinces? If it does not violate the equality principle to support the physically disabled, then why should it violate the equality principle to support cultural and demographic minorities, recognizing that this challenge may require non-identical treatment in some form or another?

I have put this argument in my own voice, but others have made it as well.[33] Indeed, as he searched for a way to move beyond the post-Meech constitutional stalemate, even Wells began to toy with the possibility that Quebec's constitutional demands, properly understood, need not contradict the equality principle. In a speech before Newfoundland's legislature in October 1991, he reiterated his commitment to the "three equalities" and continued: "While these precepts emphasize the equality of citizens and the equality of the provinces, Newfoundland has never maintained that every constitutional provision must be precisely the same in respect of every province. We have, in the past, suggested variations that are appropriate to the circumstances. Any special accommodation, however, must result in a fair and balanced treatment of all Canadians of whatever language, race or place of residence. Canadians may not insist on absolutely identical or equal treatment for individuals and provinces but I believe that they will insist that preferential treatment for any province is unacceptable." Wells drew out the implication for the distinct society clause: "While philosophically I personally, and perhaps the vast majority of Canadians, would prefer to see the Charter apply to every part of the country and to each individual in exactly the same manner, if the majority of citizens of Quebec want their individual Charter rights to be somewhat subordinated to their collective rights, then it is difficult for the citizens of any other province to say we don't want to see that happen in Quebec." And he concluded: "Some limited subordination of individual rights to collective rights within Quebec, if that is what the people of Quebec want, may not be an unreasonable concession to accommodate the legitimate concerns of a province that is, by reason of its culture, language and legal system, distinctly different from any other province in the country."[34]

This is a remarkable statement and, despite Wells's disclaimer about continuity, one that moved significantly beyond his position throughout the Meech debate. The admission that a substantive distinct society clause is essentially consistent with the principle of equality is striking, coming from the man who argued throughout the Meech debate that "recognition of Quebec as a distinct society in the preamble to the Constitution, would not and should not, impact on the Charter of Rights and Freedoms."[35] Having proposed that the equality principle is essentially inconsistent with creation of a "special legislative status different from that of the other nine provinces,"[36] he now suggested that Quebec ought to be able to act in certain ways that other provinces cannot – if that is necessary to preserve and protect its distinctness.

Now, one can explain the premier's shift in a number of ways. He may have softened his position when he saw that the post-Meech version of the distinct society clause was weaker than the original[37] or when he realized that Newfoundland had less leverage in the "Canada Round" of negotiations. Still, I think it important to understand him on his own rhetorical terms. His shift may have something to do with his thinking through the implications of provincial equality in the same way that many liberals have thought through individual equality. And that means that any attempt to realize equality among the provinces has to acknowledge differences among them – which is, as it happens, the nub of the theory of provincial autonomy.

So Wells ultimately came round to support inclusion of the same distinct society clause supported by Quebec. He signed on to the Charlottetown Accord. After a slow start he went on the road to defend it as "a fair and honourable compromise." And it may not be coincidental that of all the provinces Newfoundland voted most heavily in favour of the accord on 26 October 1992.

Yet in retrospect what seems most significant is both how hesitant[38] Wells was in embracing the 1992 agreement and how carefully circumscribed his position was. As noted above, he typically applies the equality principle both to individual rights and to provincial powers. His remarks of October 1991, however, were directed only to the Charter. Thus where he suggested that Quebec may be allowed to define individual rights differently as a way of protecting what is "distinctly different" about that province, he said nothing about granting Quebec different or more powers than other provinces to achieve the same goal. In other words, where he was prepared to talk about an asymmetrical regime of rights protection, he would not sanction asymmetrical federalism.[39] This was a crucial qualification, for by it he closed off one potential avenue for constitutional reconciliation that enjoyed a certain support among constitution-watchers. More important, in setting out his reservations he managed to articulate what turned out to be the most powerful objection to the accord as a whole.

Wells's public agonizing over the distinct society clause showed the real limits of attempting to defend Quebec's aspirations as if the constitution were an affirmative-action program. Caught between the liberal ideal of "fairness" and the liberal distaste for "preference," Wells's approach to the clause betrays the same deep ambivalence that informs Canadian attitudes to affirmative action. It is quite elastic and potentially sympathetic but, when push comes to shove, still largely hostile to anything that smacks of "special treatment" – which is exactly why Wells thought it necessary to qualify his support so carefully.[40] From his perspective, it is permissible to allow Quebec to limit specified individual rights in the name of some larger collective goal. Such action is "fair" in light of Quebec's deeply held belief that its cultural integrity depends on such actions. Besides, such policies really affect directly only the people of Quebec, and it is reasonably easy for the premier of another province to regard this as a purely internal matter that does not affect his own interests directly.[41]

But it would be quite "unbalanced" and "unfair," according to Wells, to give Quebec a "special" status that would allow it to legislate on matters over which other provinces have no jurisdiction, for that would impinge on the interests and, more decisive, the sensibilities of other Canadians. To recognize the special constitutional status of Quebec would be to grant a "preference" to one part of the community that is not available to others, and that flies in the face of liberal justice, which requires that political goods be distributed "fairly" and in a "balanced" way – that is, according to "objective criteria"[42] such as merit or need. Some of the early versions of the distinct society clause upset the liberal balance by creating special legislative status for Quebec. Having argued that it was perhaps reasonable to allow "some limited subordination of individual rights to collective rights in Quebec," Wells proceeded, in the same speech, to worry about the implications of allowing that the government of Quebec had a "special responsibility ... to preserve and protect its distinct society." "Again, much will depend on the form this statement ultimately takes. One has to be concerned about how a court will interpret this in the future. Would the court conclude that this responsibility is limited to the extent to which it can be discharged within the existing provincial powers of the government and legislature in Quebec or would the court see it as a separate responsibility beyond the existing responsibilities and find that Quebec must, therefore, have whatever additional governmental or legislative jurisdiction is necessary in order to enable that responsibility to be discharged?" The possibility of such an expansive interpretation was clearly troubling. "If successful this could result in a special legislative status for Quebec that no other province would have."[43]

For Wells, it would seem, any deviation from the principle of equality bears the burden of proving that such special consideration is necessary. As he told the Beaudoin-Dobbie Special Joint Committee (of the House and Senate) in January 1992, the onus is on those who would "temper" the principle of equality understood as equal treatment to show that their approach will produce "fair and balanced treatment for all Canadians wherever they live or whatever their racial origin or language." "Constitutional provisions cannot result in special status or legislative power for one province or territory that others do not enjoy, and cannot result in a privileged position or superior benefits for one group of citizens over others. There must be no constitutionally provided unfairness or imbalance between Canadian citizens or Canadian provinces."[44] And it is clear that, from Wells's perspective, Quebec's case for a strong distinct society clause with broad legislative implications fails the fairness test.

Moreover, in his view, the creation of a "preferential position" for Quebec would create a system of first- and second-class citizenship in Canada. And that, he says, would be an affront to citizens in the rest of the country, who have "a sense of their culture and their personal worth" and who would be "personally offended by any suggestion that in any degree they are somehow ordinary and Quebec is distinct."[45] Nor is that merely an abstract consideration. Like many opponents of social equity programs, Wells argues that "preferential treatment" of Quebec would be counterproductive, because it would create resentment, and that in turn "would serve only to increase prejudices and drive an even bigger wedge between English and French Canadians."[46] So Wells wanted to accommodate Quebec; but – and here is a classic example of conflating individual and governmental – "the people of Quebec must also understand the rest of the country has a soul too."[47]

Wells was certainly right about one thing. He predicted that a constitutional proposal that "results in unfairness or imbalance will not ... be accepted by the majority of the Canadian people," and the 1992 referendum proved him right. The Charlottetown Accord, which he ultimately defended as a "fair and honourable compromise," apparently was judged to be neither fair nor honourable by most Canadians. Having let the genie of "fairness" escape, neither he nor anyone else on the "yes" side could control it.

CONCLUSION

Recent constitutional debate in Canada has been constructed around the principles of equality and fairness, including a form of federal equality, that evokes the same deep hostility that affirmative action does.[48] And whatever its source, this way of framing the debate over federalism feeds and reinforces a politics of deep regional and cultural resentment. Matters that might otherwise be passed off as the routine (if somewhat messy) business of democratic politics – assigning defence contracts or bailing out airlines, for example – have now been elevated to questions of high liberal and constitutional principle. And once there, they move into the rhetorical rut created by the debate over affirmative action. That is one of the things that makes the current constitutional debate so difficult, and it is one of the reasons that prospects for a mutually acceptable solution seem so bleak. It is hard enough to reform the institutions of federalism without having to confront all of the baggage associated with opposition to affirmative action as well. To that extent, the discourse of provincial equality has transformed – and I think actually hobbled – Canadian constitutional discourse.[49] As important as the principles of fairness and equality may be for organizing a liberal polity, it is unclear that it is either efficient or ultimately just to expect a federation as diverse as Canada's to put these principles first. Perhaps the original autonomists got it right after all, and perhaps it is time for Canadians to brush off that older understanding of liberal federalism that sustained the country for the larger part of its history. Whichever way the Quebec referendum goes, we could well use a little of their practical wisdom.

NOTES

1 See Robert C. Vipond, *Liberty and Community: Canadian Federalism and the Failure of the Constitution* (Albany, NY: SUNY Press, 1991), chap 2.
2 This section summarizes the argument that I make in greater length in ibid., chap. 5.
3 Think, for instance, about the treatment of language and religion in the late nineteenth century. The federal government ducked responsibility for protecting minority religious rights in the 1870s in New Brunswick, stating that this was a wholly provincial matter. Parliament essentially caved in on language rights in the North West in the 1880s, ceding major responsibility to a territorial assembly, even though Parliament acknowledged that it had clear authority to act. Only in Manitoba, in the 1890s, did minority rights become a major issue – and even there the federal government declined to act vigorously. As well, there are all the cases in which Ottawa simply refused to use its veto power to vindicate individual rights.
4 Again, this is a brief summary of an analysis presented at much greater length in Vipond, *Liberty and Community*, chaps 3, 4, and 5. For a more elaborate and elegant presentation, see Paul Romney, "The Nature and Scope of Provincial Autonomy: Oliver Mowat, the Quebec Resolutions and the Construction of the British North America Act," *Canadian Journal of Political Science*, 25 no. 1 (March 1992), 3–28.
5 See Canada, Parliament, *House of Commons Debates*, 2 May 1894, 2298–332 (Charlton), for one example.
6 Ibid., 30 May 1894, 3404 (Amyot). Opponents included a broad range of English- and French-Canadian parliamentarians – among them, Casey, Chapleau, Langellier, Laurier, Mills, and Tisdale.
7 Again, Amyot's argument is the clearest and most colourful on this point. See *House of Commons Debates*, 30 May 1894, 3399–404.
8 *Globe and Mail*, 1 March 1992.
9 Quebec Liberal Party, *A Quebec Free to Choose: Report of the Constitutional Committee* (Montreal: Quebec Liberal Party, March 1991).
10 Ibid., 4.

11 "Under the proposed reorganization, Quebec will move resolutely towards political autonomy, Quebec will exercise exclusive, discretionary and total authority in most areas of jurisdiction" (ibid., 37). The report is laced with similar statements strongly reminiscent of the provincial-rights rhetoric.

12 Ibid., 56.

13 Ibid., 44.

14 The points and quotations in this paragraph are taken from ibid., 31–2.

15 In a poll taken in the spring of 1992, for instance, Canadians were asked which politicians had credibility in handling constitutional issues. Wells scored near the top, with 41 percent of respondents answering in the affirmative. Only former Prime Minister Pierre Trudeau – with whom Wells shares a basic philosophical approach – scored over 50 percent. By contrast, Don Getty (who was also associated with the Triple-E Senate proposal) scored 28 percent; Robert Bourassa, 29 percent; and Brian Mulroney, 20 percent. *Globe and Mail*, 6 April 1992.

16 That is how the us Articles of Confederation arranged matters, for instance.

17 See Clyde Wells, *Submission to the Special Joint Commission of Parliament on the Constitutional Amending Process*, 9 April 1991.

18 See Clyde Wells to Brian Mulroney, 6 Nov. 1989, copy in Premier's Office, St John's.

19 Wells would have matters concerning French language and culture pass a "double majority" in the Senate – that is, a majority of both francophones and anglophones.

20 See, for instance, Wells's oral testimony to the Beaudoin-Dobbie Committee, 14 Jan. 1992, in *Minutes of Proceedings and Evidence of the Special Joint Committee of the Senate and of the House of Commons on a Renewed Canada*. Engaged by committee member Jean-Pierre Blackburn to explain how Quebec is to protect those interests vital to it unless it has more autonomy, Wells shifted the discussion to the double-majority Senate proposal. He concluded: "I think that fairly provides for the differences that exist between Quebec and the rest of Canada" (40:25).

21 Province of Newfoundland, General Assembly, Verbatim Report, 20 June 1990, L17–L18 (Wells).

22 Wells to Mulroney, 18 Oct. 1989, Premier's Office.

23 Ibid.

24 Ibid.

25 Ibid.

26 This cataloguing of the species of equality has become a standard part of his major constitutional speeches. For starters, see Assembly, Verbatim Report, 20 June 1990, L17–L18 (Wells), and compare the slightly different list in Wells's submission to the Beaudoin-Dobbie Committee, 14 Jan. 1992, *Minutes*, 40:5–40:6.

27   But since representation by population exaggerates the power of central Canada, one needs another principle and another institution – namely a Triple-E Senate – to ensure "balanced" representation of the whole country.

28   Wells to Mulroney, 18 Oct. 1989, Premier's Office. Provision of equal opportunities requires a strong national government.

29   Again, this is a characteristic phrase of his; see Assembly, Verbatim Report, 20 June 1990, L18 (Wells). He has repeated it several times, most recently before the Beaudoin-Dobbie Committee, 14 Jan. 1992, *Minutes*, 40:5.

30   See Ronald Dworkin, *Taking Rights Seriously* (Cambridge, Mass.: Harvard University Press, 1978).

31   Constitution Act, 1982, sec. 36.

32   See the headnote for ibid., sec. 6.

33   In response to the federal proposals of September 1991, Judy Rebick, president of the National Advisory Committee on the Status of Women (NAC), made this argument explicitly. "For example, employment equity is something we've understood that we need to correct historical disadvantages of women, visible minorities and disabled people, and we would say that we also need special powers ... for Quebec to recognize the fact that they have a disadvantage in being the only French-speaking nation or province in the whole of North America." "NAC Responses to Federal Constitutional Proposals," 25 Oct. 1991.

34   Wells's commentary on the federal government's proposals, "Shaping Canada's Future Together," Assembly, Verbatim Report, 22 Oct. 1991, 8.

35   Wells to Mulroney, 18 Oct. 1989, Premier's Office.

36   Proposal for Amending the Meech Lake Accord, in Wells to Mulroney, 6 Nov. 1989, 4, Premier's Office.

37   When it came time to defend the distinct society provision in the Charlottetown Accord, Wells said explicitly that he was able to support this version, though he had been unable to support the Meech version, because the Charlottetown text was significantly watered down.

38   Thus he was hostile to the Meech Lake version, reacted more positively to the federal proposals of September 1991, sounded more negative in his testimony before the Beaudoin-Dobbie Committee in January 1992, seems to have opposed the various versions of the distinct society clause circulated in the early months of 1992, and then signed on to the so-called Pearson Accord of 7 July 1992.

39   Thus, logically, Wells could support reform in which powers were devolved uniformly to the provincial governments. This possibility, however, is precluded by his conviction that the national government needs to be strengthened, not weakened.

40 On Canadian attitudes to affirmative action, see Joseph Fletcher and Marie-Christine Chalmers, "Attitudes of Canadians toward Affirmative Action: Opposition, Value Pluralism, and Non-Attitudes," *Political Behaviour*, 13 no. 1 (1991), 67–95.

41 This interpretation is consistent with Wells's anxiety about non-Quebecers who reside temporarily in Quebec. See Assembly, Verbatim Report, 22 Oct. 1991, 8 (Wells).

42 The argument about "objective criteria" comes from his testimony to the Beaudoin-Dobbie Committee, 14 Jan. 1992, *Minutes*, 40:22. His references to fairness, balance, and preference appear as leitmotifs throughout the testimony.

43 Assembly, Verbatim Report, 22 Oct. 1991, 11 (Wells).

44 Wells, testimony to Beaudoin-Dobbie Committee, 14 Jan. 1992, *Minutes*, 40:6.

45 Ibid., 40:26.

46 Wells to Mulroney, 18 Oct. 1989, Premier's Office.

47 Wells, testimony to Beaudoin-Dobbie Committee, 14 Jan. 1992, *Minutes*, 40:26.

48 It would be interesting to conduct a thorough empirical study to find if attitudes to affirmative action correlate directly with attitudes to the distinct society clause. Fletcher and Chalmers's study – which shows support for affirmative action toward French Canadians to be significantly lower than support for gender equity programs – may give us insight about the connection. See Fletcher and Chalmers, "Attitudes," 95.

49 On this point, see also Alan C. Cairns, "Constitutional Change and the Three Equalities," in *Options for a New Canada*, ed. Ronald L. Watts and Douglas M. Brown (Toronto: University of Toronto Press, 1991), 77–100; and Charles Taylor, "Shared and Divergent Values," in ibid., 53–76, later republished in Charles Taylor, *Reconciling the Solitudes: Essays on Canadian Federalism and Nationalism*, ed. Guy Laforest (Montreal: McGill-Queen's University Press, 1993), 155–86.

CHAPTER FIVE

Decline of Procedural Liberalism: The Slippery Slope to Secession

Janet Ajzenstat

PROCEDURAL AND SUBSTANTIVE LIBERALISM

In "Shared and Divergent Values," Charles Taylor argues that there is "a remarkable similarity throughout the country, and across the French/English difference," in adherence to such liberal values as "equality, nondiscrimination, the rule of law, [and] the mores of representative democracy."[1] English-speaking Canadians who remember the intolerance of political dissent that characterized Maurice Duplessis's era in Quebec may harbour suspicions about Quebec's liberal credentials, but their fears are unjustified: "both parts of Canada have been swept up into the liberal consensus that has become established in the whole western world in the wake of World War II."

Taylor is not alone in suggesting that Quebec's political culture increasingly resembles that of North America and the industrialized West. In this volume Howard Adelman argues in chapter 3 that Quebec's immigration policy and treatment of refugees are proof that its political culture and government are liberal. Joseph Carens, in chapter 2, describing the multicultural character of life in Quebec, comes to a similar conclusion. In chapter 8, Reg Whitaker suggests indeed that today "the distinctiveness of Quebec society [is] marginal." As late as the 1940s and 1950s, he says, one might have detected in francophone Quebec a culture that was genuinely distinct, but today "the Québécois way of life has come to represent a regional variation of North American mass culture."

These observations raise a question: if cultural differences between Quebec and the rest of Canada are disappearing, why are the two political societies now farther apart than ever on constitutional issues? In the 1960s, Quebec bargained for reform of the division of legislative powers. Today the possibility of secession looms. Moreover, the argument for political autonomy assumes that Quebec must control the levers of government in order to protect and promote a distinctive way of life.[2]

Kenneth McRoberts observes that at the time of the Quiet Revolution English Canadians welcomed the "conversion of French Canadians to English goals and values," on the assumption that ideological convergence would foster national unity – "a unity that had been impossible as long as French Canadians subscribed to traditional values."[3] But, as he adds, it soon became apparent that ideological convergence would not make unity more likely. After the Quiet Revolution, Quebec more often took a posture of confrontation on constitutional issues and increasingly couched demands vis-à-vis Ottawa and the other provinces in nationalist terms. As Taylor says: "We have never been closer to breakup in our history, although our values have never been so uniform."[4] We are left with our question: if cultural differences are decreasing, what explains the demand for autonomy?[5]

We can imagine someone arguing that though differences are fading Quebec still maintains a core of distinctiveness – something worth protecting, which may require protection by enhanced powers exactly because it is vulnerable in the face of the "consensus that has swept the western world since World War II." Taylor inclines to this explanation.

His discussion turns on the distinction between "substantive" and "procedural" liberalism. Quebec adheres to the former, and the rest of Canada to the latter. Quebec is as liberal as the rest of the country, but in a distinctive way.[6]

Substantive liberalism, in Taylor's description, subscribes to collective ideas about "what a country is for." Quebec is not "neutral between remaining true to the values of our ancestors and those who might want to cut loose in the name of some individual goal of self-development." The collective goal is *survivance*; Quebecers are collectively devoted to ensuring that coming generations go on identifying themselves as francophones.

Procedural liberalism, in contrast, is avowedly and proudly neutral with respect to ideas of social and political good. This is not to say that the procedural republic never gives rise to ideas of social good. Taylor does not elaborate on the theme in this essay, but what is usually said is that ideas about the good are tolerated when they emerge from political debate and the political process. The central tenet of procedural liberalism is that notions about what is best for society must always be open to challenge through the political process.[7] Laws and policies express the will of an ever-changing majority that is likely to comprise a different aggregate of views after every election. The procedural liberal maintains that democratic rights – the right to majority government, the alternation of parties in office, and the right to political opposition and dissent – are possible only where no prior idea of the good is tolerated.[8]

It is not always easy to see how substantive liberalism in Taylor's schema differs from the illiberal, closed regime. But Taylor maintains that its collective goals are not "seen as a depreciation of those who do not personally share the definition."[9] He depicts the substantive liberal as firmly committed to procedural principles such as equality of right and the rule of law; moreover, he believes that Quebec's substantive liberalism could flourish in a federal system such as Canada's.

To illustrate the way in which Canada accommodates diversity, Taylor notes that "someone of, say Italian extraction in Toronto ... might feel Canadian as a bearer of rights in a multicultural mosaic."[10] In contrast, Québécois, or Cree, or Dené are more likely to feel that they belong to Canada "through their national communities." Multiculturalism is an example of what Taylor calls "first level diversity." Membership through national communities results in "deep diversity."

Can a country accommodate both first-level and deep diversity? Procedural liberals may have their doubts. Even Taylor admits that immigrants to Quebec may feel less than fully committed to survivance as the national goal of a people that has lived in the area for centuries. Nevertheless he believes that Quebec's record today on treatment of minorities is good – as good as that of most liberal democracies. That there is evidence to support the contention, I have suggested. Quebec's commitment to the protection of minorities and immigrants is asserted repeatedly in both the Bélanger-Campeau report and the Allaire report – documents that also set out Quebec's challenge to the rest of Canada.[11]

Taylor's argument in brief is that Quebec can allow collective goals for the majority while ensuring procedural freedoms for all. Quebec is both like the rest of Canada and yet distinctive, distinctive enough to require a degree of political autonomy. His discussion of substantive and procedural liberalism appears to tell us why Quebec should demand enhanced powers.

Or does it? If Taylor is right, it appears that Quebecers have been supremely successful within the federal system in protecting what is most dear to them – survivance – as well as the procedural principles that they also value.[12] Our question becomes even more urgent. Why the continuing drive for more powers, and the ever-growing belief that only sovereignty will protect and promote the essential Quebec?[13]

The subject of language requires special mention. That Quebecers regard French as requiring protection hardly needs to be said.[14] But it is difficult to imagine what steps an independent state could adopt to protect French that Quebec has not already taken. Whitaker, for one, suggests in chapter 8, below, that under the existing federal system Quebec could attain all its material objectives.

Reflection on use of state powers during the Quiet Revolution poses our question in different terms: if Quebec had the powers of government to transform society in the 1960s, why the demand for still more? The Quiet Revolution utterly changed the province's character, erasing the old way of life, with its dedication to spiritual values, rural attachments, classical education, and church-controlled and -inspired social welfare institutions, and erecting in its place secular institutions, state-run welfare programs, an educational curriculum that is oriented to the needs of a technological society, and a modern economy.[15] Taylor and others find it ironic that this transformation made Quebec more like other jurisdictions on the continent.[16] What cannot be denied is that it was the product of the exercise of state power on a grand scale.

In an essay first published in 1979, "Why Do Nations Have to Become States?" Taylor addressed the demand for sovereignty by arguing that Quebec was a nation and that nations gravitate toward statehood.[17] He did not need to posit a core of distinctiveness for Quebec. A nation, according to the definition in this essay, is a people that has a collective sense of identity. McRoberts argues in similar fashion that Quebec "meets many of the definitions of a nation," because it comprises "a French-speaking population with a centuries old history of seeing itself as a people, even as a nation."[18] I have shown that Québécois do not in fact define themselves primarily in terms of a centuries-old idea. What is valuable in McRoberts's definition is the idea that Quebecers are a nation because they "see themselves" as a people and nation. We don't have to suppose that the politics of Quebec is characterized by pursuit of collective, substantive goals in order to explain the drive toward sovereignty. It is enough to say that Quebecers have a sense of themselves as a people entitled to sovereign institutions.

In "Why Do Nations Have to Become States?" Taylor suggested that although nations tend to move toward statehood, there is no absolute requirement that they become states. He believed that federation remained "an important option" for the nation that is Quebec.[19] Today he still hopes for some form of federal association between Canada and Quebec; he believes that Canada could learn to accommodate "deep diversity." Our original question still has force. Describing Quebec as a nation does not give a sufficient explanation of the demand for sovereign institutions.

The picture of Quebec that emerges from the Bélanger-Campeau and Allaire reports of 1991 is in accord with Taylor's in so far as it suggests that Quebecers have a well-entrenched sense of identity. But whereas Taylor says that the demand for autonomy emerges out of the sense of national identity, the reports argue that Quebecers' present sense of national identity emerged from the étatisme of the Quiet Revolution. Taylor is suggesting that nations may have to become states; Bélanger-Campeau and Allaire, that states become nations. The reports depict two kinds of Québécois national identity. One, now a thing of the past, was associated with the traditional Québécois way of life. The other is the product of the collective assertion of francophone rights, and the building of state institutions, during the 1960s; it is modern, open to the world, and informed by the principles and values of procedural liberalism.[20]

Thus the defining characteristic of Quebec as a nation, according to Allaire and Bélanger-Campeau, is not survivance, but the triumphant emancipation brought about by the Quiet Revolution. The transformation that made Quebec virtually indistinguishable from other jurisdictions on the continent was exactly what made of the people a nation – "maîtres chez eux." Quebec is not a vulnerable polity needing enhanced powers, but a strong one with such a well-defined sense of self that it can in fact be open to the world.

Our original question remains. We can imagine a triumphant Quebec finding it appropriate to sever the last connections with Canada, but we can also conceive of its opting for association with Canada exactly because it has already achieved an unquenchable sense of national identity. The conception of Quebec as a people that now sees itself as a nation provides a good, but not entirely satisfying, answer to our question: why sovereignty?

It is impossible to escape the idea that there is some as-yet-unexplained factor at work promoting the idea of Quebec's secession, making it appear not merely feasible and attractive, but necessary at all costs. In the next section I suggest that this factor comes to light when we see how negotiation of political objectives in the arena of constitutional reform undermines the principles of the procedural constitution. What is heightening contestation in constitutional negotiations, I argue, is not tension between the procedural constitution and Quebec's pursuit of collective goals, but erosion of confidence in procedural institutions. The breakdown of the procedural constitution is provoking immoderate opposition to Quebec's aspirations and creating the conviction in Quebec that only secession will remedy grievances.

CONSTITUTION-MAKING AND THE PROCEDURAL CONSTITUTION

If cultural differences between English Canada and Quebec are decreasing, if the government of Quebec does not lack the power to effect social changes, and if it is not obvious that an independent state could better protect the Québécois way of life, why does secession loom? The clue lies in the story of the constitutional negotiations over the past twenty-five years.

Jean Lesage's confident Quebec government of the early 1960s demanded reform of the division of legislative powers in order to provide Quebec with enhanced powers. A new division of powers required agreement among the eleven governments, precipitating the first ministers into the search for a home-grown

amending process.[21] No amending formula emerged from the
constitutional meetings of those years. But under pressure from
Quebec, Ottawa introduced the policy of allowing provinces to
"opt out" of joint federal-provincial programs, and Quebec took
full advantage of it to secure new powers.[22] McRoberts argues
that in doing so Quebec demanded and received "de facto particular status."[23]

Courchene and McDougall note a "growing feeling that Quebec has had more than its fair share of influence in Ottawa, and
is the spoiled child of the Canadian federation."[24] They are
speaking of the period since the demise of the Meech Lake Accord in 1990, but the sentiment they describe had already begun
to surface in the 1970s. The jockeying among governments in
the 1960s and early 1970s taught a lesson: there are political
gains to be made in constitutional negotiations. The fact that
Quebec made its real gains through bilateral negotiations with
Ottawa rather than through the formal amendment process only
increased the resentment felt by other governments and interests.

The process that in the 1960s and early 1970s involved discussions among governments was soon challenged by political
interests anxious to make sure that the club of eleven did not
strike a constitutional deal that left them out. By 1980–81, the
interests jostling the governments in the constitutional bargaining arena included the northern territories and organizations of
the Aboriginal peoples; special interests of many descriptions,
such as civil liberties groups, bar associations, research institutes,
minority-language groups, women's groups, and associations
representing the handicapped, the gay community, and ethnic
groups; and committees of the various parliaments, ad hoc
groups, and numbers of constitutional experts and academics.
Constitutional reform became a forum in which to advance
concrete, partisan, political objectives.[25]

According to David Milne, it is now routine for Canadian
political leaders to look to constitutional change to remedy
grievances whose cause lies in the complexities of a modern
political economy.[26] Donald Smiley tells us that this intrusion of
political issues into the constitutional debate is a novel phenomenon; it began, he says, with pressures emanating from Quebec in
the years after the Quiet Revolution.[27]

Quebec's manoeuvring for new powers opened the constitution-making door. What came through were interests that in the

end proved hostile to Quebec's aspirations. In the constitution-making arena resolution of political issues is difficult; contestation rather than compromise is the usual outcome.

The Constitution Act of 1982 is regarded by Quebec's elites as an insult – proof positive that the constitutional process has worked to Quebec's disadvantage.[28] At first reading it is not obvious why it is so offensive. It is true that it was adopted without the consent of Quebec's national assembly, and true as well that it curtails Quebec's powers in the area of language education. But the act entrenches a vision of Canada already expressed in the Official Languages Act and in Ottawa's policy of building up francophone representation in the public service – measures acceptable to most Quebecers. Why should Quebecers object to the opening of opportunities to French Canadians in other provinces and in the federal government? Pierre Trudeau meant his program of bilingualism as an alternative to the aggrandizement of the province of Quebec; he intended it to challenge Quebec's *étatisme*. But Quebecers for some time before 1982 had refused to find a contradiction between Trudeau's vision of a Canada for French Canadians and Quebec's vision of a strong provincial state. They voted for Trudeau's Liberals in federal elections and for the Parti québécois in provincial. What changed after 1982?

What changed is that the 1982 act is no mere program of the federal government, but part of the constitution, the supreme law of the country. Quebecers might very well welcome Trudeau's program in the form of federal law and policy. They have every reason to reject it as constitutional law.

To see what is at issue we must take another look at procedural liberalism. Procedural liberalism was said not to tolerate a prior idea of the good in politics – the constitution, the system of government, should be neutral with respect to ideology and political interest. The constitution is the rule book for the game of politics. The fact that it does not prefer one way of life, one political ideology or program, is what enables parties to come and go in office, secures respect for political opposition, and enables marginal groups to bid for influence. The procedural constitution is supposed to be above politics, immune to political manipulation, in order to make politics possible.

It cannot be said that liberal democratic constitutions such as Canada's are always in fact free of ideological bias. But the perception has been that the standard of constitutional neutrality was well-enough established that groups and interests offensive to the majority were tolerated and could even hope in time to persuade the majority. Support for the idea that the Canadian constitution was believed neutral in this respect can be found, for example, in the Regina Manifesto of 1933. The Co-operative Commonwealth Federation (CCF) did not opt for revolution in 1933, nor did it reject the form of government that sustained political parties deemed unjust by socialists. The expectation was that the system would in time allow socialist programs and policies their due.

From the point – some time prior to 1981 – at which it became standard practice to press political and ideological arguments in terms of proposals for constitutional amendment, the idea of the unbiased procedural constitution began to lose credibility. Political contestants in the constitutional arena are not competing for benefits under the political rules of the game in the ordinary way of politics. Nor are they merely proposing constitutional amendments – changes in the rules. It is understood that a procedural constitution will require amendment from time to time. What is novel about constitutional bargaining in Canada today is that groups make bids for concrete political benefits in terms of demand for constitutional amendment; they put forward proposals for amendment in order to advance concrete interests. The result is to call in question the distinction between amendments meant to maintain or improve the neutrality of the constitution and those intended to promote particular interests or ideologies. The very idea of the neutral constitution is challenged.

What Quebecers see in the 1982 act is that it entrenches Trudeau's pan-Canadian ideology, his particular – contestable – vision of Canada. The constitution of 1982 is a statement to the effect that the two visions of French Canada in relation to the rest of Canada – the one favouring the opening of more opportunities for francophones across the country, and the other, a strong Quebec – are no longer compatible.[29] Trudeau's has been given the constitutional imprimatur. Quebecers cannot enjoy both; they can no longer pursue their happy policy of endorsing Canada as well as Quebec while playing federal and provincial elites against each other. They have to choose and, if they choose Quebec, have to reject the constitution of Canada. In short, the federal government's injection of a particular political conception into the constitution has forced Quebecers to adopt a more aggressive, less conciliatory posture vis-à-vis the rest of Canada.

The ideological character of constitutional politicking and the level of contestation advanced by quantum leaps with the debate over Meech Lake. Among the most vocal opponents of Meech were groups, such as feminists and Aboriginal peoples, that had influenced the form of the 1982 act. Their success of 1982 did not make them more conciliatory and certainly did not dispose them to welcome Quebec into the constitutional fold.

Many of those opposed to the Meech Lake Accord said that its "distinct society" clause would endanger the rights of individuals in Quebec; the Quebec government's use of the Charter override to forbid English on business signs was seen as an intolerable invasion of citizens' rights. The National Action Committee on the Status of Women called up the idea of a Quebec trampling on the rights of women (curtailing access to abortion, or sale of contraceptives), though organizations representing Quebec feminists were overwhelmingly in favour of the distinct society clause, even describing it as essential to feminism. In other words, the opposition to Meech painted the Quebec of today in the colours of the Duplessis era. In vain were protests from Quebec that its provincial human rights code is as liberal as the Charter, or more so.[30]

Taylor maintains that there was something exaggerated, even silly, about the objections to the distinct society clause. I agree that the portrayal of Quebec as a closed society lacked credibility and that the concern for Quebecers' rights had a hollow sound. The true – and, I would argue, sad – fact about Canada today is that the rest of Canada is not vitally concerned about Quebec's treatment of its citizens, or any other issues relating to that province's internal policies.[31] What those opposing Meech feared was not that Quebec would act autocratically, but that its gains in the constitutional area would be their loss, that Quebec would recover its "favoured-child" status. Women's groups, multicultural groups, and Aboriginal people believed that the distinct society clause would detract from or dilute the constitutional status that they and their clients and members had acquired in 1982. In the unmaking of Meech Lake we see the evil genius of constitutional politicking working hard, heightening the contestation, and inviting all participants to take a more aggressive posture.

That constitutional debate encourages contestation is evident in the case of Aboriginal claims vis-à-vis Quebec. Quebec's assertions about distinctiveness call forth protests from Aboriginal groups, which argue, surely with justice, that their history, languages, and present way of life make them truly unique in Quebec and Canada. It would take a longer essay to explore the way in which the claims of native peoples for territory and for special privileges under the constitution are a challenge to Quebec's ambitions. My point here is simply that in order to influence debate in the shrill forum of constitution-making, those claiming status as distinct societies must emphasize their distinctiveness; each must appear less able to compromise, more like a self-sufficient political entity, and consequently less in need of the give-and-take of debate to establish rules for ongoing life with the other governments, groups, and peoples of Canada.

Let me focus on the idea that competition of interests in the constitutional arena is harmful. Procedural liberals maintain that competition is inherent in politics and indeed leads to a positive outcome. The jockeying among parties, groups, and interests – during elections, in the media, and in the legislatures and representative bodies – is regarded as the lifeblood of the system. It furthers the aggregation of diverse interests, producing legislation for the common good, and confers legitimacy on the outcome.

Procedural liberalism posits that open debate on proposed legislation aggregates interests exactly because under a neutral constitution laws are always open to challenge. Its boast is that it does nothing to limit complaint and debate and nothing to prevent opposition groups and parties from organizing to plot the overthrow of particular laws and policies. As decrees of the executive branch, laws must be obeyed, but as measures emanating from the legislature, they may be endlessly contested. The fact of debate and popular participation does not undermine the requirement to obey; and the fact that obedience is required enables continuing debate. No political loss is entirely without remedy. If interests remain unaggregated and the players retain their energy, the game can be virtually endless. Those who fall rise to fight again.

Thus the contestation inherent in day-to-day politics is manageable because, or if, political actors assume that no party or interest is constitutionally privileged, because they believe that certain expectations about fairness and neutrality inform the constitution. Only when the assumption of neutrality is undermined does contestation become unmanageable.

Because constitution-making arena is now a forum for political demands in Canada, participation is increasingly portrayed as a democratic right, comparable to the citizen's right to have a say in the ordinary business of politics. It is assumed that the competition of interests in the constitutional forum is like that in electoral and legislative politics. The distinction between constitutional law and ordinary legislation is eroded, and as a result the idea grows that constitutional reform can never be anything but a battle of ideological and particular interests.

In most procedural democracies, constitutional reform is carried on at a moderate pace. A distinction between constitutional law and the ordinary business of politics is observed; special majorities and special procedures are required for amendment of the constitution. Even in Britain, where in theory the legislature can amend any constitutional document on a majority vote, the fundamental principles of the procedural constitution are entrenched de facto, beyond the reach of the government of the day, and relatively immune to corrosive debate.[32] Canada's wholesale embrace of constitutional reform is unusual. In the text book definition, constitutions define the form of government, determine relations between levels of government in a federal system, protect individual and political rights, and provide for the amendment of the constitution.[33] Canadians are demanding changes in all four dimensions. There is scarcely an aspect of our political system that is not today described as flawed, elitist, discriminatory, and unjust.

The irony is that constitutional participants continue to appeal to "justice," as if it were a constitutional absolute that would permit neutral adjudication of their claims, while the effect of their appeals is to erode all idea of constitutional neutrality and neutral adjudication. In procedural liberalism, justice takes its meaning from the constitution; it is assumed that the requirements for justice have been met when the procedures set out in the constitution have been adhered to.[34] When it is those very procedures that are being called in question, when indeed the very idea of a procedural constitution is questioned, what can "justice" mean? In effect, justice becomes the pronouncement of the strongest.

Consider the demand for constitutional recognition. Quebec argues that the province has been unjustly denied even the kind of constitutional recognition that in 1982 was acccorded Aboriginal peoples, the multicultural associations of English Canada, women, and the other interests that left their mark on the Charter. Aboriginals say that they received only minimal recognition in 1982, and that centuries of injustice give them every reason to be dissatisfied with their position in constitutional law. The Charter groups claim that the status that they won in 1982 is threatened; justice requires reaffirmation of their rights. The constitutional players speak of what "justice demands," but the quarrel is not really about the requirements that will satisfy justice. It is about what justice *is*. To be treated justly now means being first in a constitutional pecking order, and each group advances the definition of justice – that is, the scheme of ranking – that gives it pre-eminence.

THE SLIPPERY SLOPE TO SECESSION

The Bélanger-Campeau report notes that public opinion in Quebec and in the rest of Canada is becoming increasingly polarized: "Public debates surrounding the 1987 Agreement on the Constitution have shown that it is becoming increasingly difficult to reconcile the various political visions, aspirations and national identities inherent in the Canadian federal regime."[35] Are the sharp differences of political opinion "out there" part of the Canadian political landscape, as this statement suggests? Or are they, as I have suggested, given shape and strengthened by the fact of being argued in the constitution-making arena?

My argument in this chapter is that an important component in the quarrel between Quebec and the rest of Canada is the contestation inherent in endless constitution-making. What we are seeing is not a battle between two forms of liberalism – substantive and procedural – but the breakdown of the procedural constitution.[36]

The demand for reform of all aspects of the constitution undermines the idea that constitutional law can be impartial, or can be used to adjudicate claims. All proposals for reform now appear arbitrary; all are open to attack as unjust. Because there is so little common ground to which participants can appeal (the common ground, and the grounds for resolving disputes, are part of what is at issue), resentments flourish, small disagreements are magnified, and grievances of substance are advanced in terms of appeals to deep-seated nationalism or a charge of centuries-old injustice – language that admits of few compromises.

The sense that the constitution is now the product of battling interests surely contributes to the feeling among Quebecers that Quebec would be better off out of the constitutional debate altogether. If all assumptions about the Canadian way of doing things are open to contest, if a new accord would be likely to come under siege immediately, there can be no lasting guarantee of Quebec's interests. Secessionist movements have surfaced in the Canadian west and among Aboriginal peoples for similar reasons.

What could possibly weigh against the factors promoting contestation in today's constitutional negotiations? We can hope that the habits of more than 125 years of settled political life under the procedural constitution will suffice.

NOTES

The author acknowledges the assistance of the Social Sciences and Humanities Research Council of Canada (Strategic Grant 806-90-1002).

1 Charles Taylor, "Shared and Divergent Values," in Charles Taylor, *Reconciling the Solitudes: Essays on Canadian Federalism and Nationalism*, ed. Guy Laforest (Montreal: McGill-Queen's University Press, 1993), 155, originally published in *Options for a New Canada*, ed. Ronald L. Watts and Doulas M. Brown (Toronto: University of Toronto Press, 1991), 53–76. Taylor adds that Canadians agree about "social provisions, about violence and firearms, and a host of provisions."

2 The Allaire report recommends a massive transfer of governmental powers from the federal level to Quebec, claiming that "under the existing federal structure the Quebec government lacks the essential tools to allow it to secure the future of the French fact in North America." The Constitutional Committee of the Quebec Liberal Party, *A Quebec Free to Choose: Report of the Constitutional Committee* (hereafter Allaire report) (Montreal: Quebec Liberal Party, 1991), 35. The Bélanger-Campeau report says that sovereignty will enable Quebecers to "assume their own destiny ... and assure their economic, social and cultural development." Quebec, Com-

mission on the Political and Constitutional Future of Quebec, *Report of the Commission on the Political and Constitutional Future of Quebec* (hereafter Belanger-Campeau report) (Quebec City: Editeur officiel, March 1991), 4.

3 Kenneth McRoberts and Dale Posgate, *Quebec: Social Change and Political Crisis* (Toronto: McClelland and Stewart, 1976), 100.

4 Taylor, "Shared and Divergent Values," 54.

5 See Stéphane Dion, "Le nationalisme dans la convergence culturelle: Le Québec contemporain et le paradoxe Tocqueville," in *L'engagement intellectuel: Mélanges en l'honneur de Léon Dion*, ed. Raymond Hudon and Réjean Pelletier (Ste Foy, Que.: Les Presses de l'Université de Laval, 1991), 291: "Le sens commun voudrait pourtant que plus deux populations se resemblent culturellement, plus elles devraient s'entendre politiquement. C'est le contraire que s'est passé au Canada." Dion tackles the question through a sympathetic exposition of Tocqueville on cultural convergence, in relation to Canada today.

6 Taylor, "Shared and Divergent Values," 175–6.

7 On procedural liberalism in Canadian history, see Janet Ajzenstat, "Canada's First Constitution: Pierre Bédard on Tolerance and Dissent," *Canadian Journal of Political Science*, 23 no. 1 (March 1990), 39–57, and Rainer Knopff, "The Triumph of Liberalism in Canada: Laurier on Representation and Party Government," *Journal of Canadian Studies*, 26 no. 2 (Summer 1991), 72–86.

8 Compare with John Locke on the reasons for not tolerating the intolerant in his *Letter Concerning Toleration* (1689).

9 Taylor, "Shared and Divergent Values," 176.

10 Ibid., 183.

11 Bélanger-Campeau report, 2, 3, 18–19, 20–1, 69; Allaire report, 4, 6, 25, 31, 32, 56.

12 For similar observations, see André Ouellet's dissenting comments in the Bélanger-Campeau report, 25.

13 According to Guy Laforest, there were only two questions before the Bélanger-Campeau commission: "What are the powers required by Quebec to preserve and promote its distinctiveness? and, How can these powers be attained?" Guy Laforest, "Quebec beyond the Federal Regime of 1867–1982," in *Options for a New Canada*, ed. Ronald L. Watts and Douglas M. Brown (Toronto: University of Toronto Press, 1991), 103–22, 107.

14 "Québec has recognized that Quebecers wish to see the quality and influence of the French language assured"; Bélanger-Campeau report, 2. The status given to multicultural groups in the Charter of Rights and Freedoms is resented because it is taken as evidence that the rest of Canada is coming to regard French as merely one more of Canada's many heritage languages; Allaire report, 23. See Dion, "Le nationalisme," 304.

15 William D. Coleman, *The Independence Movement in Quebec, 1945–1980* (Toronto: University of Toronto Press, 1984); Marcel Rioux, *Quebec in Question* (Toronto: Lorimer, 1971). See also Kenneth McRoberts, *Quebec: Social Change and Political Crisis*, 3rd ed. (Toronto: McClelland and Stewart, 1988).

16 Taylor, "Shared and Divergent Values," 156. Coleman argues that the steps taken by Quebec to protect the French language have severed the connection between the language and the particular culture of Quebec: "French, in becoming an improved medium for technological and scientific discussion, is also moving away more and more from its traditional roots and becoming more like the language of advanced capitalism in North America, English." Coleman, *The Independence Movement in Quebec*, 209.

Quebec's civil law tradition, often considered a cornerstone of its distinctiveness, is now being revised in ways that will bring its laws on family relations, inheritance, property ownership, contracts, abortion, surrogate motherhood and similar "new social issues" into line with the laws of other jurisdictions on the continent. Patricia Poirier, "Civil Code Revisions Reflect Societal Change," *Globe and Mail*, 21 Dec. 1991, A4. That the government of Quebec can make these changes is evidence of its ability to alter fundamentals of the society; but, as in the case of language, the result of the changes is to make the society less distinctive.

17 Charles Taylor, "Why Do Nations Have to Become States?" in Charles Taylor, *Reconciling the Solitudes: Essays on Canadian Federalism and Nationalism*, ed. Guy Laforest (Montreal: McGill-Queen's University Press, 1993), 40–58.

18 Kenneth McRoberts, *English Canada and Quebec: Avoiding the Issue* (Toronto: York University, Robarts Centre for Canadian Studies, 1991), 9.

19 Taylor, "Why Do Nations Have to Become States?" 35.

20 "The 1960s saw Québec take charge of its development and affirm its uniqueness." Bélanger-Campeau report, 12. In the Quiet Revolution, "Quebec was ... affirming itself as a distinct society." Allaire report, 10. Compare Peter Russell's suggestion that Canadians (in the old coast-to-coast sense) never constituted themselves as a people. Russell, "Can Canadians Be a Sovereign People?" *Canadian Journal of Political Science*, 24 no. 4 (Dec. 1991), 691–709.

21 On the search for an amending formula, see Peter H. Russell, *Constitutional Odyssey: Can Canadians Be a Sovereign People?* 2nd ed. (Toronto: University of Toronto Press, 1993).

22 David Milne, *The Canadian Constitution: From Patriation to Meech Lake* (Toronto: Lorimer, 1989), 23–48.

23 McRoberts, *English Canada and Quebec*, 11.

24 Thomas J. Courchene and John N. McDougall, "The Context for Future Constitutional Options," in *Options for a New Canada*, ed. Ronald L. Watts

and Douglas M. Brown (Toronto: University of Toronto Press, 1991),
33–51.

25 Every political scientist who writes on this topic is indebted to Alan
Cairns. See, for example, Alan C. Cairns, *Disruptions: Constitutional
Struggles from the Charter to Meech Lake*, ed. Douglas E. Williams
(Toronto: McClelland and Stewart, 1991).

26 Milne, *The Canadian Constitution*, 19.

27 Donald Smiley, *The Federal Condition* (Toronto: McGraw-Hill Ryerson,
1987), 68.

28 Bélanger-Campeau report, 28 ff.; Allaire report, 3.

29 David M. Thomas, "Turning a Blind Eye: Constitutional Abeyances and
the Canadian Experience," *International Journal of Canadian Studies*,
Special Issue, no. 7–8 (Spring-Fall 1993), 63–79.

30 Bélanger-Campeau report, 19.

31 See David J. Bercuson and Barry Cooper, *Deconfederation: Canada without
Quebec* (Toronto: Key Porter, 1991).

32 Michael Foley argues that the British turn a deliberately blind eye to what
he calls constitutional "gaps" or "abeyances" – areas of constitutional law
that if closely examined would provide fertile ground for political
contestation. Michael Foley, *The Silence of Constitutions: Gaps, "Abeyances"
and Political Temperament in the Maintenance of Government* (London:
Routledge, 1989).

33 Mark O. Dickerson and Thomas Flanagan, *An Introduction to Government
and Politics: A Conceptual Approach*, 4th ed. (Scarborough, Ont.: Nelson,
1994), 62.

34 See Janet Ajzenstat, "The Campaign against the Constitution," *Policy
Options*, 15 no. 3 (April 1994), 22–5.

35 Bélanger-Campeau report, 33, 41.

36 Endless constitutional wrangling is not the sole factor breaking down of
Canada's procedural constitution. In recent years, powerful theories in
political science, law, and philosophy have suggested that constitutional
law cannot be distinguished from ordinary legislation, that it is always the
product of political forces, and that the notion of the neutral constitution
was never anything more than an argument to bolster the privileges of
society's economic and political elites. Richard Rorty, *Contingency, Irony,
and Solidarity* (Cambridge: Cambridge University Press, 1989). See, on
post-modernism, Thomas L. Pangle, *The Ennobling of Democracy: The
Challenge of the Postmodern Age* (Baltimore, Md.: Johns Hopkins University
Press, 1992), 56–68.

CHAPTER SIX

The Ideology of Shared Values: A Myopic Vision of Unity in the Multi-nation State

Wayne Norman

Canada has had serious unity problems for three decades, and they may very well continue for three decades to come. Even if Quebecers decide to remain within the fold, it would take some time before they could be expected to embrace Canada with "honour and enthusiasm." And should Quebec leave, there is no telling how the rest (or rump, as it may then be called) of Canada will deal with its existential angst. In either case, we can expect Aboriginal Canadians to demand increasingly the trappings of nationhood, and eventually even the status of statehood. For many people, the prospect of continual rear-guard action to preserve the integrity of the federation is not inviting. We are consoled only in the thought that, as the world becomes more democratic, the trials and tribulations of multinational federations may become the norm. In the emerging global economy, Canada may find a niche as an exporter of constitutional expertise.

In this chapter I discuss a peculiar (in both senses: characteristic and queer) bit of constitutional theorizing that Canadians should neither export nor continue to dump on the home market. Let us call this the ideology of shared values. It can take different forms and has been developed with varying degrees of sophistication. Its core is the belief that in a pluralistic, multi-ethnic state, national unity is based in some sense on shared values. And its politics thus aims to promote national unity by identifying and reinforcing such values. As a normative theory, its central claim is that the sharing of values gives members of a federation a kind of quasi-moral reason to remain within the same country.

There is evidence that this ideology is widely held among ordinary Canadians and Québécois,[1] and it is prominently espoused by opinion leaders, politicians, and government officials. In various subtle forms it is also not without academic support.[2]

Obviously, there is something to the idea that shared values keep a country together. Disunity, instability, and even civil war can result when there is radical divergence on some questions about values. Nevertheless, I want to argue here that the assumptions and motivations behind the ideology of shared values are false or misleading. It seems more reasonable to look to a shared identity of some sort to secure a stable national unity. But, I suggest, shared identity relies less on shared values than is commonly assumed.

IDEOLOGY OF SHARED VALUES AFTER MEECH: THE OFFICIAL LINE

The ideology of shared values is clearly present in the major reports and proposals issued or commissioned by the government of Canada after the demise of the Meech Lake Accord in 1990. For our purposes here, the most interesting of these is the report of the Spicer Commission, which was based on an unparalleled sampling of public opinion. Some 400,000 Canadians were said to have participated in the commission's deliberations between late 1990 and mid-1991. The final report[3] emphasizes that "Many Canadians spoke or wrote eloquently to the Forum on the subject of the core values they see as essential elements of Canadian society ... A number of participants spoke to us specifically about the importance of shared values in building a nation" (p. 35). They "articulated a sense of Canadian identity and a set of fundamental Canadian values by which they believe we should be governed – as individuals as well as politically and institutionally" (p. 34).

From these comments, the commission distilled, in the report, a list of seven "core values which emerged very strongly, from participants in all regions of Canada, as essential elements of Canadian society": belief in equality and fairness in a democratic society, belief in consultation and dialogue, accommodation and tolerance, support for diversity, compassion and generosity, at-

tachment to Canada's natural beauty, and a commitment to freedom, peace, and non-violent change (pp. 34–44). In their recom-
mendations, the commissioners describe this list as "an impressive array of common, shared values" (p. 117) and assert that "We
must build on these shared values as we proceed to revitalize our
country" (p. 116). "Perhaps in the search for constitutional
renewal," they conclude, "we should take the time to find the
words [for a constitutional preamble] that will help to bind us, to
remind us of what we have in common, of what we cherish.
They should be modest and quiet, but they should resonate to
that most central of values we all share: freedom and dignity in
diversity" (p. 121).

The federal government's constitutional proposals, tabled
about two months after the Spicer report, in September 1991,[4]
refer explicitly to these themes. A background paper, *Shared
Values: The Canadian Identity*,[5] released with the proposals, states:

Canada is a country that believes in freedom, dignity and respect, equality
and fair treatment, and opportunity to participate. It is a country that cares
for the disadvantaged at home and elsewhere, a country that prefers
peaceful solutions to disputes. Canada is a country that, for all its diversity,
has shared values ... Although we may sometimes lose sight of this com-
monality, essential values are shared by Canadians from coast to coast to
coast, including aboriginal Canadians, Canadians in Quebec's distinct
society, and Canadians who have come to our country from other shores
and lands. (p. 1)

The document itself is described as an attempt "to discern and
set out the fundamental values and realities of Canada" (p. 2).
And it adds: "The Government of Canada believes the Constitution must be a framework that reflects our values, our aspiration
and the best of what Canadians really are" (p. 2).

The report of the Beaudoin-Dobbie Committee,[6] which studied
and recommended revisions to the government's proposals of
September 1991, also does not hesitate to sample from the ideology of shared values. It believes there has been "a noticeable
convergence at the level of fundamental values" among Canadians. And it cites approvingly from the barely federalist Allaire
report: "Québécois share fundamental values of the Canadian
people, including respect for human rights, freedom of expres-

sion, unity and harmony between fellow citizens, and the right of every individual to fulfil his essential needs" (p. 9).

The Beaudoin-Dobbie report goes further than the government's proposals in giving constitutional expression to Canadians' shared values in at least two ways. First, it recommends including a non-justiciable social covenant in section 36(1) of the Constitution Act, 1982, which would commit governments to fostering social commitments to health care, adequate social services and benefits, high-quality education, the rights of workers to organize and bargain collectively, and the integrity of the environment (87f). This recommendation appealed to many Canadians, as well as to the Ontario government, which had explicitly evoked the ideology of shared values in its cases for some form of social charter.[7] And second, the report assents to the view that "the Constitution must include a statement that describes who we are as a people and what we aspire to be" (p. 21). Such a statement should be "a 'written flag,' flying in our hearts and minds. It must unite us with the history and values that we share, not merely containing something for everyone, but rather expressing what we *together* recognize and hold dear." (pp. 21f). To this end, it recommends a Canada clause to be included in section 2 of the Constitution Act, 1867 (giving it interpretive effect), which is to suggest "poetically," among other things, that "Canadians all, we honour our roots and value our diversity" and that "We affirm that our country is founded upon principles that acknowledge the supremacy of God, the dignity of each person, the importance of family, and the value of community" (p. 23).[8]

Now while all of the statements about shared values cited above come from official government reports (and we could have referred to constitutional reports produced by most provincial governments of the time) they accurately reflected the views of a great majority of Canadians with an active interest in their country's future. Never before in the nation's history have governments paid so much attention to the views of their citizens on these matters. Even if use of the ideology of shared values in these reports is primarily lip-service, it is still an excellent indicator of what Canadians were telling the various commissions and committees that canvassed the country after the death of the Meech Lake Accord and of what, in effect, must be a key component of Canadian political culture.

SHARED VALUES AND NATIONAL UNITY

In this section, I begin by sketching a brief argument for why shared values are not nearly as relevant, empirically or normatively, for national unity as the ideology of shared values presumes. I next discuss some of the subtle but pervasive implications of this ideology for our ability to think clearly about constitutionadl and political issues and policies.

The Irrelevance of Shared Values

The first step in my argument consists in highlighting the obvious fact that shared values or principles are neither necessary nor sufficient for national unity of the sort relevant in the Canadian context. Whether or not Canada should remain united is, at bottom, a question of why two or more polities should want to share the same country. My argument is simply that the ideology of shared values is, by itself, a hollow and disappointing answer to that question.

Let us imagine that there is a remarkable convergence in the political and social values held by the citizens of, say, Norway and Sweden. We might imagine further (though this element is probably irrelevant) that these values distinguish Norwegians and Swedes to some significant degree from citizens of other neighbouring countries. Now I don't think that anyone believes that these facts would constitute any reason whatsoever for Norway and Sweden to (re)unite within the same country. Of course, were there other reasons for uniting then this convergence of values would make things easier; but that is not itself a reason why these two polities ought to form a single country. Similarly, if there were a reliable study revealing that New Englanders were much closer in their basic social and political values to Canadians than they were, say, to Americans in the us south, it would not inspire anyone to advocate that New England should join Canada or that it should become its own country. I need not belabour the point.

Ideologues of shared values must also be baffled by another striking empirical phenomenon in recent Canadian history. It is well documented that there has been a pronounced process of convergence in the social and political values of French- and

English-speaking Canadians over the last two or three decades.[9]
But, paradoxically for our ideologue, this process has been
accompanied by a rise rather than a decline in nationalist sentiments in Quebec. Now explaining the forces behind Québécois
nationalism, and of its increased or decreased intensity at any
given moment, is, of course, a complex task.[10] There may, however, be a general lesson of special relevance to the ideology in
question. Stéphane Dion reminds us of a rarely discussed paradox, first noticed by Tocqueville, whereby the more the values of
groups converge, the more likely they are to emphasize and
identify with those differences in values that remain.[11] If this
theory is correct as an empirical generalization, the politics of
shared values is likely to be inherently self-defeating.

Clearly something vital is being left out of the intuitively
appealing connection between shared values and national unity.
In some cases that "something," I take it, is captured by the
notion of a political or national identity. New Englanders coexist
more or less happily with southerners not because they share
values but because they share an identity: they are all Americans.[12] In many cases, polities band together or stay together for
reasons of military or economic security; if they remain together
long enough a pan-national identity may develop, even among
linguistically and culturally diverse peoples (such as the Swiss).
Now the notion of an identity is by no means a clear one, but for
all its vagueness we can appreciate immediately how it binds a
diverse country – even to the point of obviating the very question
of separatism, as is the case in the United States or Switzerland
today.

It is not my intention here to offer anything like an ideology
of shared identity (in other words, a theory of nationalism) to
replace that of shared values, though I return in the next section
to the relation between a shared identity and shared values. First,
however, I shall discuss a number of ways in which the ideology
of shared values is likely to obscure or misdirect political thinking and policy formation.

Kinds of Values

The most serious way in which the ideology of shared values
muddles our political thought is by conflating a number of

crucial distinctions between different kinds and categories of values. There are certainly some sorts of values that members of a liberal democratic society have to share, but there are also many others that we do not expect or even desire to be shared. Indeed, it is generally and rightly acknowledged that a wide diversity of values is something that enriches a modern pluralistic country such as Canada. This kind of diversity, in other words, is not something that ought to be redressed by enforcing or encouraging more uniformity of values. An ideology of shared values will be untenable unless it incorporates some bench-mark for distinguishing the values that have to be held in common from those that needn't or shouldn't be. Without such a criterion, the very idea of the value of diversity will remain paradoxical to the ideologue of shared values.

While the official sources of the ideology do not discuss such a criterion, they do for the most part seem to me to be guided by one, and a reasonable one at that. The relevant distinction, I believe, is roughly that between the two broad categories of moral concepts: the *good* and the *right*. Values of the good are involved in judgments of what is intrinsically worthy and of what adds value to life. Principles of right or justice are concerned with how we ought to treat each other and what rights and obligations we have. Thus we tolerate and even encourage a wide diversity of ideas about the good – that is, about how people find value in their lives; but we find it reasonable to demand that while being free to pursue different life-styles citizens must also agree to abide by certain principles of right or justice. In short, everybody must have the same basic rights, but how they choose to realize their good within the bounds of this scheme of equal basic rights and freedoms is their business. This use of the distinction between the right and the good is the standard way in contemporary political philosophy of explaining the core commitments of liberalism.[13] So a *liberal* ideology of shared values will insist (roughly) that only fundamental principles of justice and democracy must be shared and that in sharing them members of a country have a reason to stick together.

All the official ideologies of shared values discussed above are basically liberal in this way. Of the seven shared values cited by the Spicer Commission, for example, only the quirky but innocuous "Attachment to Canada's Natural Beauty" could be categorized as a conception of the good. The rest are all typical liberal democratic principles of justice. Now, for the reasons discussed above, a liberal ideology of shared values is not any better than any other ideology of shared values at explaining why two polities should share the same state. Again, Canadians share liberal democratic values with citizens of the neighbouring states (and Germans with Austrians, and Swedes with Norwegians, and so on), but that gives them no reason at all to want their provinces to join the United States, or us states to join Canada.

Moreover, in failing to draw explicitly the distinction between values of the right and the good, a liberal ideology of shared values risks undermining its own liberalism. Unable to explain and justify convincingly the value of diversity, it lends itself to the most reactionary of policy prescriptions. Traditionally it is conservatives who are most likely to pine for a strengthening of shared values in order to prevent the unravelling of the social fabric.[14] The sorts of values that they believe ought to be shared and reinforced are, of course, values of the good – concerning how people ought to live their lives (for example, by going to church and living in monogamous, heterosexual families). All the talk of strengthening shared values by liberals and social democrats in Canada recently may encourage this sort of politics, given that conventions of language do in fact associate the term *values* with conceptions of the good, not with conceptions of right or justice, which we generally call principles, standards, norms, rights, or obligations. Without a clear distinction between the right and the good, the liberal ideologue of shared values invites, and may have difficulty resisting, something such as the Beaudoin-Dobbie Committee's recommendation that, in the name of shared values, we embrace the supremacy of God, the importance of the family, and the value of community. Most liberals do, of course, accept at least some of these commitments, but they would be justifiably worried about how the state (including the courts) might interpret and "foster" such values.

Even a thoroughly liberal ideology of shared principles, such as that presented by the Spicer Commission, is likely to muddle our analyses about national unity in so far as it fails to distinguish what we might call different realms of principles. Consider the differences among personal principles, which guide one's daily life; political principles, which govern how society as a whole ought to take decisions; social principles, about how governments should distribute the benefits and burdens of social cooperation; and even federal principles, that special and neglected realm of norms that regulate relations among federal partners. These distinctions could be useful for a variety of practical and theoretical problems, but never have I seen it drawn explicitly in the literature on shared values. I do not discuss its implications at length here, but I would like to offer two remarks.

First, there is reason to believe that the intuition harboured by many ordinary Canadians about shared values concerns personal and social principles (such as tolerance and health care), whereas the "experts," such as the Spicer Commission, come up with lists of principles from all the above-mentioned categories – in particular, political principles. If this is true, then both the ordinary citizens and the experts may be wrong. Our real conflicts threatening national unity may take place almost entirely in the realm of *federal* principles. Consider the clash between an insistence on the alleged federal principle of equality of provinces and the demand by Quebec for a special status derived from its alleged collective rights. Or the tensions highlighted by Alan Cairns between "the old federalism, defined as an affair of governments" and "the new constitutional forces stimulated by the Charter and by the scattering of aboriginal clauses in various parts of the constitution."[15] It is evident, however, that hardly anyone has clear, let alone shared, intuitions about such abstract federal principles.

The "bottom line" for liberals and social democrats is that the ideology of shared values buys them nothing, politically or intellectually. It does not explain how a multinational federation such as Canada stays together, nor why it ought to. It doesn't even explain why liberals are committed to the social and political principles that they believe ought to be shared – since they believe that such principles, such as fundamental civil, political, and social rights, should be enforced even if they are not (yet) shared. Indeed, they must surely believe that basic liberal democratic principles (such as the self-determination of peoples and the equality of basic individual rights) must be adhered to even if they undermine national unity. Yet while buying nothing, the ideology costs liberals and social democrats in terms of their ability to praise the virtues of pluralism and diversity, and it encourages a political discourse that can only aid their conservative opponents.

IDENTITY AND VALUES

I suggested above that if one is looking for "national-unity glue" that is (as the *Economist* has put it[16]) somewhat stickier than maple syrup, but still based on some form of shared feelings or collective conscience, one might consider the bonds of shared identity rather than the muddle of shared values. Again, I do not intend to develop a rival ideology of shared identity, but I do believe that it is worth our while to explore at least some of the relations between values and identity, in part because this exercise will reveal some of the misdirected motivations for the popularity of the ideology of shared values. And also, as I point out in the final section, one of the most interesting national-unity strategies in Canada's history had remarkable success through a unique way of merging the ideas of shared values and shared identity.

What is the relation between shared values and shared identity? The answer is as discouraging for the ideologue of shared values as it was for Marxists during the First World War. To the dismay of the latter group, members of the working class in the nations of Europe – who clearly shared more values with each other than they did with their own bourgeoisies – nevertheless fought each other in defence of their nations. Their national identities and sense of solidarity with fellow citizens whose social values they loathed were stronger than their sense of solidarity with fellow proletarians (of other nations) whose values and interests they shared.[17]

Though there may be no strong relation between *shared* values and *shared* identities, there are important links between identities and certain values. People identify with various collectivities, including their country or nation, to different degrees. And these degrees vary with, among other things, the value that a person attaches to her being a member of that collectivity. For most people, one or more of their identities can have a pervasive and integral role in the very structure of their well-being. In a partial, but very real sense one's major identities define who one is. For many Canadians – but probably not for most Québécois, not even federalists – being Canadian is significant in this way.

Losing their status as Canadians would be a blow – a value loss – that could not be accounted for merely by changes, if any, in material circumstances. (Or think of the same relation between identity and value from the other side: for sovereigntist Québécois, losing their status as Canadians because of Quebec's secession could be an exhilarating experience despite, say, negative effects on material circumstances.) For many people, Canada would not be Canada without Quebec, even if after separation there were still a country called "Canada." So should Quebec separate, these people would literally lose their country and hence their identity (though they would simultaneously gain another, in their eyes inferior, country and identity). Thus there are indeed some important relations between (some) people's national identities and what they value; but these connections do not seem to be illuminated in any way by the ideology of shared values.

The ideology of shared values gets the connection between shared identity (in so far as it takes account of this) and shared values backward. It is not typically common values that lead to a common identity, but vice versa. Consider another source of identity that is often used as an analogy for the nation – namely, the family. The bond and special friendship that exist among family members (and I am thinking in particular or a family whose children have grown up and moved away) have relatively little to do with shared values. (Of course, there are kinds of value differences and failures to follow standard norms that can test the bonds of a family, but we can ignore these for present purposes.) We enjoy and cherish the company of our siblings or parents or children even when, say, they are not the sort of people – in terms of interests and values – that we would normally include among our close friends. A sort of family identity and family culture binds us together despite our lack of shared values or interests. As with national identity and culture, this family identity and culture derive partly from the context of our birth, but primarily from our shared history. Now this latter factor gives family members a rich pool of common experiences, memories, and, in various senses, values. Its history together allows members of a family, among other things, to value each other and their mutual company. This, then, is a special set of shared values that is made possible by a common identity and history – not, as the ideology of shared values might sometimes lead us to believe, the other way round.[18]

Canadians share many memories and value many of the same things as a result of living together. At one time they shared a certain relation to the land and the climate. Out of this, arguably, evolved a fairly widely shared fondness for hockey. A great many Canadians take pride in some of Canada's international achievements – for example, as a founder of the UN or as a peacekeeper. For my generation, growing up with universal social programs has also engendered widely shared beliefs about social entitlements. It is worth making two points about the relevance of these shared values that arise out of a shared history. First, to reiterate the main argument above: these shared values, like any shared values, do not necessarily give peoples and polities a reason to share a country. As Philip Resnick has recently explained: "Young English Canadians and young Québécois, even when they do have some inkling of the language of the other, have not necessarily grown closer together. They may share dress codes, taste in music, career aspirations, concern for the environment … but group sentiments tend to be articulated locally, not globally, and ties that bind are most often forged with those one has gone to school with, lived next door to, or worked beside. For most Québécois that means fellow francophones; for most English-speaking Canadians elsewhere in Canada, fellow anglophones."[19]

Second, shared history is of little value in cementing a shared identity and values if there are radically different interpretations of that history (was Riel a traitor? was Quebec "betrayed" by the patriation of the constitution in 1982?); if the same historical episodes have had different effects on different communities (for example, the role of the Canadian armed forces in the world wars, and the conscription crises); or if there have been different historical episodes within different communities (such as the settling of the west or the Quiet Revolution). I return briefly to these themes below.

The spectacular irrelevance of shared values to national unity permits some otherwise gratuitous speculation. It may well be that when ordinary Canadians and not a few poets told the Spicer Commission that they believed that our shared values could keep us together, they were thinking of something more like the tightly woven tapestry of values, identity, and unity sketched above in the analogy with the family – and not particularly of Canadians' shared belief in democracy, universal health care, and VIA Rail. The thought may have gone like this – "Most of us really do value being Canadian; our politicians are placing the very existence of this thing we value in jeopardy; and we ought therefore to warn them in no uncertain terms that we want to keep the country together because we all share this identity, this value of being Canadian." For all its quaintness, such a thought process is at least coherent. It is, however, manifestly false. Canadians have a "national unity" crisis precisely because they do not all value being Canadian. And again, one will not give Québécois indépendantistes a reason to value being Canadian and to remain in Canada merely by pointing out that they share with anglophones the basic social and political values of Spicer's list.

FORGING A NATIONAL IDENTITY: THE TRUDEAU ERA AND BEYOND[20]

In this section I discuss another important theory about the relation among national unity, national identity, and shared values. The motivations and shortcomings of this more sophisticated (and plausible) ideology of shared values are captured in the ambiguity of the first word of the section heading: "forging" as creating from raw materials, and "forging" as faking.

In countries lacking some of the usual bases of a strong national identity – for example, shared myths, symbols, and values arising out of a common heritage; or a common ethnicity, religion, language, or external enemy[21] – some form of national identity must be forged, in the sense of created and shaped, more or less intentionally, from some design. The pressing need to forge an identity is likely to be felt in New World countries (which are populated largely by descendants of recent immigrants), ex-colonies, and federations – especially federations characterized by diverse languages, religions, peoples, and regions. Canada is a challenging case for nation-builders because it has, at least in some periods, been an example of all of these conditions, which make establishing a national identity difficult.

At least since the union of Upper and Lower Canada in 1841, if not to some degree since the British Conquest of New France, Canadian nation-builders have appealed to numerous visions,

ideals, and rationales to get Canadians (especially, during most of
this time, English and French Canadians) to be loyal to and to
identify with Canada as a whole. We may recall, for example,
Mgr Joseph-Octave Plessis's exhortation in 1799 for French Canadians to recognize the happy fortuity of British rule (as opposed
to rule by republicans and revolutionaries from the United States
or France) because of its wholehearted support of throne and
altar. Or consider the vision advanced early in this century by
Canadian nationalists such as Wilfrid Laurier and Henri Bourassa – of Canadians exploiting and taking pride in their unique
ability to build a country that takes the best from, while rejecting
the worst of, two of the world's great cultures.

In the remainder of the chapter I would like to consider a
more modern and liberal ideal of the basis for a shared Canadian
identity that for better or worse we might call the "Trudeau
vision."[22] It is probably the most sophisticated and plausible
version of the ideology of shared values that has ever guided
official attempts to forge a Canadian identity. The core of Trudeau's vision is the idea that social unity in a modern liberal
state must be founded on a shared conception of justice.[23] Unlike
other, failed liberal versions of the ideology of shared values,
however, it recognizes the need for a shared identity, which it
aims to (re)generate through a national project of creating a just
society. Let us consider how Trudeau himself was led to this idea,
how he and a generation of Canadian "nationalists" breathed life
into it, and, finally, why we should not be surprised if it turns
out to be not much better a basis for Canadian unity than other
ideologies of shared values.

There seems to have been more development on Trudeau's
views about national unity than he recalls in "The Values of a
Just Society," his 1990 piece of intellectual autobiography.[24] I
believe that in particular something interesting happened to his
"vision" between his "functionalist" period, in the early and mid-
1960s, and his first few years in government, from around 1965
to 1968. Trudeau's entire intellectual and political career was, of
course, marked by an irredeemable hatred of nationalism. By
"nationalism" he means not (what he considers to be) the perfectly respectable feeling of belonging to a nation – something
akin to national identity – but rather a more primitive, exclusive,
often chauvinistic or racist desire to preserve the integrity of the

nation.[25] Not the least (but also not the only) of his worries about nationalism was that in a state with more than one national group, nationalists would never be satisfied until their nation was a state of its own, thus destroying what might be an otherwise rationally ordered state for the sake of what he would call "emotionalism."

In 1965, during his functionalist period, Trudeau considered two ways of controlling ethnic and regional nationalism in a federal state such as Canada. Though he rejected the first and accepted the second, both would later become associated with the cuddly Canadian nationalism of the Trudeau era. The first way "of offsetting the appeal of separatism is by investing tremendous amounts of time, energy, and money in nationalism, *at the federal level*." To do this, he continues:

A national image must be created that will have such an appeal as to make any image of a separatist group unattractive. Resources must be diverted into such things as national flags, anthems, education, arts councils, broadcasting corporations, film boards; the territory must be bound together by a network of railways, highways, airlines; the national culture and the national economy must be protected by taxes and tariffs; ownership of resources and industry by nationals must be made a matter of policy. In short, the whole of the citizenry must be made to feel that it is only within the framework of the federal state that their language, culture, institutions, sacred traditions, and standard of living can be protected from external attack and internal strife.[26]

Even though "national unity" policies during Trudeau's years in power would later embrace every single one of these initiatives (except the new flag, which was already in place), Trudeau himself recognized before entering government that they were, in themselves, no match for a sub-nationalism bent on separation: "Any expenditure of emotional appeal (flags, professions of faith, calls to dignity, expressions of brotherly love) at the national level will only serve to justify similar appeals at the regional level, where they are just as likely to be effective. Thus the great moment of truth arrives when it is realized that *in the last resort* the mainspring of federalism cannot be emotion but must be reason."[27] Trudeau believed that "separatism would remain a recurrent phenomenon" and that "massive investment in flags, dignity, protectionism and Canadian content of television" might hold Canada together only a few more years.

This first way of fighting separatism fails for Trudeau because it tries to fight a deeply entrenched emotionalism with a newly devised, and presumably weaker emotionalism. His solution in those heady days of functionalism – the second way – was to fight emotionalism with reason, pre-modern romanticism with rationality. "Thus there is some hope that in advanced societies, the glue of nationalism will become as obsolete as the divine right of kings; the title of the state to govern and the extent of its authority will be conditional upon *rational justification*; a people's consensus *based on reason* will supply the cohesive force that societies require; and politics both within and without the state will follow a much more functional approach to the problems of government."[28]

Trudeau believed that federalism had "all along been a product of reason in politics. It was born of a decision by pragmatic politicians to face facts as they are, particularly the fact of the heterogeneity of the world's population."[29] The Canadian constitution of 1867, with "its absence of principles, ideals, or other frills," was a model of such pragmatic federal reason. "If reason be the governing virtue of federalism," he added, "it would seem that Canada got off to a good start."[30] The essay concludes with Trudeau's suggestion "that cold, unemotional rationality can still save the ship."[31]

Though Trudeau is still inclined to see the attraction of nationalism as largely emotional, he no longer contrasts it with reason per se. What, after all, could he have meant by "reason" and "rational justification"? He seemed to have in mind the use of "political instruments which are sharper, stronger, and more finely controlled than anything based on mere emotionalism: such tools will be made up of advanced technology and scientific investigation, as applied to law, economics, social psychology, international affairs." It is hard to believe that less than thirty years ago intelligent people could still be titillated by such positivist, technocratic fantasies.[32] But it is not hard to imagine what would have happened to his first campaign as Liberal leader, just three years after writing this paper, had he not come up with a more attractive vehicle for national unity. That vehicle, which we might consider his third strategy for national unity, was the ideal of the Just Society.

Trudeau recalls that "the dominant theme of the election campaign in the spring of 1968 – a strong and united Canada founded on a policy of equal opportunity for all – was the one I approached with the greatest conviction and the one to which others responded with the greatest enthusiasm."[33] And he describes how, between 1968 and 1984, his government tried to counterbalance "the centrifugal forces that were threatening to break the federation apart ... by implementing policies whose goal was to create a Just Society."[34] Not surprising, Trudeau sees the Constitution Act, 1982, as the crowning achievement of his efforts to forge a Just Society.[35] With its equality of opportunity and regional equalization provisions in section 36, and its Charter of Rights and Freedoms, which included provisions for the equality of French and English, the constitution "was a new beginning for the Canadian nation: it sought to strengthen the country's unity by basing the sovereignty of the Canadian people on a set of values common to all, and in particular on the notion of equality among all Canadians."[36]

In Trudeau's own mind and writings, this idea of the Just Society retains some of the remoteness of his earlier pitch for reason. The "common values" to which he refers are, of course, quintessentially liberal principles of justice, including redistributive justice. As such, they remain vulnerable to our earlier criticism directed against this version of the ideology of shared values. What we often refer to as the "Trudeau vision," however, has clearly developed a life of its own, moving beyond some of its author's own intentions and objectives for what we might call the ideology of the Just Society – or better yet, the Canadian Just Society, for this ideology is idiosyncratically Canadian. What makes it more effective and interesting as a strategy of national unity is that it incorporates the more traditional elements of national identity: a shared mythology and a national project or destiny. The idea is not merely that Canada is a relatively just society and that Canadians by and large, as the Spicer Commission reports, are just and democratic citizens. This again, in itself, would give English Canadians and Québécois no more reason than it gives Swedes and Norwegians to cohabit within the same state. The ideology of the Just Society goes further in seeking to get Canadians to identify with and be proud of the

Just Society that they have all supposedly helped to create. For many, the Charter, official bilingualism, and multiculturalism are important symbols for this identity.

But the identity and pride have also been sustained by not a little mythology and revisionist history. The mythology is nourished in part by the fact that most Canadians are blissfully ignorant of their own history, and in part by their obsessive gazing at the United States of America's navel. National health care and relatively safe cities look like unique achievements to take special national pride in only if one ignores the fact that they are taken for granted in virtually every Western country except the United States. Similar mythology overplays the success of bilingualism and multiculturalism. The absence of nation-wide official bilingualism for the entire century after Confederation, and the continuing, not-always-benign decline of francophone communities outside Quebec, should be sources of national shame. So should the reception, official and unofficial, of most non-British immigrants, as well as the treatment of Aboriginal peoples, throughout Canadian history. Even the much-heralded achievement of a "mosaic," in contrast with the US-style "melting pot," is almost certainly overdrawn.[37] In so far as immigrant communities have retained their identities (especially in the west), this result may have more to do with the fact that Canadian governments did not have the resources to assimilate them. These remarks are meant only to suggest how powerful the widely shared but quite recent mythology of the Just Canadian Society must have been in order to have overcome so much contrary historical fact.

As a basis for forging a national identity and national unity, the ideology of the Canadian Just Society was a bold and surprisingly (if incompletely) successful idea. It is also morally attractive. As long as some form of strong national pride and national identity are necessary for political stability, it is much better to develop this out of commitment to creating a just society than from an appeal to shared ethnicity, a glorious past, or a belligerent present. This is, as noted above, the utopian liberal ideal. It just may, however, be an ideal ahead of its time.

Though it is encouraging that such a recently conservative country as Canada could make such a good "go of it," one must also be discouraged by the fact that, even in as liberal a country as Canada is now, it may not succeed. Its weakness is derived from the inherent weakness of any ideology of shared values. Citizens of polities within the larger state have no special reason to want to share a state with other polities simply because they have the same basic political and social values. And further, it is always possible that members of the "nationalist polity," whom the ideology of the Just Society is trying to integrate, will identify with their own polity as the force behind their own Just Society. This is of course exactly the point that Trudeau raised against the forging of a pan-regional identity through pan-regional symbols: any given region is likely to adopt similar symbolism, which will turn out to be more attractive.

Arguably, this tendency of nationalists to take credit for their own social achievements also explains why the ideology of the Canadian Just Society has manifestly not succeeded in binding Quebec to the rest of Canada. Quebecers too take justified pride in turning a conservative society into a modern liberal one. And they see this accomplishment as largely their own doing: from the Quiet Revolution in the 1960s and the social democracy of the Bourassa and Lévesque governments of the 1970s, to Quebec, Inc., and the made-in-Quebec "boom" of the 1980s. And along with these advances goes a mythology that remembers fighting *les Anglais* and Ottawa for every opportunity, as well as the "betrayal" by English Canada over the constitution of 1982, the "humiliation" of Quebec from the refusal to acknowledge its distinct society in the Meech Lake Accord, and the "mutual rejection" of the Charlottetown referendum. Add in memories of the Conquest, the conscription crisis, and the treatment of French Canadians outside Quebec, and it is little wonder that many Québécois are more inclined to see their Just Society as something that they got in spite of, rather than in concert with, English Canadians. Of course, much of this mythology is forged, in the sense of faked, just as is that of the rest of Canada. But this fact just serves to emphasize how powerless the ideology of shared values remains in the face of the traditional role played by myths, symbols, and ethnicity in the moulding of a national identity.

NOTES

I am grateful to Hilliard Aronovitch, Allen Buchanan, Théo Geraets, Patricia Ivan, Will Kymlicka, Guy Laforest, Don Lenihan, Michael Oliver, and Don Ross for comments on earlier drafts of this chapter.

1 Federalists in Quebec often cite the convergence of basic values, of the sort discussed below, as a reason for Quebec's remaining in Confederation. Similarly, many separatists support their beliefs by emphasizing the alleged lack of convergence between some fundamental values in Quebec and those in the rest of Canada (e.g., concerning the importance of collective rights or the state's role in supporting culture and economic development) while trumpeting the "consensus" around the Bélanger-Campeau report as evidence of Quebec's readiness to assume the challenges of statehood.

2 See, for example, Charles Taylor, "Shared and Divergent Values," *Options For a New Canada*, ed. Ronald L. Watts and Douglas M. Brown (Toronto: University of Toronto Press, 1991), 53–76, republished in Charles Taylor, *Reconciling the Solitudes: Essays on Canadian Federalism and Nationalism*, ed. Guy Laforest (Montreal: McGill-Queen's University Press, 1993), 155–86; William Kaplan, ed., *Belonging: The Meaning and Future of Canadian Citizenship* (Montreal and Kingston: McGill-Queen's University Press, 1993). In Europe, similar views have been espoused by Jürgen Habermas and his followers in their defence of post-nationalism and constitutional patriotism. I discuss these theories and their relation to what I am calling the ideology of shared values in "Unité, identité et nationalisme libéral," *Lekton*, 3 no. 2 (1993), 35–64.

3 Citizens' Forum on Canada's Future, *Report to the People and Government of Canada* (Ottawa: Ministry of Supply and Services, 1991).

4 Government of Canada, *Shaping Canada's Future Together* (Ottawa: Ministry of Supply and Services, 1991).

5 Government of Canada, *Shared Values: The Canadian Identity* (Ottawa: Ministry of Supply and Services, 1991).

6 Beaudoin-Dobbie Committee, *Report of the Special Joint Committee on a Renewed Canada* (Ottawa: Ministry of Supply and Services, 1992).

7 See, for instance, the Ontario government's discussion paper, *A Canadian Social Charter: Making Our Shared Values Stronger* (Toronto: Ministry of Intergovernmental Affairs, Sept. 1991). This document discusses at length the "Canadian social contract" and the "values which underlie it" and how entrenching these values and principles will give "formal recognition of a part of what defines and holds us together as Canadians." This is why Premier Bob Rae states in his introduction that "a social charter can be an important part of nation-building." On the nation-building argument for a social charter, see L. Osberg and S. Phipps, "A Social Charter for Canada,"

in *A Social Charter for Canada? Perspectives on the Constitutional Entrenchment of Social Rights*, ed. L. Osberg and S. Phipps (Toronto: C.D. Howe Institute, 1992); and for a critical discussion, see W. Kymlicka and W. Norman, "The Social Charter Debate: Should Social Justice be Constitutionalized?" *Network Analysis No. 2* (Ottawa: Network on the Constitution, 1992), 6–7.

8   Many of these phrases and ideas would eventually appear in the Charlottetown Accord, the gargantuan constitutional agreement signed by the eleven first ministers, as well as Aboriginal leaders, in August 1992, and defeated, for reasons too numerous and complex to mention here, in a referendum two months later.

9   For a useful list of studies supporting this view, see Stéphane Dion, "Explaining Quebec Nationalism," in *The Collapse of Canada?* ed. R. Weaver (Washington, DC: Brookings Institute, 1992), 99 n 44. Other important recent studies of the evolution of Quebec nationalism include: Christian Dufour, *Le défi québécois* (Montreal: L'Hexagone, 1989); Michael Oliver, *The Passionate Debate: The Social and Political Ideas of Quebec Nationalism, 1920–45* (Montreal: Véhicule Press, 1991); and Gilles Gougeon, *A History of Quebec Nationalism*, trans. Robert Chodos (Toronto: Lorimer, 1994).

10 For an impressive recent attempt, see Dion, "Explaining Quebec Nationalism."

11 See Stéphane Dion, "Le nationalisme dans la convergence culturelle: le Québec contemporain et le paradox de Tocqueville," in *L'engagement intellectuel: mélanges en l'honneur de Léon Dion*, ed. R. Hudon and R. Pelletier (Ste-Foy, Que.: Les Presses de l'Université Laval, 1991), 291–311; and "Explaining Quebec Nationalism," 101.

12 This example reminds us that shared values are not completely irrelevant to questions of national unity. The US Civil War was, after all, fought primarily over a disagreement on values. Nevertheless, it is an underlying assumption here that that kind of diversity is not at stake in Canada, nor probably in any Western country at present.

13 The loci classici here are John Rawls, *A Theory of Justice* (Cambridge, Mass.: Harvard University Press, 1971), and Ronald Dworkin, "Liberalism," in *Public and Private Morality*, ed. S. Hampshire (Cambridge: Cambridge University Press, 1978), 113–43.

14 As Lord Devlin puts it: "Without shared ideas on politics, morals, and ethics no society can exist ... For society is not something that is kept together physically; it is held together by the invisible bonds of common thought. If the bonds were too far relaxed the members would drift apart." Patrick Devlin, *The Enforcement of Morals* (Oxford: Oxford University Press, 1965), 10.

15 Alan Cairns, *Disruptions: Constitutional Struggles from the Charter to Meech*

Lake, ed. Douglas E. Williams (Toronto: McClelland and Stewart, 1991), 27.

16 In a special report on Canada, *Economist*, 29 June 1991.

17 Just as Tocqueville had foretold in 1840 in *De la démocratie en Amérique* (Paris: Flammarion, 1981), 289; as discussed in Dion, "Le nationalisme," 292–4.

18 Though I am naturally suspicious of arguments by analogy – since every analogy is by definition a disanalogy, for otherwise it would be an identity – I believe that a comparison of this sort is relevant, even though the thumbnail sketch above is surely inadequate. For one thing, people really do conceive of their country as a kind of family. And in Canada we can never resist describing our national unity traumas with marital and family metaphors. Even more important, families and countries provide very similar exceptions to a whole range of intentional attitudes. For example, normally it does not really make sense, conceptually or psychologically, for one to be proud of, or ashamed of, an event or achievement that one did not help to bring about and that one could not have helped to prevent. Yet we do feel a natural sense of pride or shame for the actions of family members and, in the right circumstances, of our fellow citizens (as when they win an Olympic medal, or a war – even one that happened before we were born). Václav Havel links one's various forms of identity with the notion of one's home: "home is a basic existential experience. What a person perceives as home (in the philosophical sense of the word) can be compared to a set of concentric circles, with one's "I" at the centre ... My home is the house I live in, the village or town where I was born or where I spend most of my time. My home is my family, the world of my friends, my profession, my company, my workplace ... the country I live in, my citizenship, this world ... my home is also my education, my upbringing, my habits, my social milieu." *Summer Meditations*, trans. Paul Wilson (Toronto: Alfred Knopf Canada, 1992), 30–1.

19 Phillip Resnick, *Toward a Canada-Quebec Union* (Montreal and Kingston: McGill-Queen's University Press, 1991), 39.

20 This section borrows from my "Unité, identité et nationalisme libéral."

21 For similar lists, see Anthony D. Smith, *National Identity* (London: Penguin, 1991), 14, 175. See also P.E. Trudeau, *Federalism and the French Canadians* (Toronto: Macmillan, 1968), 189, 193.

22 For the most thorough recent evaluation of this "vision," see D. Lenihan, G. Robertson, and R. Tassé, *Canada: Reclaiming the Middle Ground* (Ottawa: Institute for Research on Public Policy, 1994).

23 This is a central tenet of modern liberal theory. See Rawls, *A Theory of Justice*, 120–9.

24 In T. Axworthy and P.E. Trudeau, *Toward a Just Society: The Trudeau Years* (Markham, Ont.: Viking, 1990), 357–85. For his more detailed account of

these years, see P.E. Trudeau, *Memoirs* (Toronto: McClelland and Stewart, 1993).

25 Trudeau, *Federalism*, 189–90.

26 Ibid., 193. In a recent article, Andrew Stark misreads Trudeau as having been advocating, rather than criticizing, this strategy. See Stark, "English-Canadian Opposition to Quebec Nationalism," in *The Collapse of Canada*, ed. R. Weaver (Washington, DC: Brookings Institute, 1992), 128.

27 Trudeau, *Federalism*, 194.

28 Ibid., 196, my emphasis.

29 Ibid., 195.

30 Ibid., 197.

31 Ibid., 203.

32 On Trudeau's fascination, and subsequent falling out, with functionalism, see Reg Whitaker, *A Sovereign Idea: Essays on Canada as a Democratic Community* (Montreal and Kingston: McGill-Queen's University Press, 1992), 155–6.

33 Trudeau, "Values of a Just Society," 359.

34 Ibid., 361. It is a significant mark of the theoretical or ideological nature of Trudeau's concept of a just society that he cannot refer to it without an upper-case "J" and "S," as if it were a proper name.

35 Ibid., 362.

36 Ibid., 363.

37 See G. Horowitz's classic analysis, "Mosaics and Identities" (1965–6), in *Canadian Political Thought*, ed. H.D. Forbes (Toronto: Oxford University Press, 1985), 359–64.

CHAPTER SEVEN

Quebec:
The Morality of Secession

Howard Adelman

Canada is on the brink of a bust-up. It teeters there for reasons peculiar to itself, but the forces that will push it over or pull it back are at play in almost every corner of the world. "The Canadian model" – whether of disintegration or of holding together in some new, post-modern version of the nation-state – is going to be an example to avoid or follow for all but a few federations, for all multicultural societies, especially immigrant ones, for countries whose borders reflect conquest more than geography, and for all states riven or driven by nationalism.

"Survey of Canada," *Economist*, 29 June 1991, 3

I am not concerned here with the domestic forces that will push Quebec into separation or prevent it from separating. Nor do I consider the international forces that might or might not give legitimacy to separation if Quebecers support secession in a referendum in 1995. I am not undertaking a political or economic analysis. Nor am I looking at whether the process under way for Quebec separation – a referendum within Quebec alone – provides legal legitimacy for separation. I am focusing rather on the morality of nationalist secession (as distinct from territorial populism) as a theoretical option in opposition to the contractarian state. This study analyses the general moral principles underlying and binding on nationalist secession in Quebec.

First, I define the essence of nationalist secession and posit that Quebec's separatist movement is as close as one is likely to get to a pure example of liberal rather than nativist nationalist separatism. Second, I examine both the ideology of statism and the character of state authority in dealing with the obligations of citizens. Only then can we probe the issue of sovereignty. Third,

I distinguish between the sovereignty of a nation, or people, and that of a state (in contrast to those who believe that sovereignty is a conception restricted to states) and then argue that a sovereign people takes moral and political precedence over the sovereignty of a state. Canadians, I believe, accept that priority. I set out the parameters for a legal and non-violent nationalist separatism to be exercised without arguing about whether or not the actual process under way is legal. Since our main concern is with the role and treatment of minorities and their rights within Quebec, I take up that issue – specifically, the rights of Anglo-Canadians, immigrants, and the Cree and Inuit of northern Quebec.

This is an analytic exercise. I am not advocating nationalist secession. I do attempt, however, to defend nationalist separatism as a moral option when it respects liberal norms. I do not argue about whether nationalist separatism is the best rational choice for Quebecers or whether it is a choice that will fulfil their emotional sense of who they are. What I do, however, is set out the moral constraints for exercising such a choice if one is committed to liberalism. If Quebecers choose nationalist secession, I maintain, they should do so within the dictates of morality and the liberal constraints of exercising the nationalist-separatist option. This does not imply that legal and economic norms and constraints may not also be applicable.

NATIONALIST SECESSION, TERRITORIAL POPULISM, AND THE STATE

Secession has become an endemic problem around the world.[1] The list of peoples, republics, provinces, territories, and areas aspiring toward secession covers the globe. In addition to Quebec in Canada as well as the vast number of potential and actual situations in sub-Saharan Africa, there are the Basques and Catalans in Spain, the Corsicans in France, the Scots[2] and Welsh in Great Britain, the Sikhs in Punjab and the Muslims in Kashmir of India, the Tamils in Sri Lanka, the Inner Mongolians and Tibetans in China, and the Kurds in Turkey, Iraq, and Iran. There were the Slovaks in Czechoslovakia, the Slovenes and Croats in Yugoslavia, the Turks in Cyprus, the Latvians, Lithuanians, and Estonians, Ukrainians, Armenians, and Georgians[3] in what was the Soviet Union, and the Eritreans in Ethiopia. Even the Palestinians in the West Bank and Gaza share some kinship with separatist movements that have seceded or are in the process of achieving de facto and even de jure secession.

The above list, which is not even comprehensive, focuses on nationalist separatist movements. There are also purely territorial populist movements, some of which advocate secession:

Territorial populists rally supporters in reaction to the fragmentation of social cohesion for which reformist policies are blamed. They claim to simultaneously fight for jobs at home, scrape away encrusted bureaucracies and overcome social fragmentation. Whether through xenophobic appeals, regionalism or a rejection of supranational economic commitments, they reaffirm the validity of a bounded political domain. They contest the perceived diffusion of decision-making to supranational authorities or offshore enterprises. They promise to restore a sense of identity and to repatriate decisions to a cohesive community on a familiar home territory.[4]

Territorial populists sometimes manifest themselves as separatists. The rise of the Reform party in western Canada is a relatively mild example of territorial populism, but it is not the same thing as western separatism. Territorial populism is distinct from but can encompass separatism.

Similarly, nationalism need not be equated with separatism. The Liberal party in Quebec has a strong nationalist strain, whereas the Parti québécois advocates nationalist separatism. In periods of state disintegration, nationalist movements of minorities within a state almost inevitably express themselves as separatist movements.

Further, just as territorial populism can manifest itself as separatism, nationalist secession movements are sometimes based on or at least borrow from and overlap with territorial populism. Still, the two are not the same. We thus have the following options:

- territorial populism
- territorial populism that is separatist
- nationalism
- nationalism that is separatist
- nationalist separatism using territorial-populist appeals

Here I am concerned with nationalist separatism that does not primarily or even significantly appeal to territorial populism. This,

I believe, is the primary character of Quebec nationalism today. Nationalist separatism begins with the concept of a people and its desire for self-determination through state institutions that are sovereign and govern a specific area of territory. Territorial populism begins with the desire for a more bounded and localized political domain. The key distinction is whether the primary appeal is to nationalism or localism, to preservation and continuity of a people or to proximity of the exercise of political authority to the territory occupied, to a temporal or a spatial rationale.

Territorial populism is not a significant force in current Canadian politics.[5] Jacques Parizeau, after he became premier of Quebec, articulated a temporal rationale for Quebec nationalist separation rather than territorial populism in his speech to the Canadian Club in Toronto: "Quebec is our community. Our society. Our identity. When we think of ourselves, we don't think of Quebec, in Canada, in the world. No. We think, more and more, of Quebec in the world ... We are members of the international community as Quebecers ... Quebec nationalism accepts as an ideal the functional integration of regions and even of whole continents. It is the reflection of the desire for a personality in an increasingly impersonal world."[6]

The confusion between territorial populism and nationalist separatism is understandable, since the two sometimes overlap on the basis of their appeal and both have the identical targeted enemy. The enemy is not the state per se, but a specific state and a conception of that state. The conception is based on a premise that the state is merely the result of an implicit contract among individuals and that order has been established through that social contract.

DEFINING NATIONALIST SECESSION

"The secessionist does not deny the state's authority as such, but only its authority over her and the other members of her group and the territory they occupy."[7] If that was all there was to secession, dealing with it would be much easier. Allen Buchanan does note the three essential components of secession – that it is an issue having to do with state authority, nationalism, and territory. However, that is all in his definition that is correct.

With respect to state authority, secessionist movements do not necessarily or even usually deny state authority over their group;

they merely desire to have a different state assume that authority. In other words, Quebec separatists do not deny the authority of Canada in governing them; they merely want to shift the authority of the federal government to Quebec. Separatists, at least nationalist liberal separatists, reject the authority of the existing state itself only when the coercive forces of the state are used to suppress articulation of a separatist vision and organization of the political instruments to achieve that goal. Though some separatists may engage in revolt and actually deny state authority (the Ibos, the Kurds, the Tamils), most usually begin by establishing that the representative group seeking to negotiate separation is recognized as legitimate and has the backing of the majority of the population on behalf of whom it seeks separation. In fact, it is usually only when the opportunity is unavailable for elections or referenda and the will of the people cannot be legally expressed that the leadership advocates violence. When there are elected representatives, but they are totally frustrated in their attempts to advance their separatist position and are even denied representative status in a parliamentary body because of their advocacy of autonomy, as was the case of the Tamils, separatist leadership generally shifts to militants.

Not all secessionists apply their beliefs only to members of their own group, though nativist nationalists do. If they are motivated by nationalism but committed to liberal principles, they have to consider the situation of individuals and groups within the territory who do not identify with that nation or people, whether it be the Serbs in Croatia, the Russians in Lithuania, the Cree, Inuit, Mohawk, and Anglo-Canadians in Quebec, and so on. In other words, a realignment of the state authority over the Québécois is not sufficient. The state authority over all Quebecers is at issue. And it is all Quebecers, not just the Québécois, who must determine whether separatism is in order. Nationalist secessionist movements may be nativist and non-liberal, but they also may be liberal. Here I am concerned with the morality of liberal nationalist separatism.

Finally, with regard to territory, secession is not simply a matter of the territory that a particular group occupies but includes all the territory of an existing political jurisdiction. For Quebec, the Eastern Townships, where English Canadians predominate; the island of Montreal, where English Canadians and immigrants are dominant; and the northern arctic regions, occupied mostly by the Cree and Inuit, are all included within the territory to be severed politically from the rest of Canada.

The Canadian Case

Canada is a test case for a liberal theory of secession not simply because it can set a model for the rest of the world but also because it is one of the purest cases of nationalist liberal secession. There are several reasons to claim purity for the Canadian case.

First, the issue of rectificatory justice – that is, where secession is justified because a nation's territory was illegally annexed by force, as in Latvia, Estonia, Eritrea, and Tibet – is minimal.[8] Quebec joined Canada of its own free will. It was not raped or tricked into joining, though the sense of Quebecers having been a conquered people is a crucial historical memory. French-Canadian history begins with *La conquête*. It reads totally differently from English-Canadian history. However, though memory of historical trauma is critical, it is not the memory of a historical injustice currently in need of rectification.

Second, the issue of distributory justice, which is sometimes used to justify secession, is also minimal. The rest of Canada can no longer be accused of continuing to exploit a minority, denying it a fair share of the proceeds. This might perhaps have been the case when Quebecers were paying 25 percent of the taxes and receiving 16 percent of the benefits, but in recent years the benefits to Quebec have been roughly proportionate to its tax base (22 percent), and some observers have even argued that the province has received extra benefits to help bribe it into staying in Canada. The mass of Quebecers are no longer hewers of wood and drawers of water for the *Anglais*; they earn 92 percent of the average income and produce 40 percent of Canada's business graduates, and Quebec business has developed a self-assurance and global reach that is often the envy of the rest of Canada. Some commentators have said that it is precisely this record of economic success and reduced economic fear that has allowed Quebecers increasingly to imagine themselves as existing separately from the rest of Canada. In fact, in the current political context, this perception by others that Quebec unfairly benefits rankles Quebecers more than any belief that they are the victims of an in-appropriate application of the principles of distributive justice.

Third, in Quebec there are no problems in deciding who represents the group that wishes to secede, as there is a proper and constitutional basis for selecting representatives. Virtually everyone agrees that a referendum is needed to back a decision to secede. Further, few individuals of influence opposing separatism have proposed creating constitutional impediments – such as the agreement of the majority in Canada as a whole or of three-quarters, or seven, of the provinces backed up by a two-thirds vote in the House of Commons – as a condition for permitting secession,[9] though recently more people have been advocating such a stance. Nor have there been any serious proposals for imposing a financial exit cost to secession over and above Quebec's assuming its rightful share of assets and debts. There are none of the constitutional barriers to secession that exist or have been proposed in other jurisdictions where the will of the majority is able to impose and restrict the rights of a minority.

Of course, constitutional changes have affected the separatist case, such as the loss of the constitutional veto when the constitution was patriated. "The two-nations concept came to an abrupt end in 1982 when Quebec found out that the most significant amendment to the Constitution did not require the consent of one of the founding nations. That year was also an important milestone for interpreting the Constitution as a compact among provinces."[10]

However, the constititional disputes do not seem to be the essence of the secessionist problem. There was full agreement by the other provinces on several formulas to allow Quebec to retain a veto. Given the notwithstanding clause in the Charter of Rights and Freedoms, there is no real impediment to Quebec's setting aside a ruling of the Supreme Court of Canada. At worst, such an action might be embarrassing and humiliating. Further, the rest of the country seems agreeable to ensuring that Quebec is represented disproportionate to its percentage of the population in the Supreme Court, even though the Charlottetown Accord entrenching this provision was defeated in the 1992 referendum.[11]

An important argument used by separatists is that Quebec needs to be separate in order to preserve its language, distinctive society, and culture. "There can be circumstances under which a group living within the jurisdiction of the state may reasonably seek to achieve political autonomy for a quite different reason: to be able to express and sustain values other than, though not opposed to, justice, such as a distinctive conception of community or a particular conception of the religious life ... perhaps an ethnic group believes (as many in Quebec apparently do) that forming its own sovereign state is the only way to preserve its distinctive culture."[12]

My own conviction, however, is that the issue in Canada is not unwillingness to allow Quebec to retain sufficient state powers to preserve its distinct society – though certainly some anglophones refuse to guarantee that such powers be retained by Quebec. Rather, the debate was and is over the impact of granting such powers in a system that those anglophones think is based on the equal status of all the provinces. The problem was recognition of a distinct identity and devolution of political authority to Quebec to correspond with that recognition.

Many argue that Quebec already has all the necessary constitutional tools to preserve its distinct society. Further, there is a great deal of evidence to suggest that there is very little danger in this regard if Quebec remains part of Canada. French was made the sole official language of the province in 1974 in the same decade when New Brunswick decided to become officially bilingual, when there were pressures on Ontario and Manitoba to do the same, and when it became *de rigueur* for many middle-class, upwardly mobile Canadians in the rest of Canada who have aspirations for their children to send them to bilingual schools or to enrol them in French immersion classes. French has become the language of Montreal and of business. The Québécois control their own television, radio, and other forms of culture. Though a higher percentage of Quebecers are bilingual compared with the rest of Canada, most francophones in Quebec do not speak English.

In other words, for the three arguments related to preserving a distinctive society, few in Canada deny Quebec that right, and many argue that it already has the constitutional tools to do so. Furthermore, most non-Quebecers are willing, if necessary, to grant other tools for it to achieve that goal within an existing constitution that insists on symmetry of powers among the provinces. In addition, there is much evidence to suggest that cultural preservation is not threatened by Quebec's continuing presence as part of Canada.

The same, of course, except in New Brunswick, cannot be said for the French residing in other provinces. Not only have the numbers of those who claim French as their mother tongue declined to 4.3 percent, but francophones in Ontario who speak French dropped from 73 percent in 1971 to 63 percent in 1991. At the same time, French has become just the language of school – francophones in the rest of Canada have far greater access to French schools than ever before; English increasingly takes the place of French at work and at home.

Quebecers, too, like everyone in today's modern world of multinationals, satellite communications, and the domination of Hollywood, are pressed by the forces of cultural homogenization that prevail throughout the world. Drinking Coke and Pepsi, eating pizza, wearing Wrangler, Levi, or Lee jeans and Benneton sweaters, and listening to the same rock music have become universal. Quebecers are no exception. Nevertheless, they are relatively more insulated from the pressures of Americanization than other Canadians, including francophones who use in everyday speech the English language which dominates international culture.

Nor are Quebecers motivated primarily by a desire to preserve values different from those of other Canadians. Though Quebecers *may* have more of a Gallic flair in their clothes and speech, though they *may* have preferred leaders with more pizazz, or at least more love of pomp and ceremony, the two peoples share a predisposition to humane attitudes, tolerance, and civility in public discourse and a preference for relative equity. The values that unite Canadians still seem much more similar than any that divide them. And those values are distinctively different than those of Americans. Canadians as a whole value peace, order, and good government and have none of the built-in antipathy and suspicion toward the state that are part of American ideology. Precisely because virtually all Canadians value order, Canada presents one of the purest examples for examining the case for secession.

The single and strongest motive for Quebec nationalism is that the French Canadians in Quebec want to be "maîtres chez nous" – masters in our own house. If they decide to secede, several factors – historical grievances, unfair allocation of resources because of lack of distributive justice, the absence of the province of Quebec's consent to the patriated constitution with its provisions that deny them a veto and transfer some control to the judiciary – all may have provided impetus to the separatist dream, but none of these is the essence of why Quebec may decide to separate any more than it is a rule for a spouse who decides to leave his or her partner. There may have been adequate consultation, not only in key decisions but in the rules for making those decisions. There may have been equitable arrangements for distribution of powers and responsibilities. Income and assets may have been more or less fairly apportioned. A spouse may simply want to leave a marriage because of feeling unfulfilled in it. There may be no incompatibility in values; the spouse may simply believe that it is time to enter the world stage alone. There need be no sense of injustice or grievance in the decision – merely a belief about what maturity, individuality, and autonomy entail.[13]

A nationalist in Quebec leans toward separatism if he or she believes that the existing political arrangements with the rest of Canada do not permit enough scope for the Québécois to achieve recognition on the world stage and that those restricted powers allocated to the province are insufficient to guarantee the continuity of the Québécois culture in the future. To opt for separatism, the nationalist may also need to be convinced that the choice is also prudent at this time.

To summarize, my claim is that Canada is probably as close as one gets to a pure case of separatism unencumbered by such issues as various forms of social injustice. Further, there are very few issues of process (though, as I contend below in the discussion of minorities, there is a critical one with respect to the Cree and Inuit). There is no difficulty in identifying the people who may decide to separate even if there is a great deal of debate over the tactics and the wording of any referendum question. Nor is there controversy over the mode by which that determination will be made. Affirmation of separation by a simple majority of Quebecers who actually vote will set Quebec on the path to negotiating the terms of separation.

In the 1980 referendum in Quebec, though a majority vote would have been required to begin separation, the support of 40 percent of the voters would have appeared sufficient to set Quebec down the path toward separation, since 40 percent would have represented the majority of French Canadians in Quebec. The failure to obtain even a majority of French Quebecers in support of separation cast a pall over the separatist forces, though successive failures at constitutional reform to incorporate Québécois nationalist concerns reinvigorated them. A vote of a majority of French Canadians in Quebec does not legitimize separation, but it would provide an enormous psychological boost for the separatist forces, for it would indicate that a majority of the Québécois, not Quebecers, favour separation.

Similarly, though historically there may have been many motives based on alleged and real injustices, and though current alleged injustices and humiliations may be cited as a catalyst, these are not the main motives. Nor are there procedural impediments to a "no-fault divorce." Canada is a case in which we can bracket issues of injustice and thus can find one of the purest and uncontaminated cases for separatism and a procedure for overcoming the main hurdle – determining whether Quebec wants to separate.

In Quebec, consent will not be the central issue, though it will be a procedural prerequisite. Injustice also will not be the primary issue. Collective identity, collective autonomy, and collective fulfilment will be. The key elements in the primary impetus to separatism are not unjust use of state authority or inadequate representation of the minority in the executive, legislative, and judicial branches, even if there remain some points of dispute in these areas. The key elements are not defects in civil society and the role of the state in creating distortions that hurt a minority; in fact, Quebec's economic success has inceased the potential for separatism. Central components of nationalism are at the heart of the move toward separatism. For it is only when the French Canadians moved from becoming a minority in Canada to developing an identity as Québécois that separatism became a powerful force. "A defensive minority had been turned into a nation, or a Staatsvolk – the ethnic group that defines the state."[14]

THE DYNAMICS OF NATIONALIST SECESSION

There are three countervailing factors that oppose nationalist separatism of even the most liberal variety: stability and order;

fear of militant majoritarianism and expansionist nationalism; and the social contract assumed to be at the root of the contemporary state itself.

Defenders of statism insist that separatism is not only impermissible but morally repugnant, an irrational disease that enhances disorder and chaos. Secession is treated as a recipe for limitless fragmentation and conflict and a resurgence of an irrational, tribalist instinct.[15]

Western European countries have been reluctant to support separatism even in the most heinous cases of brutal victimization of minorities by the state. Though the United States, Great Britain, and France were allied in providing a safe haven for the Kurds, they desperately opposed Kurdish separatism and vowed that they were not out to destroy the territorial integrity of Iraq. The European Union attempted to broker the Serbian/Slovenian and Serbian/Croatian dispute without explicitly endorsing separatism. The various countries of Europe were all ambivalent, but some ended up opposing separatism, while others finally supported it. Spain and France initially opposed the independence movements, while Germany was somewhat sympathetic. The European states, in general, seemed to be wary of separatist trends, despite the evidence of Serb interest in creating a greater Serbia in the name of state sovereignty. They characterized separatism and/or nationalism as an irrational disease in their attempt to defend the ideology of the post-Second World War order – the territorial borders of existing states were to be inviolate, against both outside aggression and attempts to redraw borders from within. Only thus could peace be preserved.

The existing order was threatened not only by internal secessionist forces but by expansionist nationalism and the willingness of majorities to suppress the rights and even the existence of minorities. Nationalist secession was regarded as a danger to itself because it could release an even more dangerous pathogen – militant, expansionist nationalism, which could use the existing state system to quash other minorities. The Serbian army seemed willing to facilitate the slaughter of civilian populations and immolate Croat villages in Serb areas of Croatia, motivated by the memory of Croat Nazis slaughtering Serbs during the Second World War. They then went on to do much worse to the Muslims of Bosnia-Herzegovina; without the excuse of recent inflicted horrors, they substituted, among other factors, the imagined vision of Muslim fundamentalists seeking hegemony in Bosnia and the memory of Muslim invasions centuries ago.

But if defence of the existing order provides a superego-style resistance to nationalist secession, and the threat of a potentially even more irrational force sets off deep fears, the response poses a conceptual difficulty. Secession or devolution of responsibility and authority of the central state is a confession that the social contract is fractured and may even have broken down.

Order is the goal of the social contract, which is associated with state building. Secession is linked with disorder and disintegration, at least by defenders of the status quo. More fundamental, secession challenges one of the basic premises of modern theories of the nation-state – that parties to the social contract have committed themselves in perpetuity. The state, as the political community par excellence, was, conceptually at least, founded on a social contract made among individuals in a state of nature to form a political union. According to the classical contractarian theorists (Hobbes, Locke, Rousseau, and Kant), that union, once formed, was indivisible. The resultant sovereignty accorded to the state was inalienable.

Secession is so feared that it is depicted as a disease even in cases where there clearly was no social contract. When a nation and a state were conquered and annexed in the recent past – as in the Baltic states, Eritrea, and Tibet – the West, with fear and trepidation, avoided any support for separatists, even if they felt some sympathy, lest such actions be interpreted as encouragement to separatism elsewhere. However, that was until 1991. That was while the Cold War lasted and before the demise of the Soviet Union.

In the changing context of global politics, secession has become not only a movement but an actuality. Nevertheless, the fear of secession – of violence and war that threatens to arise in the wake of secession and nationalist passions – runs deep. It is at the foundation of Western statist ideology and practice. It is rooted in the conception of the social contract, which forms the ideological foundation for the modern state system.

The conceptual root of the difficulty is the issue of consent. In social contract theory, consent was a prerogative of individuals. Once consent was given in the innocence of the state of nature, there was no return. The process was irreversible. For some contractarians, this meant that if the state imposed order unlawfully consent could be withdrawn and rebellion could ensue. Not secession, but rebellion. The state remained indivisible, and sovereignty was inalienable. This was held true whether the consent theory was based on a social contract of "self-interested reciprocity" – a bargain among rationally self-interested individuals – or on "subject-centred justice which is non-strategic."[16]

There is, however, an alternative foundation to consent theory, one that Buchanan and others omit – a communitarian basis rather than a social contract among individuals founding a state. The consent of the community rather than of the individuals within it is the key element. The community's consent – the consent of *a people* – authorizes union or federation. It also permits separation. It does not endorse or entail separation. The principle of community consent, taken on its own, only permits separation.

The rationale for secession in communitarian consent, however, is not the same as that for rebellion in a social contract. In the latter, political obligations must be rooted in the will of individual members. They can rebel if they decide that the state no longer represents their will or governs with their consent. But then illegitimacy is attributed not to the state as such but only to those who exercise authority within it. Communitarian secessionists want to change the state that exercises that authority – not because it governs without their consent or no longer allows expression of their will (though this may be the case with rebellious secessionists) but because it is no longer perceived as the best means of expression of a collective will.

When a state is seen as not representing the will of "a people," even though the state represents the majority of "the people," we have the beginnings of a separatist movement. The sine qua non for foundation of a modern state is the will of a people, and not just the will of the people. A people insists that it is sovereign. For instance, the us Declaration of Independence may state that the government derives its legitimacy "from the consent of the governed," and the Preamble to the us constitution may embody the principle that governmental authority derives from the will of the people, but the American state became a powerful entity by creating a unified people through the force of the state crushing a secessionist movement in the south.[17]

Furthermore, "a people" is not necessarily equivalent to "the people." Where a state consists of more than one people, it has a built-in schizophrenia, for the will of the people will not necessarily be the will of each of the peoples that constitute the state. Modern political theory assumes either that a contract is made by an agglomeration of individuals, in which "the people" then is simply the collective expression for the members of the state, or that "the people" is an organic collectivity without individual wills that count, so that mystic forces and a moral vision of destiny determine the will of a people, as expressed in the "vision" of a prophetic leader. Further, where the people are totally identified as "a people," leaders (some would cite Abraham Lincoln[18]) feed on that alleged equivalence of "a people" with "the people" to suppress any regional separatism and forge the members into a single people through civil war, bloodshed, and sacrifice of many of its members.

In the social contract theory, there are no rules of divorce built into the political marriage contract. Individuals and groups may be allowed to leave, but they cannot stay in the house in which they live and simply demand that the territory be governed by a new constitutional authority. If they were present at and participated in the founding of a state, in contractarian theory there is no provision to cancel or withdraw that agreement. The Catholic-style politics of the modern world seemed to demand that political marriages were made for ever.

Who make up the "people"? Is there a people? How can a people decide that it wants to be governed by a different state authority and seeks not just a change in those who exercise that authority? And if the people can be designated, and the process defined to permit separation, how can the territorial assets be divided?

The need to divide assets sets off enormous fears. On this issue, an amicable agreement to separate may often lead to a dirty divorce. Even when heartfelt sympathy is extended to separatists, separatism twists the guts of otherwise powerful nations into knots of fear, not only because the existing order is threatened, not only because the spectre of expansionist nationalism looms in the background, but because secessionism threatens the social contract presumed to be at the foundation of the state system. The roots of that fear in the ideology of the social contract need to be probed, but only after the authority of the state in dealing with separatist nationalism is clarified.

THE AUTHORITY OF THE STATE

Separatists may argue that the other party fails to recognize who they are; they may even insist that they are demeaned by their partner. Jacques Parizeau, in his speech to the Canadian Club in Toronto, depicted a growing trend toward bashing Quebec: "I am truly saddened to say that respect for Quebec and Quebecers has been a disappearing feature of Canada's life."[19] But this does not mean that Parizeau bases his case for separatism on the contempt of the other.[20] Rather, creative expression of the power of the nation is at the fount of the separatist dynamic.

Though the expression of creative power may be the most important motivating factor, and though an absence of coercive power by the other party may be critical in making Quebec an ideal case for analytical examination[21], neither factor addresses the morality of separatism.

As well as ignoring issues of power, we can also set aside the importance of "influence" in the current debate.[22] Separatism has gained momentum as two conceptions recede in their persuasive power. The Tory vision of a state based on a multi-communitarian foundation – a community of communities – is widely viewed as a major cause for the fissures in Canada. Since Ottawa's ability to induce Quebecers to remain in Canada through generous distribution of economic benefits under the rationale of a community of communities has greatly diminished because the power of the state has declined with the rise of globalization and regionalization, this combination of territorial populism and fiscal bribery has receded as any basis for keeping the federal state together. Intellectual as well as material influence has also declined as a force. For example, the widespread Whig vision of a state, constructed on the basis of protection of the rights of individuals, with the French and English in Canada having equal rights and opportunities across the country (to the greatest extent possible) to participate in government and have access to services in their own language, has not helped preserve unity either. In fact, the new belief in individual rights is now seen by some as the ideology of English Canada, as distinct from that of French Quebec.[23]

Furthermore, the Tory and the Whig visions both addressed the authority of the state by considering the mode of exercising authority – that is, division of roles and assigning of responsibili-

ties for each of those roles between provincial and federal jurisdictions. Generally, the Tories were willing to delegate far more
powers to the provinces while trying to retain the economic clout
of the central state, while the Liberals saw the federal state,
following the American model, as the protector of individual
rights, including assuring individuals from both language groups
of access to services and participation in government in their
own language.

Separatists, however, play down the issue of role or formal
authority. They do not focus on the division of roles and responsibilities; indeed, it is theoretically possible (though practically
difficult) that a separatist and a federalist could propose similar
divisions of powers between the two levels of government. Separatists, however, value authentic authority[24] rather than role
authority and division of powers. Authentic authority is not
rooted in one's role in an institutional structure but comes from
an authentic source, either because that source is the ground of
other authority or because it is the one most knowledgeable
about an entire situation. "It is political authority as authority-
over ["role authority" in my terminology], i.e. as a right to obedience of one's fellow citizens with their correlative obligation to
obey, which is the traditional philosophical problem of political
authority."[25]

Role authority is the central issue of traditional politics.
Authentic authority, the authentic ground for assigning role
authority, is the central issue for separatists. Once the authentic
ground is established, division of roles and responsibilities can
be subdivided in numerous ways to suit contemporary realities
and a wide variety of conditions and circumstances. As Leslie
Green argued so clearly and convincingly,[26] the need to command obedience is not the norm of the operations of a state but
the confession of its failure. A state truly has authority to the
extent that its decisions are willingly complied with without any
resort to commands. That requires recognizing an authentic
source of authority for the state.

Willing compliance is not reducible to habitual obedience. It
involves willing and implicit assent to the rules established and
the decisions of the state. Tax revolts frequently make clear that
this assent cannot be assumed to be merely habitual. Nor does
the right to command because of one's position or role in a

hierarchy explain the fundamental authority of the state. For the basic question is who has the right to decide how its powers are divided up. Who are the people who delegate powers to different levels of government? The question of why the roles are divided the way they are and how those responsibilities are to be exercised is less important than determining the authentic source of authority.

The nature of that authentic source shapes the role authority that follows from it, for those assigned roles can normally expect compliance from fellow citizens in the decisions made by those who occupy authoritative positions. Some exceptions are forbidden, and some are granted. If my taxes are raised significantly in one year, I cannot refuse to pay them because I do not like paying taxes or because they were too great for me to pay, given other financial obligations. I can refuse to pay them if I believe that an error was made or if they were assessed inequitably and appeal to someone in higher authority to overrule the decision. But if I believe that the government that assigned those roles to determine the taxes of individuals was itself corrupt, unrepresentative, or ideologically unsound in raising taxes whenever it decided that it needed money to do something, I can try to replace the highest authorities by appealing to the authentic source of any delegated authority – which in the modern Western world is the people. I can call on my fellow citizens to "throw the buggers out."

That is why the issue of separatism is not about the theory of consent (wherein "separatists should be permitted to specify the territory in which the secessionists' referendum is held"[27]). Consent must be obtained from the majority within a political jurisdiction. Separatists accept the liberal principle that the consent of the majority within a political jurisdiction is a necessary requirement to govern.

Nor is separatism about recognizing a distinct community and assigning that community more powers. Separatism is not primarily about how government or its assignees exercise their authority. It is about who is to be accepted as the definitive group for selecting a government to decide our fundamental obligations and which groups should assign roles. Separatists subordinate the division of roles and responsibilities to recognition of a people as a primary source of authentic authority.

This is where the problem begins. In liberal theory, consent is the basis of political obligation and the formal authority exercised by the state. In communitarian theory, determining the nation as the authentic source of authority is the basis of deciding whose consent is needed to choose those assigned sovereign authority. Separatists accept the requirement of the consent of the majority of those within a political jurisdiction to make fundamental determinations. But they insist that the most basic decision to be made is whether a nation should be a "staatsnation" within a political jurisdiction, and they insist further that the "staatsnation" should be the primary source for authentic authority, even when the majority's consent is still a requirement. "When you have 70 per cent of your French population that feel in their hearts that they are Quebecers first; and when they want all decisions taken in Quebec city, only two things can happen. Either they leave and give themselves a real country; or they stay and they provide you with a never-ending visit to the dentist."[28]

The Sovereign State

The sovereign authority of government can be divided between two or among three levels. The same can be done with administrative authority. But the two types of authority are distinct. The authority delegated by a province or state to a municipal level of government is administrative in character. A municipality is not sovereign in any of its powers. The authority at any level of government can be divided among executive, legislative, and judicial branches, or between a municipal council and a board of education, but such divisions tell us nothing about where sovereign authority resides. Authority at any level can be divided and can be delegated downward and upward.

This is what has happened in the formation of the European Union (EU) as the authority over economic matters, and such issues as human rights have been delegated upward to its parliament, administration, and judiciary. But the EU has not itself become a sovereign level of government, even though it has been delegated sovereign powers and exercises authority in a number of jurisdictions. Why? Because a level of government has sovereign authority only if another level of government cannot take that authority away without its consent. The legislature of a prov-

ince or a state can take away the authority of a municipal government without its consent. Member states can take away the EU's
authority. A state or a province, and a country that is a sovereign
federation, have sovereign power because no other level can
assume their authority without their consent. That level of government is deemed to have received its sovereign authority directly from the people, not from another level of government.

The EU may indeed have been assigned sovereign powers.
Nevertheless, it is not a sovereign government – at least not yet.
"Nations have the legal power necessary to institute 'fractional'
commonwealths, such as the European Economic Community,
and to invest the government of those fractional commonwealths
with legal powers superior to those of the governments of national states."[29] Thus the basic sovereign authority is not necessarily
the one that exists at the highest level – traditionally the state.
For example, the state has less and less to do with determining
fundamental economic issues on its own as economic matters
become delegated to higher interstate government authorities.

The European Court ruled in *Van Gend en Loos v. Nederlandse
Administratie der Belastingen*: "the Community constitutes a new
legal order in international law, for whose benefit the States have
limited their sovereign rights, albeit within limited fields, and the
subjects of which comprise not only the Member States but also
their nationals."[30] The subjects of this higher level of government
include not only member states but nations as well. Why?
Because the EU can then develop into a sovereign government in
its own right. How? A sovereign level of government does not
obtain its sovereign authority from a social contract among
individuals but from the people that constitute it. The basic
sovereign authority is the one that represents a people – the
French, the British, the Americans, the Canadians, the Québécois, the Walloons, the Flemish. If Europeans begin to see
themselves as Europeans first and only then as English or
French or German, just as Americans began to see themselves as
Americans first and not as Virginians or Texans or New Yorkers,
then the EU may emerge as a sovereign authority and no longer
see itself as having received its authority from the states that
constitute it. The sovereign authority that it exercises will be seen
as deriving directly from the people. To the extent that a group
begins to envisage itself as a people and sees a government as

representing that people, that government has received its sovereign authority from the people, even if it once obtained its powers through delegation from other authorities.

The process may work in the reverse direction. If the majority of the people in Wales ever begin to see the Welsh government and its capital in Cardiff as representing the will and sovereign authority of the Welsh people, then Wales will have sovereign status and not simply be a level of government that has authority delegated by the British government in London. England conquered Wales in 1282 perhaps because the Welsh were unable to unite against an external enemy. Wales may even have forfeited any sovereign authority as a political unit in the Tudor acts of union in the mid-sixteenth century, after the allegedly Welsh house of Tudor took the crown of the realm and Wales was incorporated within England, retaining only delegated powers in its council and law courts.[31] But sovereignty is decided by allegiance and identity. If the Welsh begin to see themselves as Welsh first and only then as British, perhaps propelled initially by endemic economic depression and the dramatic decline of coal, and if Cardiff begins to acquire real sovereign authority in some jurisdictions, then the potential for separation from Britain exists.

In Canada, Quebec's government already exercises sovereign authority in a number of areas. If the majority of the people of the province now regard themselves first as Quebecers and only secondarily as Canadians, then the ultimate sovereign authority for the Québécois has become their province, even if Ottawa exercises sovereign authority in a number of areas. If that is indeed the case – and I believe that it is – then the issue is Quebec separatism not as a goal but only as a procedural matter. National separation may have already taken place. Quebec's government is then the ultimate sovereign authority of its people, even if Ottawa continues to exercise sovereign authority in a number of jurisdictions. The referendum may determine only whether the majority of Quebecers are willing and ready to have that fact recognized legally, with all the economic and legal disruptions that such a shift entails.

This is the argument that Jacques Parizeau uses to defend fulfilment of separatism by Quebecers' taking the formal authority of the state into their own hands: "Your national will and ours no longer converge."[32] It is also the position that Richard Gwyn takes in insisting that this step need not be taken, since Canada is already evolving into a postmodern state: "The essential reason Quebecers no longer feel the need to separate is because they are already separate, culturally and psychically and in almost all practical respects. Rather than a distinct society, Quebec is a distinct nation within Confederation. It's one of the ways we have already become a post-modern state."[33]

Gwyn's argument, however, is based on a false premise – that there is a Canadian people, which includes Quebecers, that is defined primarily by a common sensibility: "We don't really know what it is: Some blend of civility, tolerance, a readiness to compromise, an eagerness to engage in dialogue, an appreciation of ambiguity, a fear of extremes, although, as critics have rightly pointed out, a fear also of excellence; plus a certain passivity and smugness. But we know that we've got it, and we don't want to give it up."[34]

The issue is not, despite Gwyn's claim, whether the Quebecois and the rest of Canadians by and large share a common sensibility, which I believe they do, but whether they see themselves as a unit for expressive purposes. It is not their sensibilities but the collective basis for their action – the authentic authority of a people – that is at stake. That authority may decide where formal authority for expressing that will may be located, but separatists see this as principally a decision for Quebecers to make.

The Québécois seem willing and eager to delegate definitive decisions in some areas upward to the Canadian federation and even to North American institutions administering a free trade deal. But because many if not most of them see Quebec, not the government of Canada, as representing the people, their people, the areas of authority that they are willing to delegate upward are no longer congruous with those that Canadians outside Quebec wish to preserve at that level. Even if they were congruous, the locus of basic sovereign authority would remain undecided. Canadians outside Quebec want a federal government to embody their ultimate sovereign authority, even though many also want to limit its powers. Many, and perhaps now most, Quebecers, in contrast, do not want Ottawa to play that role.

The sovereign state is that level of political authority that represents the will of the people who are viewed as the nation, the Staatsvolk, the ethnic group that defines the character of the state. However, it is not necessarily the highest level of political authority; it is just the most basic and ultimate one when it represents the will of a people. If most people in Quebec think of themselves now primarily as Québécois and only secondarily as Canadians, then, in one important respect, separation has already taken place, even if the division of powers sought by the Québécois could be reconciled with that desired by other Canadians. However, the fact that the psychological separation, at the source of authentic authority, has already occurred does not necessarily entail institutional separation.

Separatists insist that it would be better if there were congruency between the authentic source of authority and the formal institution charged with defending and expressing it; if a nation is sovereign, it should have a sovereign state. Unification, in contrast, can go in the opposite direction. Many southerners before the Civil War, and, subsequently, Texans and Californians, thought of themselves primarily as Georgians, say, or Texans or Californians. Only gradually did the conception of themselves as Americans replace their national identities as members of the sovereign state that subsequently (re)joined the union. The historical remnant of that memory lingers in such institutions as presidential nominating conventions, when the delegates from "the sovereign state of Virginia" announce that they have cast their ballots for candidate "A." Similarly, if or when most Europeans think of themselves as Europeans first and foremost, then Europe will have become a sovereign state. If most Europeans do not develop such a conception, then even if the institutions of Europe exercise the highest and most extensive authority and make definitive judgments in those areas, then Europe will not be a sovereign state. It will be a confederation of sovereign states.

In addition to presupposing jurisdiction over a clearly demarcated territory (the sovereignty bill that Parizeau introduced in the national assembly reads in clause 4: "Quebec shall retain the boundaries it has within the Canadian Confederation at the time section 1 comes into force"), sovereign statehood depends on two additional requisite conditions. First, the majority of individuals within a designated political jurisdiction must consent to a state as representing the will of the people. Second, the majority of the people within the state jurisdiction must identify themselves as a distinct nation. Exercising sovereign authority, whether through a provincial or local state government or through an interstate government council, administration, and judiciary, does not make that level of government a sovereign state. It does not matter whether that authority is exercised over such crucial matters as monetary policy, foreign policy, and defence. As long as the sovereign state has delegated that authority and can retract it, perhaps at the risk of losing its membership in the confederation of states, that level of government has ultimate sovereignty.

Sovereignty as herein described is rooted in three factors. First, there is the collective will of a people with which an individual identifies. Second, though the collective will is not reducible to the self-determination of individuals who have collectively taken up membership in a state, consent of the majority of those within that political entity is required for determining the collective will. Third, there must be a political entity with authority in a designated territory in which that majority voice can be exercised. Otherwise, any concentrated group can exercise its right to self-determination at any time and has the option of seceding from the state.

This analysis of sovereignty avoids the immutability of contractarian theory, which assumes that once the state is formed self-determination is resolved once and for all. It also avoids the danger that any group in any concentrated territory can secede. We are then not forced to choose between stability at the cost of self-determination (and generally construct a higher moral purpose, such as the laudable aim of distributive justice, as the mode of keeping the state together and forging unity) and self-determination at the cost of stability.

MEMBERSHIP IN A STATE OR IN A NATION?

What about the minorities in Quebec – Anglo-Canadians, immigrants, and Aboriginal peoples? Each poses different sets of problems. And these problems become clearer if we first clarify the difference between membership in a people or nation and membership in a state.

For most individuals, membership in a state comes as a birthright. No contract, consent, or promise is made. As a natural citizen, an individual has rights and duties. They did not follow from a voluntary act by the individual. But an individual can voluntarily give up that citizenship. Or that individual may acquire another citizenship and retain the original one if permitted to do so by the laws and rules of the state of his natural birthright and the state in which he was offered and agreed to take citizenship.

For most individuals, membership in a nation also comes as a birthright. Again, no contract, consent, or promise is made. However, as a natural member of a nation and a people, an individual has only obligations, but no rights or duties. Those obligations are not assumed as a result of a voluntary act by the individual. Nor are they part of the birthright. As the child matures and begins to accept his or herself as part of the nation, the sense of what those obligations entail begins to assume some content.

For some members of a nation, the obligations assumed are few; for others, they are extensive. For still others, no obligations are assumed and membership in the nation may become a nominal rather than a substantive matter. Or the individual may renounce his or her membership in a people/nation. This is not done simply by acquiring membership in another people. For it is possible to assume memberships in two different peoples and extensive obligations toward each, or memberships in two peoples with minimal obligations to either of them. It is possible to be a member of both the Estonian and the Canadian people. It is more difficult, however, to be members of two peoples with the same sense of extensive obligations where the states that represent the collective wills of these two peoples have jurisdictional conflicts, or, at the very extreme, engage in conflict and war with one another. Difficult but not impossible. It was possible for a Japanese Canadian to retain both a sense of strong obligation to the Japanese people and to his or her sense as a Canadian during the Second World War, but then the obligation to each would have required making a decision to support or oppose the Japanese state's war aims. The same dilemma faced many other nationals in Canada, such as Croats and Serbs during 1991.

Membership in a state entails rights and duties and, in certain situations, choosing between membership in one state and membership in another. Membership in a people, in contrast, entails obligations that go beyond duties. In certain situations, possessing memberships in two peoples may face an individual with difficult choices, but not the duty of choosing between memberships. One may indeed make such a choice, but it is not a duty. Because it is an internal decision about identity, there is no method of imposing such a duty unless the devices of a totalitarian state are employed to control the thinking and beliefs of its members.

If one is a member of two nations, in which two states, representing the will of each nation, have overlapping jurisdictions, one may sometimes have to choose which state is one's sovereign state for that jurisdiction. Service in the armed forces is a case in point. This is conceptually no different than the requirement that citizens within the United States must choose (and prove their choice) that they are residents of a specific state for tax purposes. Florida, for example, has no state income taxes or estate taxes, and it is necessary to register and prove that one is a resident of that state to escape paying those taxes in another state.

Further, unlike membership in a state, membership in a nation is not a choice made at a definitive point in time, though the aggregate of choices of members of a political jurisdiction in a referendum may be used to record which state should have the basic sovereignty in representing the will of the nation at a definitive point in time. The obligations that one assumes as a member of a nation grow, develop, and alter over time, refined through public discourse and debate. It is in this context that the options available to Anglo-Canadians, immigrants, and Aboriginal peoples in Quebec need to be examined.

Minorities and Membership Rights

Anglo-Canadians in Quebec have three choices available. First, they can remain a minority within the Québécois nation and continue to reside in Quebec; if they do so, they have two sub-options: they may support Quebec separatism because they decide that it is in the best interests of the Québécois or the Canadian people or both, or, more likely, they can oppose separation because they do not want to live outside the state of their national allegiance. Second, they can migrate to the political jurisdiction in which their fellow nationals are the majority. Third, they can acquire Québécois nationality. This will not necessarily entail supporting separation. They may argue, as Québécois nationals, that it is in the best interests of the Québécois to remain within the bosom of Canada because the Québécois are better protected and can achieve greater self-realization within Canada than apart from it. Most individuals who make that choice, including many French Canadians in Quebec, do so because they may want to remain both Canadian and Québécois.

How does the contention that most Québécois see Quebec as the sovereign state representing their nation fit in with the possibility of being a separatist and a Canadian at the same time? Many separatists were able to join and vote for the federal Tories. Though they were Québécois first and foremost, they decided that they could also be Canadians, provided that Canada were restructured to recognize that Quebec represented the will of the Quebec nation and was given the jurisdiction and powers to represent that reality. That is why some Quebec federalists can also be Québécois – they believe that such a restructuring is both possible and feasible. They also may believe that any precipitous move to separation would endanger the economic well-being of the Québécois. Still, separatists who entered federal politics or joined the federal public service and federalists who are primarily Québécois share one common conviction – Quebecers are a sovereign nation, with Quebec as the political jurisdiction that primarily represents that nation and is responsible for securing its future. In that sense, to the degree that most French Canadians in Quebec are Québécois, they already perceive Quebec to be a sovereign state. If that perception is to become a formal reality, if that perceived sovereign state is to become independent, a majority vote of its residents is required.

If the majority of Quebecers (as distinct from Québécois)[35] vote for separation, the one option that is neither legitimate nor realistic for Anglo-Canadians in Quebec, even where they are a clear and concentrated majority, as in west Montreal or in the Eastern townships, is to create a separatist movement themselves. At least, they do not have that choice, given an understanding of their moral and political duties and obligations, though, of course, as individuals they are free to try. There are two reasons for this situation. First, their ethnic group already has a state in which it constitutes the Staatsvolk; therefore their obligations to their nation do not entail the territorial division of an integral political unit in order to ensure the existence of a state that represents and protects that ethnic group. Second, they do not belong to a political jurisdiction with clear boundaries and with any degree of sovereign authority allocated to it; duties to the state, both to Canada and to Quebec, for reasons of peace, order, and good government, forbid division of an integral political unit, unless, of course, it is with the consent of the majority within that jurisdiction. They lack, as a group, the moral imperative, the residual sovereignty, and the political institutional instruments for such a quest. Nevertheless, clause 3 of the separatist bill introduced by Jacques Parizeau states: "The constitution shall include a charter of human rights and freedoms. It shall guarantee the English-speaking community that its identity and institutions will be preserved."

What about immigrants in Quebec? First, they can remain a minority within the Québécois nation and continue to reside in Quebec; if they do so, they have two sub-options: they may support separation because they decide that it is in the best interests of the Québécois or the Canadian people or both, or, more likely, they can oppose separation because they want to have the widest number of options available to decide on their new nationality, assuming that they want to acquire a new nationality as well as citizenship. Second, they can migrate to the political jurisdiction in which the nationality that they wish to join is in the majority. Third, they can acquire Québécois nationality. This will not necessarily entail supporting separation. They may argue, as Québécois nationals, as explained above, that it is in the best interests of the Québécois to remain within Canada because the Québécois are better protected and can achieve greater self-realization within it than apart from it. In sum, their choices are similar to those of the Anglo-Canadian minority.

The Aboriginal peoples are a different case altogether. They call themselves First Nations, but they have only a few minimal accoutrements necessary to preserving nationality in the modern world. What they primarily lack is support of a political jurisdiction with at least minimal sovereign powers. As a people, they may be sovereign. They may even have that sovereignty recognized by such jurisdictions as that of Ontario. Jacques Parizeau's separatist bill may "recognize the right of Aboriginal nations to self-government on lands over which they have full ownership."

But clause 3 continues: "Such guarantees and such recognition shall be exercised in a manner consistent with the territorial integrity of Quebec." The First Nations of Quebec lack a political entity governing a territorial jurisdiction with definitive sovereign rights on at least a number of minimal levels. Recognition of self-government and of landownership is not the same as recognition of the sovereign rights of a people that can be exercised over a specific terriory.

If the Cree are recognized as a sovereign people, if the Inuit are recognized as a sovereign people, if both groups obtain sovereign rights, however minimal they may be, with a territorial jurisdictional base, such as over Nunavut, extending northward from the Beaufort Sea to the North Pole and southward to the Labrador Sea and the southernmost reaches of Hudson Bay, and if they are the majority of the population there, then they can develop their legal jurisdiction so that it evolves into a separate state if and when the people in that sovereign nation determine that they wish to be Cree or part of Nunavut and/or Canadian and not Québécois, if Quebec votes to separate.

The Aboriginal groups in Quebec have a potential for separation depending on three parameters: the nation with which they principally identify; development of a sovereign polity to represent that nation; and staking out of territorial boundaries over which that polis has jurisdiction.

Separatism and Territory

Normally, you can't take your little piece of territory with you when you opt out of the state or a nation. My family has a six-acre island in Georgian Bay. We cannot declare it a sovereign state, not simply because realpolitik would not permit such an act. For a territory to declare itself as desiring to be administered by a government that represents the sovereign will of a people, there must first be "a people" and, second, that people must vest its will in one level of state authority viewed as representing its collective will. Unless a group views itself as a nation and has a political unit with jurisdiction over a specific territory that it entrusts as the embodiment of that will, the political unit is not sovereign and the group is not truly a nation, but a minority within a nation. The degree of sovereign authority exercised by the state is of secondary importance to having a state that can exercise sovereign authority in the first place. It is to that state that an individual delegates ultimate authority for the definitive decisions on what levels of government are to exercise which levels of authority, and not to reserve to itself the highest, in the sense of the broadest, levels of authority.

First, the necessary condition for separation is the existence of a sovereign people. It is not a sufficient condition. Second, it must also have a polity that has the mandate to exercise the will of the people. Third, the sovereign people and the sovereign political unit must have a clearly demarcated territorial base. Further, it must be the majority population in that territorial base. With a majority vote among all members (not just the nationals) within that territorial base, that sovereign entity has the right to separate and designate itself as the fundamental sovereign state for that national group. It is then free to delegate whatever sovereign powers to another state or a higher international entity that it chooses and that are acceptable to that other state or states participating in the larger, supra-national political unit.

CONCLUSION

To conclude, the implications of this analysis are quite clear. If the majority of French Canadians in Quebec already regard themselves as Québécois first and Canadians second, and if the polity of Quebec is given the mandate to negotiate on its behalf to determine which level of government to assign role authorities to, then Canada has already been separated in spirit. To separate in law is morally permissible, provided that separation is supported by a majority vote of Quebecers (not just Québécois). But such a legal separation is not morally obligatory or even clearly desired, even if the separation in spirit has already occurred.

However, the quid pro quo is that minority ethnic groups without a state of their own anywhere, who are a majority in a relatively defined territory, if they have a conception of themselves as a sovereign people, and if they develop the political institutions to govern a boundaried territory, also have the right to decide whether to join one political jurisdiction or another or to insist that their own is sovereign.

NOTES

1 Cf. Ernest Gellner, *Nations and Nationalism* (Ithaca, NY: Cornell University Press, 1983), who thought that secession had become virtually extinct as a political issue. In January 1991, Allen Buchanan, referring to Gellner, wrote, "Nevertheless, in spite of the fact that both the potential number of secessionist groups is huge and that there is no small supply of moral slogans to justify secession, serious secessionist movements have been very few indeed." Allen Buchanan, "Toward a Theory of Secession," *Ethics*, 101 (Jan. 1991), 338.

2 "A large majority of voters now favour the creation of their own parliament. ... If Scotland were not a nation, this might matter less. But it is, and the demands of the Scots cannot be swept aside." *Economist*, 6 July 1991, 14.

3 Cf. Ronald Grigor Suny, *The Making of the Georgian Nation* (Bloomington, Ind.: Indiana University Press, 1991).

4 Charles S. Meier, "Democracy and Its Discontents," *Foreign Affairs*, 73 no. 4 (July/Aug. 1994), 61.

5 "Another poll finds 83 per cent of all Canadians say their commitment is to all of Canada rather than 'just the area where you actually live,' 78 per cent of Quebecers say the same thing." Richard Gwyn, "The First Borderless State," *Toronto Star*, 26 Nov. 1994, B5, reprint of an edited version of the D.G. Wilmot Distinguished Lecture at Brock University in St Catharines given on 23 November 1994.

6 Jacques Parizeau, *Toronto Star*, 23 Nov. 1994, A32.

7 Buchanan, "Toward a Theory," 326.

8 Cf. Lea A. Brilmayer, "Consent, Contract, and Territory,'" *Minnesota Law Review*, 39 (1990), 1–35.

9 "The U.S. Constitution ... stipulates that a proposed amendment must receive a two-thirds majority in Congress and be ratified by three-quarters of the states ... to strike an appropriate balance between two legitimate interests: the interest in providing flexibility for change and the interest in stability. Similarly, the point of erecting inconvenient but surmountable obstacles to secession is not to make secession impossible but to avoid making it too easy." Buchanan, "Toward a Theory," 337.

10 Thomas J. Courchene, "After the No: The Search for a New Order," *Globe and Mail*, 27 Oct. 1992, A4.

11 This, of course, suggests that the argument that the 1982 changes buried a view of an asymmetrical Canada once and for all in favour of a compact among equal provinces is seriously flawed (cf. ibid), including the belief that the 1992 referendum not only interred that concept but did so in favour of the position that a constitution is a compact among citizens.

12 Buchanan, "Toward a Theory," 325.

13 The marriage analogy should be used with great caution. Not only are

gender assignations controversial, but nations do not "marry" one another. Individuals do. Most important, separation need involve no divorce per se. The two nations may continue to live side by side and inhabit a larger political entity, but it will be on the basis of equality and not the aggregate number of individuals belonging to each nation.

14 "Survey of Canada," *Economist*, 29 June 1991, 7.
15 "Yugoslavia is a potentially infectious carrier of a virus that risks becoming the AIDS of international politics – lying dormant for years, then flaring up to destroy countries. It is the virus of tribalism." *Economist*, 6 July 1991, 13.
16 Cf. Allen Buchanan, "The Morality of Inclusion," *Social Philosophy and Policy*, 10 no. 2 (Summer 1993), 51–64.
17 When Parizeau set out his program for independence, the sovereignty bill that he introduced began with a reference to "We the people," and Parizeau explicitly referred to the preamble to the US Declaration of Independence.
18 Buchanan, "Toward a Theory."
19 *Toronto Star*, 23 Nov. 1994, A32.
20 This was the contention of the *Toronto Star*'s editorial (ibid., A24), which contended: "With national unity almost a non-issue these days, with no more Brockvilles to broadcast on the nightly news in Quebec, a desperate Parizeau has discovered and declared a crisis in human relations between Quebecers and the rest of the country. By fabricating and fomenting a climate of mutual suspicion and resentment, he wants Quebecers to believe that only he – and a separate country – can rescue them from the contempt of Canadians."
21 The resort to violence cannot be ruled out altogether. W.L. Morton and Jack Granatstein believe that the potential for resort to force is much more proximate than most Canadians (including me) would like to and do believe. They may be correct. But it is a probability impossible to calculate. In any case, because the belief prevails that violence is remote, we need not consider it, and the fear of it, as a serious factor when we consider the right to secession. And if violence does stir its ugly head again in Canada over secession, this time it will ensure the permanent irreconcilability of the English and the French.
22 For a more extensive analysis of the three concepts, see Howard Adelman, "Authority, Influence and Power," *Philosophy of the Social Sciences*, 6 (Dec. 1976), 335–51.
23 Cf. Kenneth McRoberts, *English Canada and Quebec: Avoiding the Issue* (North York, Ont.: Robarts Centre for Canadian Studies, 1992). McRoberts argues that, though Québécois and the rest of Canadians by and large share common values, this is one major area in which a divergence emerged during the 1980s. The English Canadians seem to have made protection of individual rights a cornerstone of the Canadian federation while the

Québécois, both federalists and separatists, have held the collective survival of the Québécois to be a higher principle. Blindness to this point led Richard Gwyn in "The First Borderless State" to conclude: "Nor are we without the vital interconnecting sinews of a nation. The Charter of Rights regulates the behaviour of all of us, and influences significantly the attitudes of all of us." Gwyn was taking the "sinews" of English Canada to be equivalent to those that also bound the Québécois to Canada.

24 Some commentators confuse authentic authority with influence – the effect of money or ideas. "Authority-with is readily accepted influence by virtue of leadership qualities or office or expertise"; Harry Beran, *The Consent Theory of Political Obligation* (Sydney, Australia: Croom Helm, 1987), 9. Aside from its awkwardness and its poor fit with everyday usage, this definition reduces "authority-with" to either influence of some sort (leadership quality) or the two other types of authority – that which comes from one's role (office) or that which stems from something fundamental, such as expertise, if the reference is to cognitive knowledge, or will (individual or national), if the reference is to an action.

25 Ibid, 10.

26 Leslie Green, *Authority of the State* (Oxford: Clarendon Press, 1990).

27 Beran, *The Consent Theory*, 39.

28 Jacques Parizeau, *Toronto Star*, 23 Nov. 1994, A32, from his speech to the Canadian Club in Toronto.

29 Haskell Fain, *Normative Politics and the Community of Nations* (Philadelphia: Temple University Press, 1987), 75.

30 [1963] 2 CMLR 129. Cf. Anthony Perry and Stephen Hardy, *EEC Law* (New York: Mathew Bender, 1973), and L.N. Brown and F.G. Jacobs, *The Court of Justice of the European Communities*, 2nd ed. (London: Sweet and Maxwell, 1983). See also Fain, *Normative Politics*, 72–6.

31 Cf. John Davies, *A History of Wales* (London: Allen Lane/Penguin, 1994).

32 Ibid.

33 Gwyn, "The First Borderless State," B1.

34 Ibid. Gwyn also contradicts himself by defining himself as a humanist, one who regards "humanity itself, or individuality, as the single essential, common, distinguishing characteristic of us all," in contrast to identity politicians. But he defines the Canadian identity in terms of sensibilities rather than cultural expression.

35 Jacques Parizeau, while leader of the opposition, told English-speaking Quebecers not to "block Quebecers' wish to live a normal life" (*Toronto Star*, 25 June, 1993, A30). He thereby excluded anglophones as Quebecers. This may have been a slip, or it may have been a revelation that Parizeau equates Quebecers with Québécois. If the latter, this is a dangerous position. Other actions and words of Parizeau suggest that this may have been a slip.

CHAPTER EIGHT

Quebec's Self-determination and Aboriginal Self-government: Conflict and Reconciliation?

Reg Whitaker

Quebec has repeatedly asserted its right to national self-determination. In 1980 its provincial government unsuccessfully asked Quebecers to give it a mandate to negotiate sovereignty along with an economic association with Canada. An act passed by the national assembly in 1991 specified that a referendum on sovereignty was to be held in 1992. In the event, a referendum was instead held on 26 October 1992, to coincide with a parallel referendum held throughout the rest of Canada, asking for ratification of the Charlottetown Accord on constitutional reform. The referendum failed. The Parti québécois, victorious in the 1994 provincial election, has introduced a bill declaring Quebec a "sovereign country" following ratification in a referendum to be held within the first year of its mandate. The Bloc québécois, which emerged from the 1993 federal election not only as the pre-eminent party in Quebec but as the official opposition in Ottawa, has premised its very raison d'être on achievement of sovereignty in Quebec. The Quebec Liberal party, while officially opposed to sovereignty, has endorsed Quebec's right to national self-determination.

Many important sectors of Canadian society outside Quebec (including the major political parties) have either tacitly or explicitly recognized that Quebec does indeed possess a right to national self-determination, though many, if not most, would prefer that it not exercise the right.

What is the "right" to national self-determination'? This is a question that could be explored on various levels; the philosophical and legal dimensions are matters of considerable controversy and complexity, which will be touched on here only superficially.[1] What I propose is a political analysis of the claim to national self-determination: what is the politics of national self-determination and of the language of rights in which the claim is cast?

Another kind of national claim was highlighted in the Charlottetown round of constitutional reform. The inherent right to self-government of the Aboriginal peoples was recognized in the Charlottetown Accord, which envisaged native self-government as a "third order of government" alongside the federal and provincial. Though this was not a claim that, in this form at least, could encompass independence or complete political separation from Canada, it was a national claim in that it posited a relatively high degree of political autonomy for groups based on their nationality, the First Nations or Original Peoples. This claim remains alive today.

If Quebec's right to national self-determination and the Aboriginal peoples' inherent right to self-government had represented parallel paths of constitutional discourse, exploration of each would have been important enough. The paths have, however, not merely been convergent but often seen, both by Quebec and by Aboriginal spokespersons, as contradictory, antagonistic, even incommensurate with one another. Why this should be so is addressed below, as is the difficult issue of possible reconciliation of the two sets of claims.

The chapter falls into four parts. In the first, I look at national self-determination in the historical context of the 1980 referendum. The second outlines the ways in which the issue is now being posed. In the third, I consider how national self-determination has clashed with the more recently enunciated principle of Aboriginal self-government. I suggest, in the fourth part, the need for reconciliation of the two types of claims if political disaster is not to follow from any move by Quebec toward sovereignty.

NATIONAL SELF-DETERMINATION AND THE 1980 REFERENDUM

The Parti québécois (PQ) government elected in 1976 was dedicated to achieving sovereignty for Quebec but declined to interpret its election as grounds for initiating separation proceedings.

It had pledged that before its mandate ended it would consult the people of Quebec through a referendum. A specific democratic mandate would be sought for a constitutional change, thus allowing for a separation between the party and its central idea. In the event, the referendum lost but the party was subsequently returned to office. The advantage of a referendum is that it allows voters to focus attention on the issue, not distracted by considerations of party politics.

Unfortunately for purists and rationalist thinkers, the referendum of 1980 did not pose the question of independence clearly. Its ambiguity took two distinct forms. First, it sought only a mandate to negotiate with the national government and promised further referenda after negotiations had produced an agreed-on plan for Quebec's assuming sovereignty that could be submitted to the people for ratification. Though this approach bespoke admirable democratic respect for popular consultation, it rather muddied the waters – how could one interpret a "yes" vote? What would a "yes" vote be for, exactly? It might be a vote for sovereignty, or perhaps only for giving the government a negotiating mandate to see what it could come up with, which itself might then be turned down in a subsequent "no" vote. This is a problem that I (along with many other analysts) simply ignore, by assuming that most people who chose to vote "yes" were indeed voting on behalf of sovereignty. Nevertheless, the problem of the second-round referendum is related to the other, more serious, difficulty with the PQ's lack of clarity.

The deeper difficulty lay in the PQ's insistence – which went back to the party's founding – that it would present political sovereignty only when that idea was linked with some continued form of economic association with Canada. In fact the original grouping that became the PQ was called the mouvement souveraineté-association. This tack was clearly chosen for reasons of political expediency, to mollify fears of economic disruption and loss of capital attendant upon a sudden political shift toward separation. But it perhaps also expressed a dominant understanding among péquistes that independence was to be understood only in a political sense, while economic independence was relatively meaningless in a world of increasingly internationalized capital. The PQ was in no way a vehicle for a socialist or state-centred nationalism, which might have posed at least a theoretical alternative to capitalist interdependence and interpenetration. The PQ clearly did not share a Marxist belief that economics was the foundation for a political superstructure. Rather, the spheres of politics and economics were separate, though interrelated. The PQ appeared to believe that political sovereignty would be a superior position from which to bargain for a better set of economic relationships with the rest of Canada. This belief seems to me a dubious proposition from a number of perspectives, but the one that I address is that of the mutual rights and obligations obtaining between those who share membership in a community in which they hold common citizenship.

The PQ's proposition in a nutshell was that an economic community could be maintained at the same time as the political framework of that community was being demolished. This theory seems to run counter to the fundamental basis of the modern state. If the PQ had envisaged some basic alteration in the form of the state, one could discuss alternative visions of political order. But this approach was not part of the PQ's agenda. It adopted instead an entirely conventional notion of the state and political system.

Behind this acceptance of the democratic capitalist state form lay a deeper compromise of Quebec nationalism with North American modernity. One might have detected in francophone Quebec as late as the 1940s or the 1950s elements of a society and culture that were genuinely distinct from that of English Canada; they were traditionally Catholic, illiberal, paternalistic, and fixated on cultural and ideological symbols of a rural, hierarchical past, elements given official expression in the provincially sponsored Tremblay Commission of the 1950s. After the Quiet Revolution of the early 1960s and the profound changes set in train in Quebec society, this distinctiveness rapidly declined. By the 1970s it could be said with confidence that the distinctiveness of Quebec society was marginal (measured most importantly in slight variations in life-style and consumption preferences in corporate marketing surveys), except in one fundamental aspect – the primacy of the French language. Otherwise, Quebec society had come to represent a regional variation of North American mass culture. This transformation was the ironic result of a strong thrust in the early 1960s to preserve a traditional society by adopting modernized means (to keep everything the same, everything would have to change). The result was ironic because the means overwhelmed the ends: Quebec preserved itself at the cost of becoming like its antagonist – a modern, urban, corporate-capitalist, and liberal society.[2]

The PQ's vision reflected this reality. Its 1978 White Paper on Culture (written by the most traditionally nationalist of its ministers) made it clear that the sole defining characteristic of Quebec's culture was the French language. So long as participants, among them immigrants and cultural minorities, were willing to accept the primacy of French, they could contribute to the culture in any way they wished, including the expression of their multicultural heritage. Thus, far from representing an integral nationalism in which language, culture, ethnicity, religion and history form an exclusionary matrix defining the "Québécois authentique," péquiste nationalism is essentially inclusive, polyethnic, secular, and even multicultural. From time to time, older, more illiberal strains have been glimpsed beneath the surface, but these are anomalies, exceptions that prove the rule.

I make this point for a particular reason. The liberalism of the PQ meant that its sovereignty project did not challenge the fundamental nature of the liberal democratic nation-state. An exclusionary, illiberal, integral-nationalist breakaway movement from a liberal democratic polity would raise a set of particular problems, especially the claims of minorities for protection by the national majority. Even if the polity were not liberal democratic but were committed to multicultural pluralism, minorities' claims would have weight (this is the case of the successor states of the former Yugoslavia, where secession has worsened already horrendous human rights abuses). If the PQ had advocated an authoritarian suppression of individual rights and privileges in the name of the collective privileges of the majority, there might be reasonable claims for national intervention to prevent this dismantling of the law-based liberal constitutionalist state. None of these problems has been in any way entailed in the PQ project, and thus a set of credible arguments for rejection of Quebec sovereignty in the name of the values of the wider political community has not been available.

Given the business-as-usual social and political content of the PQ's vision, the arguments on behalf of separation are much weaker than if they had been predicated on the need for a separate state to guarantee the right of Quebecers to live distinctive lives and participate in a distinctive culture made impossible without its own sovereign guarantor. Since the only clear and unequivocal distinction is the primacy of the French language, the independence project has been vulnerable to a demonstration that the language could be preserved within existing political structures. This is exactly what the PQ itself, as a provincial government, did by enacting its famous Law 101, followed by the Liberals, with their Law 178, which was further buttressed by the addition of the "notwithstanding" clause to the Charter as protection against constitutional challenge.

This weak, or thin argument for sovereignty also seriously undermines the language of the right of national self-determination with which PQ claims have been advanced. Setting aside the complexities of this language, and the thorny philosophical issues involved, we might assume a broad consensus that such claims have plausibility when the following conditions hold:

1 a people has developed clear self-consciousness of itself as a distinct nation (and could potentially form a viable nation-state[3]);
2 individuals' identities as members of this nation cannot be realized in their present political and economic conditions of citizenship, because:
3 another, dominant group has imposed a state structure on them that expressly denies their identity and/or actively seeks to repress it.

Under such conditions, we might speak of a right to national self-determination, in that only independent self-government can meet the requirements of national identity. In this sense, we might speak of a right to national self-determination of Native peoples in the lands of European settlement, Palestinians, Kurds, and black South Africans until the recent sweeping changes in that country.

Application of this argument to Quebec case fails at stages 2 and 3. This is not to suggest that there might not be rational and persuasive arguments on behalf of a sovereign constitutional status for Quebec as an arrangement instrumentally advancing certain values and objectives that might be agreed on by all members of the larger community. But this would be to avoid the language of the right to national self-determination, which was posed, as rights claims most often are, as a trump that would silence conflicting claims. Suh a right presents itself here as an obstacle to evaluation of the case for sovereignty, which attempts to encompass both sides of the argument. For that reason, I simply set the right aside as a rhetorical device for political mobilization which is philosophically uninteresting.

Quebec sovereignty does not then constitute a challenge, however, to the fundamental political values of the Canadian political community. It does challenge, however, the symbolic values of "national unity" and of the continuous geographical expression of a Canada *ad mare usque ad mare*. I take it that these symbolic values are not fundamental but instrumental. To the proponents of national unity, a united Canada will arguably better advance the ends of the liberal and democratic polity than a divided state, or one in the process of disintegration. This is an empirical issue, to be settled in terms of facts and circumstances, not in theory. Indeed, national unity has never been seriously posited as an end in itself, except in rhetorical shorthand.[4] Rejection of Quebec sovereignty on the grounds that separation would break down national unity is thus tautological and, as such, just as philosophically uninteresting as the claim for secession couched exclusively in terms of rights.

We can now examine the specific issues posed by the sovereignty-association referendum in 1980. Here I want to return to the linking of political sovereignty with economic association, within the framework of the liberal capitalist state. This state form assumes separation of the political and economic spheres, but in a particular way. Economic activity is largely "private" and governed by the market, but the state, or public sphere provides a coercive framework for enforcing fulfilment of contractual relationships formed in the private sphere. The state is liberal when it sets the rules of the game according to universal principles of abstract "fairness" to all participants (the rule of law) and maximizes the freedom of individual members of the community to pursue their own ends, limited by the principle of non-interference with others. Citizenship in the state involves a set of reciprocal rights and obligations shared with fellow citizens. In the welfare state, economic rights are matched with

some economic obligations through redistribution among different classes of citizens. In a federal state, formal redistribution
also takes place among provinces and regions.

The PQ's referendum proposition did two things: it asked if
people wanted sovereignty, but it tied this status to a promise of
a particular form of economic association with Canada. While the
government could certainly ask the question, it had no business
making the promise as a corollary of the answer to the question.
In pre-referendum statements of how it envisaged this association (a document called, significantly, *Égal à Égal*, and the White
Paper on sovereignty-association), it argued that it could in fact
establish not the same relationship previously enjoyed under
federalism but a better one – that is, one more advantageous to
Quebec. To this end, it projected a series of commissions to
regulate the association, on which Quebec would have equal, or
near-equal, representation with Canada.

What claims does Quebec have to equal representation with
Canada when it in fact represents roughly one in five of the
Canadian population? Here we have to uncouple the two parts of
the referendum proposition. If Quebec were not to separate from
Canada (if the answer to 1 were "no"), then the second part
would have to be answered in the context of the existing rights
and obligations obtaining among members of the Canadian community. Arguments for binationality, special status, a distinct
society, and so on, which would have the effect of enhancing
Quebec's representation beyond its demographic proportion (and
beyond the other provinces), have been made, are made, and
have even been realized to a limited extent, but within existing
constitutional relations. Certain claims can be made by French
Canadians or by Quebec on historical grounds (for example,
minority-language rights, which cannot be legitimately advanced
by other linguistic groups such as Ukrainian or Hindi speakers)
or to control old-age pension funds (which cannot be claimed by
other provinces), but these claims are related to obligations
accepted by francophones, such as paying taxes to Ottawa, and by
the government of Quebec, in accepting the legitimacy of a federal government elected by the Canada-wide anglophone majority.
Claims for more than proportional representation would have to
be assessed according to a kind of prudential calculus involving
constitutional law, historical precedent, relative bargaining power,

political expediency, and the structure of rights embedded within the existing community.

If the answer to the first part of the question were "yes," however, the situation is radically altered. The effect of such a result would be that Quebec was renouncing its obligations by asserting a unilateral right. This right is self-referential only and is realized by its breaking away from the reciprocal rights and obligations of the wider community. Having thus snapped the bonds of the community, or signalled its firm intention to do so, which amounts to the same thing, Quebec loses its capacity to argue its claims in the same language and by the same calculus that it can use when the answer to the first part of the question is "no." A different set of parameters must now come into play – those that normally govern relations between independent, sovereign states. There is of course an abstract equality that exists between any two sovereign states that negotiate with one another bilaterally: there are two sides to the bargaining table and two signatories to a bilateral agreement. But it requires little analysis to conclude that this equality is merely formal and is often a highly misleading guide to the actual balance of power. For instance, Canada is an "equal" partner with the United States and Mexico in the North American Free Trade Agreement; but no one could seriously believe that there is substantive equality among states whose populations, power, and wealth are so different.

Relations between an independent Quebec and a Canada without Quebec, and thus the specific form of economic association, would be based on relative bargaining power and political expediency but not on constitutional law, historical precedent, or mutual rights and obligations embedded within the existing community structure. Negotiations based only on relative bargaining power and political expediency are driven by the moral calculus of self-interest and concern for consequences. Concretely, as a Canadian citizen, I would look quite differently on Quebec's claims in this case than I would in the former. I would specifically deny that citizens of Quebec any longer had valid claims on me as a citizen. My concern as a citizen would now become a concern that my government conclude a bargain most favourable to me and my fellow Canadians. To be sure, enlightened self-interest would dictate that any bargain struck be fair, so that it would not rebound against the position of my own community, and thus against myself (namely, that it not force an eventual backlash on the other side). But my calculation of fairness would be quite different than one made in relations between fellow members of the same community. In practice, it is highly doubtful that such negotiations would result in the degree of substantive equality between Quebec and Canada that the PQ promised, given the disproportion in population, resources, and so on.

The PQ's referendum question, by refusing to recognize this distinction, was presenting a dishonestly posed choice to Quebecers. It was attaching a unilaterally formulated promise of a particular form of economic association, which it could not keep, to its assertion of political sovereignty, which it could make unilaterally. But if the latter were premised on the former – that is, if Quebec's voters were to choose to demand independence because they were convinced that it would result in precisely the form of association promised by the PQ, then even assertion of a will to be politically independent was itself tainted and uncertain.

An honest approach would have been quite different. Quebec's government would have posed a simple question: do you wish to form an independent sovereign Quebec? Armed with a clear mandate based on an expressed will of the majority for independence, it could then have initiated negotiations with Canada. This would of course have been politically chancy; but 60 percent of the electorate rejected even the qualified, tortuous, and dishonest question that was posed. If most of the people who did vote "yes" were actually voting for sovereignty, *tout court*, for which there is some empirical evidence, then a "clean" question would have armed the PQ with the support of a substantial minority on which further political mobilization might build.

NATIONAL SELF-DETERMINATION AND THE 1995 REFERENDUM

A decade and a half later, the question of Quebec sovereignty has been posed once again, this time with greater clarity. First, the alternative to sovereignty of a "renewed federalism" has been closed by the successive traumas of the Meech Lake and Charlottetown failures. Then the PQ won a majority in 1994 with a promise to hold a referendum on sovereignty (not sovereignty-association) by the end of 1995. The choice before Quebec voters should thus be starkly clear: sovereignty or the status quo, despite forelorn attempts by the federal government to substitute "flexible federalism" or "le féderalisme en évolution" for the status quo.

The sovereignty option is by a number of measures actually much stronger now than it was in 1980, when the last sovereigntist government was in office. Potential support is more widely dispersed throughout Quebec society, especially the francophone business community (a most significant change from 1980). The sovereignty option was first placed on the table after the collapse of Meech Lake not by a party but by a bipartisan commission (Bélanger-Campeau), the membership of which was extended beyond parliamentarians to encompass representatives from capital, labour, agriculture, and other social sectors. More significant is an entirely new factor in federal politics: the emergence of a credible sovereigntist option in the Bloc québécois (BQ). Close to a majority of Quebec voters in the 1993 federal election voted for a party whose sole platform is the secession of Quebec; so solid was this support that the BQ became the official opposition. The effects of the Quebec government working hand-in-glove with the official opposition in Ottawa to advance the sovereigntist cause can hardly be gauged by any precedents. In no previous moment in Canadian history has the sovereigntist position had significant political strength in the federal Parliament. In 1980, Pierre Trudeau held at least equally legitimate claims to speak for "Quebec" as René Lévesque: if anything, his majority in Quebec was larger than Lévesque's. The changed political context spells a weakened federalist position.

There is significant change also in the economic context. In 1980, sovereignty was argued within the framework of the national state as the container for economic decision-making. Though allusions were cast (quite unsuccessfully) to the European Community, there was no concrete or realistic context in North America for discussion of an economic space that transcended the national state. Consequently, the PQ was limited largely to postulating mechanisms of association between two sovereign states. These devices either took the form of international coordination or involved definite derogations of national sovereignty to the other state (as with a monetary commission, on which the PQ agreed in advance to claim less than equal representation). In every case, these mechanisms clearly involved creation of another layer of (interstate) bureaucracy with regulatory and administrative powers.

In the 1990s, sovereignty takes on the colour of a very different reality: the Canada–United States Free Trade Agreement, since expanded to encompass a tripartite North American Free Trade Agreement (NAFTA) including Mexico, and now projected to extend to a hemispheric free trade zone of the Americas. NAFTA is the particular form that economic globalization – or perhaps, more accurately, economic regionalization – has taken in North America. Under free trade, continental markets take precedence over national politics. In theory, economic regulation is removed as an instrument of national policy to be replaced by regulation by international treaty, with disputes over interpretation to be resolved by tribunals. The Bélanger-Campeau report sang the praises of economic globalization as an inevitable and indeed beneficent trend with which Quebec sovereignty has no quarrel. Quebec nationalists, at least of the respectable and official variety, apparently have no intention of interfering with the free functioning of the (continental) marketplace. Sovereignty is conceived entirely in political terms, without economic-nationalist consequences. This approach is of course quite in continuity with the underlying logic of the sovereignty-association project of 15 years ago, but free trade offers sovereigntists a way out of the earlier dilemmas of economic association. Why not political sovereignty along with a place for Quebec within an expanded, four-way NAFTA or, even better, as one partner among many within a hemispheric bloc? Why not regulate economic relations by treaty rather than by the complex and politically booby-trapped process of creating an additional layer of government and administration?

There is a seductive logic to this argument, though there are a good many complex problems glossed over. Both the Liberals and the péquistes were strongly in favour of the Canada–US Free Trade Agreement during the 1988 federal election. Such a profoundly liberal view of the relationship between economics and politics does raise significant questions about the true nature and content of Quebec national self-determination, and thus about how we are to understand this "right" which is being asserted. Specifically, how strongly do the claims to sovereignty ring when the claimants apparently have so little quarrel with the existing economic arrangements that they actually wish them to be deepened and consolidated yet further? To put the matter another way: claims that take the exclusive form of political and administrative rearrangements may be legitimate enough when taken purely at the practical level (which arrangement would work most efficiently in light of mutually agreed goals of public policy), but can they assume the dignity of the "right to national self-determination"? At the practical level, the idea of political sovereignty within a wider economic environment shaped by free trade offers a more attractive post-separation scenario for both parties than sovereignty-association. But the philosophical grounding of the independence project in the right of national self-determination is correspondingly weaker.

One of the lessons of 1980 was that Ottawa tacitly agreed that a "yes" vote would have given effect to Quebec's "right" to proceed with separation. All three national parties in the House of Commons that sat 1988–93 (including the then-ruling Conservatives) either explicitly or tacitly granted that Quebec has the right (in the sense of the capacity) to quit the federation if empowered by a democratic mandate. In the current House of Commons, the official opposition, the BQ, is of course avidly pro-sovereigntist, and the Reform party, representing the effective opposition outside Quebec, has explicitly considered Quebec's departure an option. Reform Leader Preston Manning was reported in the fall of 1994 as stating: "I think it's accepted that if there was a fair, democratic referendum on a straight question that most Canadians would reluctantly accept the outcome."[5] Given a potentially more attractive post-separation scenario for maintaining economic relations, one might postulate that the entire issue has effectively been removed from the table of high principle and onto the more manageable terrain of pragmatic accommodation of pluralist interests – the familiar field of "let's make a deal."

This is not, however, the case. Another, potentially incommensurable assertion of a right of national self-determination has been placed on the table – the claim to self-government by Canada's Aboriginal peoples. Aboriginal people clearly have much stronger moral claims than the Québécois, but the latter have vastly greater political power and capacity. To an extent yet to be determined, these claims conflict, and this conflict intersects with the ambivalent feelings of English Canadians toward changes in the constitutional status of Quebec. Thus a highly explosive situation exists which could make a mockery of any pragmatic, moderate solution.

ABORIGINAL CLAIMS TO SELF-DETERMINATION

The Aboriginal peoples clearly answer much more plainly and unambiguously to the criteria that I suggested above for a credible basis for a right to national self-determination. Both they and the Québécois constitute separate national communities in the cultural, linguistic, and sociological senses in which one "people" is distinguished from another. However, the capacity of Aboriginal people to express their individual identities as members of this nation within their present political conditions of citizenship is in much greater doubt because the dominant white majorities (both Canadian and Québécois) have imposed structures of law, politics, and economics upon them that sometimes expressly deny their identity and sometimes actively seek to repress it. Most important, Aboriginal communities lack the basic instruments of self-government, both political and economic, that already rest in the hands of the government of Quebec, seen as the collective instrument of the Quebec community.

The Québécois, in contrast, have already demonstrated through the agency of the government of Quebec that their cultural and linguistic identities are hardly threatened within the current constitutional structures. When the language law was challenged by the Supreme Court of Canada (as well as the highest court in Quebec), the government simply overrode the Charter of Rights and Freedoms in passing Bill 178, which reinstated unilingual French commercial signs. This was a perfectly legal and legitimate act on its part, whatever displeasure and controversy it may have aroused in English Canada. Within the framework of the Canadian liberal capitalist state, it is difficult to see any positive discrimination against Québécois entrepreneurs operating in the North American market or abroad – especially in light of the dominant market-driven, neo-liberal ideology of Quebec nationalists. We return again to arguments about administrative efficiency and perhaps about status or symbolic politics. Certainly the latter reflects the reaction in Quebec to the failure of Meech Lake and the apparent rejection by English Canada of the "distinct society" clause. While it would be quite wrong to belittle these concerns and a grave political mistake to dismiss the significance of constitutional recognition of Quebec's distinct society (which is a sociological reality in any event), we are still far from criteria suggesting that the Quebec national identity is being actively repressed by an intolerant and dominating majority.

Aboriginal claims, at least as represented during the Charlottetown round, were different from Quebec's claims in a political sense. Sovereignty as potential national independence did not seem to be on the agenda. This is not surprising, given the practical difficulties of hundreds of relatively small bands scattered across thousands of miles of territory asserting independence – not to speak of Métis, non-status Indians, and Aboriginals living in predominantly non-Native urban settings. There had been ideas floated of an Aboriginal "province" with provincial powers based on non-contiguous territory. Interesting though such ideas might be, they do not add up to independent national statehood. The Charlottetown Accord spoke of Aboriginal self-government as a "third order of government," along with the federal and provincial levels. Further establishing this concept of a third order, the projected elected Senate would have contained equal representation from each of the provinces, as well as guaranteed seats for Aboriginal representatives (the exact number to be determined later by negotiation). In short, Aboriginal claims were directed essentially toward reconstituting the existing rules of the Canadian political community to ensure space for degrees of Aboriginal self-government. At its best, such a concept could result in a new partnership between Aboriginal and non-Aboriginal peoples, with power-sharing significantly revised in the direction of righting the historic imbalance against Aboriginal peoples.

None of this should be taken to diminish the political significance, or the moral weight, of Aboriginal claims for self-government as against Québécois claims for self-determination. To rank Quebec claims higher would be to assert that states, or potential states, are privileged over peoples. If Aboriginal peoples cannot, for practical reasons, look to independent national statehood as a viable option, this consideration does not in any way weaken the strength of the claim to self-determination. Indeed, as I argue, it may even enhance it.

In the Charlottetown Accord – negotiated by representatives of the federal and provincial governments and of treaty and non-status Indians, Métis, and Inuit peoples – the section on Aboriginal self-government opens with recognition of the "inherent right to self-government." Philosophically, the notion of an inherent right is questionable: right is relational and contextual, while inherency seems to deny both relation and context. However, the political significance of recognition of inherent right is striking. What it appears to imply is that self-government is not a grant or a gift (that is, something that carries an obligation of gratitude on the part of the recipient to the donor – and something more-over that can, under certain conditions, be reclaimed or repossessed by the donor) but a right that has always existed and is now being recognized (a prior reality acknowledged). Negotiations with federal and provincial governments over specific self-government arrangements would proceed within the framework of this constitutional recognition of inherent right, which would form the basis of justiciability in case of disagreements that ultimately came before the courts. In brief, Charlottetown, both in process and in substance, recognized the justice of the Aboriginal claims to self-determination and sought to devise appropriate mechanisms for embodying these in a third order of government within Canada. This was a clear form of what Charles Taylor has called the "politics of difference recognition."[6]

Despite the demise of the Charlottetown agreement, the constitutional status of the inherent right to self-government is hardly dead. It continues to inform all continuing debate surrounding treaty rights, land claims, and Aboriginal policy on the part of all governments, federal and provincial. The current Liberal government in Ottawa has proposed that self-government may be achieved by agreements short of formal constitutionalization, and indeed it signed an agreement on self-government with Manitoba natives in late 1994 that is expected to be paralleled in the future in other jurisdictions.[7] A Royal Commission on Aboriginal Peoples has issued an interim finding that the right to self-government already exists without its formal recognition in the constitution. And if the constitutional agenda is soon re-opened, that right will certainly be central.

From the point of view of power, as opposed to right, the respective positions of Quebec and Aboriginal peoples differ strikingly. The Aboriginal peoples have weakly articulated power bases and limited means of political influence. Scattered and divided, they exist mainly on the margin of the political system. Quebec, in contrast, has its own state, its own legislative, admin-istrative, judicial, and coercive apparatus, its own relatively well-defined economic space, and long-established forms of accommo-dation in Canadian national structures, as well as forms of inter-national recognition. While all these exist within the framework of provincial status in the federation, they could all with relative ease be transformed into the attributes of national sovereignty outside the federation. Even the tacit understanding of this potential is itself a tangible source of power and influence within Confederation: Quebec, as Pierre Trudeau used to say, has a power to break Canada that other identifiable groups (including Aboriginal Canadians) do not possess. Against this fact, the claims of the Aboriginal peoples, strong as they are in terms of justice, have been flimsy and insubstantial in power-political terms.

The contrast, however, is no longer so strong as it once was. Questions of the Aboriginal right to national self-determination scarcely came into the picture at all during the Quebec referen-dum in 1980, entered mainly as an afterthought into the struggle over patriation of the constitution in 1980–81, were ultimately a crucial factor in the defeat of the Meech Lake Accord in 1990, and then became a central element in the Charlottetown Accord. It was more than a mere accident that it was Elijah Harper's lonely veto in the Manitoba legislature that effectively scuttled Meech. His action foused not only Aboriginal opposition to Meech, but a good deal of white English-Canadian opposition as well. During the Charlottetown round, many English Canadians saw Aboriginal people as allies in a potential common front on constitutional reform. While it is unclear how much of this support was merely self-interested, if not downright mischievous (using Aboriginal people as a convenient club with which to belabour Quebec), the objective effect was to deepen the reson-ance of Aboriginal rights claims within the constitutional debate.

Unfortunately, this situation developed in tandem with a
growing alienation of Aboriginal peoples from the Québécois.
Indeed, there is a kind of "zero-sum-game" mentality that seems
to have infected participants in the debate. Some Aboriginal
spokespersons asserted flatly that that people's concerns must
take absolute priority over those of Quebec, while some Quebec
spokespersons labelled any suggestion that Aboriginal issues be
placed on the table alongside those of Quebec a "trivialization" of
the constitutional debate. Many sovereigntists have airily dismissed Aboriginal claims as of no consequence to the process of
asserting Quebec sovereignty on the international stage. At the
same time, Quebec's Aboriginal leaders, including those of the
Inuit people of the far north, have insisted that they will refuse
to recognize any proclamation of Quebec sovereignty as in any
way binding on them.

This is no trivial matter. There are not a lot of Cree in northern Quebec (some 12,000), but they outnumber non-Native
Quebecers in the region, which includes James Bay and its hydro
power, an important element of Quebec's economic viability. The
same Cree have already demonstrated their ability to undermine
Quebec's freedom of action internationally by appealing successfully to foreign opinion on environmental and human rights
issues – so successfully that they forced cancellation of the huge
"Great Whale," or James Bay II project in November 1994. If
they remain determined, they can certainly throw a large wrench
into the PQ's sovereignty project. Indeed, the same day that Great
Whale was shelved, the chief of the Cree, Matthew Coon Come,
was telling an American audience that Quebec independence
would be a breach of Aboriginal treaty rights: "If Quebec unilaterally and illegally separates from Canada, this fact of separation
will, in and of itself, constitute a violation of our treaty rights ...
It will constitute denial of our right to nationality and of our
rights as citizens of Canada."[8]

At the heart of this problem is a question posed by Aboriginal
spokesperson Mary Ellen Turpel: "Does the road to Quebec sovereignty run through aboriginal territory?"[9] If Quebec's claim for
national self-determination becomes an assertion of sovereign
national statehood, can it be imposed on Aboriginal peoples on
Quebec (provincial) territory without their express consent? This
objection has a stronger basis than the qualification noted above

to the right of national self-determination – that a secessionist national group not itself oppress its own national minorities. The latter qualification must be decided on the basis of the empirical probability of post-independence developments. I have argued that it is extremely unlikely that a sovereign Quebec would be illiberal, or less liberal than the rest of Canada, toward its linguistic and cultural minorities. On this ground, Quebec sovereigntists have promised Aboriginals that they would be generous and tolerant to Aboriginal aspirations, once independence was achieved – but that independence must come first and must not be impeded by Aboriginal claims.

While this liberal democratic argument about the priority of majorities, along with guarantees of minority rights, might be relatively strong in regard to other national minorities in Quebec, including anglophones, it simply misses the point of the Aboriginal claim. The inherent right to self-government is a national claim, in the same way that the claim to self-determination is national. If it is set aside until Quebec's claim is realized, it is no longer recognized as national but is reduced to a minority group's claim. Indeed, the very notion of the right to self-government can hardly be sustained if the bearers of this right are forced without their consent to accept a fundamental alteration in the constitution of the larger community within which self-government is to be exercised. "Trust us" as a response to Quebec's Aboriginal peoples is thus a clear denial of the principle of self-government. The Aboriginal minimal demand is that their national claims must be settled at the same moment as Quebec's national self-determination.

The sovereignty bill introduced in Quebec's national assembly in the fall of 1994 contains the following provisions bearing on this issue:

3. The Government shall, in accordance with the procedure determined by the National Assembly, see to the drafting of a constitution for Quebec and to its adoption.

The constitution shall include a charter of human rights and freedoms. It shall guarantee the English-speaking community that its identity and institutions will be preserved. It shall also recognize the right of Aboriginal nations to self-government on lands over which they have full ownership. Such guarantee and such recognition shall be exercised in a manner consistent with the territorial integrity of Quebec. The constitution will provide for the decentralization of specific powers to local and regional authorities together with sufficient fiscal and financial resources for their exercise.

4. Quebec shall retain the boundaries it has within the Canadian Confederation at the time section 1 comes into force. It shall exercise its jurisdiction over the maritime areas and the territories adjoining its coastline in accordance with the terms and conditions provided by the rules of international law.

This text makes quite clear that the sovereignist project envisages native communities as potentially self-governing minorities within the borders and under the sovereign jusrisdiction of Quebec. It is just as clear that this status is unacceptable to most, if not all, of Quebec's Aboriginal communities.

Aboriginal arguments have not always stopped at the stage of self-defence but have sometimes been expressed in more aggressive, if not provocative language that would seem to deny actively the validity of Quebec's claim to national self-determination. Mary Ellen Turpel addresses herself to the point that "Quebec" is a political unit (a province) while the right to sovereignty is predicated on a claim to self-determination of a nation (a people): "[T]he right to self-determination is not a right of the province of Quebec. In international law, provinces do not enjoy a right of self-determination, peoples do. Consequently, other peoples who may have competing claims, especially to territory, cannot be ignored. Sovereignists in Quebec have, in effect, constructed their claim on the basis of the province of Quebec as the entity which will exercise the right of self-determination. However, this would unjustly efface the competing and legitimate rights of aboriginal peoples."[10]

Though her logic cannot be faulted, there is a Jesuitical cast to this argument. Technically, "Quebec" is a province, the boundaries of which derive from internal arrangements made by the Canadian Confederation. It is true, of course, that "Quebec" territory encompasses more than francophone Québécois. Thus, in a narrow, abstract sense, an assertion of national self-determination cannot legitimately be coterminous with the boundaries of the province of Quebec. However, the political implication of Turpel's argument is actually quite perverse. She seems to be saying to Quebec sovereigntists that in order to legitimate their claim they ought to recast it in exclusivist ethnic terms. The Aboriginal question aside, this approach would presumably result in communal separatism, intricate territorial partition, and population transfers involving anglophone and ethnic minorities – a nightmare eerily reminiscent of the catastrophe of the former Yugoslavia. The important point lost in this legalistic objection is that Quebec's assertion of the right to national self-determination has been put in inclusionary, liberal democratic terms. Given guarantees of minority rights, a will of the majority on existing Quebec territory to seek sovereignty, expressed through a democratic mandate derived from a referendum, has legitimacy. To deny this is to ensure an illiberal result, since the only alternative is narrowly defined ethnic communalism.

However, for reasons given above, Aboriginal rights are of a different nature than the minority rights claimed by other groups in Quebec. But when insistence on that distinction is expanded to denial of the acceptable face of Quebec national self-determination, we face an equivalent conundrum to the reduction of Aboriginal claims to mere minority group rights by many sovereigntist spokespersons.

Of course, when political debate is couched in the language of rights, there is always a tendency to argue rights as trumps. This makes compromise extremely difficult and greatly increases the risk of failure. There is no point in deploring the discourse of rights, which now seems endemic to Canadian constitutional deate, but it is at least incumbent on observers who essay an objective stance to deconstruct the rhetoric. As I have tried to make clear, the language of the right to national self-determination contains at least two kinds of claims – of the moral sort, derived from a conception of natural justice, and of the power-political variety, derived from a conception of what is possible or realizable. Quebec's right to national self-determination is relatively strongly based on the latter kind of claim, and the Aboriginal right is more strongly grounded in the former. Both statements contain an admixture of both sorts of claims, in shifting balance. It is precisely this changeable balance that ought to force both sides to stand down from their irreconcilable, rights-as-trumps positions and into the realm of rational compromise.

When the Aboriginal right to national self-determination was almost purely justice-based, it was pretty much ignored. The reasons for its increasing centrality are not, of course, derived from some sudden accession of enlightened generosity and altruism on the part of white Canadians. It might be comforting to moral reformers to believe that white Canadian's eyes were opened to the inherent injustices visited on Aboriginal peoples by a viewing of *Dances with Wolves* or official admission of the victimization of Donald Marshall. But the real world has less time for ideals. If Aboriginal issues are today more central, it is mainly because they are supported by claims that are more power-political than before. The siege at Oka in the summer of 1990 showed that moral claims could be reinforced and strengthened by real-world power politics. To be sure, the force majeure of the Canadian state ultimately prevailed over the armed resistance of the Mohawk Warriors, as the latter always knew it would. But what Oka demonstrated was that Aboriginal resistance could impose a full-scale crisis on Ottawa and Quebec and (no small matter in the age of CNN's global television village) force Canada and Quebec into a public international humiliation. Quebec, above all, should have learned from these events that Aboriginal claims are no longer prayers to be ignored, but real properties on the Monopoly (Oligopoly?) board of politics. As noted above, Quebec was similarly humiliated by the capacity of the Cree of northern Quebec to attract highly unfavourable publicity in the United States and in Europe to James Bay II, encouraging cancellation of the project. The capacity to exploit effectively media and public relations is itself an important form of political power in a mass democracy.[11]

Morality, however, does not rest with the Aboriginals alone. Quebec's claims are not purely power-political. It is above all the legitimacy of a democratic mandate for sovereignty that would give Quebec, following a successful referendum on the issue, the power to realize a separate nation-state. A democratic mandate is a political form of a moral claim, different from a moral claim based on historic injustice, but powerful none the less.

Hegel remarked that the essence of tragedy is the war of right against right. The mutual failure of recognition on the part of the Québécois and Aboriginals in Quebec lays the groundwork for a potential tragedy, what we may call the Doomsday, or "Yugoslav" script for the near future of Quebec-Canada relations. Admittedly a worst-case version, and, we hope, unlikely, it nevertheless describes the potential dangers of mutual non-recognition of rights:

1 Quebec voters ratify the national assembly's sovereignty resolution in 1995.
2 The Quebec government begins behaving as a sovereign state, anticipating negotiations with the remaining parts of Canada on a post-separation arrangement.
3 The James Bay Cree refuse to recognize the sovereignty of the new Quebec nation over their territory.
4 Other Aboriginal communities in Quebec, notably the Mohawk and Inuit, similarly refuse to recognize Quebec sovereignty.
5 Faced with attempts by the Quebec Sûreté to enforce Quebec's sovereignty over James Bay, the Cree appeal to the federal government to protect their rights.
6 Elements of English-Canadian opinion, already angered and humiliated by Quebec's unilateral declaration of independence, press Ottawa to assert new borders, reclaiming all of northern Quebec (held by the crown until 1912, when it was ceded to the province of Quebec), as well as to demand a corridor through the Eastern Townships to connect Ontario and New Brunswick.
7 The anglophone minority in Quebec calls for Canadian intervention on its behalf, increasing pressure on Ottawa to do something.
8 The Canadian army moves into northern Quebec to "protect the rights" of the Cree.
9 Other Aboriginal communities in Quebec impose Oka-style blockades across their lands.
10 Francophone elements in the Canadian armed forces refuse to follow orders from Ottawa and begin defecting, with arms and equipment, to the new Quebec state.
11 Civil war breaks out.
12 The United States intervenes militarily to protect American interests and to restore order to the northern half of the continent.

Under the Yugoslav script, Canada would become "Balkanized." With problematic borders separating majorities and minorities, and no agreement over rights, the descent into a naked power struggle could be swift, and terrible.

No one, save a certifiable psychopath, could possibly wish to see this vision become reality. Its avoidance is certainly possible, but only on the basis of mutual accommodation of rights claims by all parties. Such accommodation should be founded on the understanding that such claims are not trumps, but mixtures of justice-based and power-political considerations. Refusal by Quebec to recognize the claims of the Aboriginal peoples would not be merely morally obtuse – it would be politically stupid. Whatever Ottawa's response to a plea by the Cree for intervention, the uncertainty and risk that such an appeal would pose for the economic climate for an independent Quebec would be disastrous. Yet whatever provocations have been posed by the arrogance of Quebec nationalists toward Aboriginal rights, the Aboriginal peoples should not shut their eyes to the moral core of Quebec's claim. To assert in advance that the legitimacy of the democratically expressed will of Quebec's people for national self-determination is of lesser dignity and significance than the equivalent will of the Aboriginal peoples is hardly helpful.

Some English Canadians have already shown an alarming tendency to project aggressive assertions about shrinking Quebec borders following independence, sometimes though not always couched in terms of democratic self-determination for minorities.[12] Use of the Aboriginals in this context is in some cases little more than cynical manipulation to deny Quebec a right in practice that can no longer be denied in theory. Indeed, the Aboriginal peoples of Quebec have already assumed a role as a bargaining chip for federalists against the sovereignty project, even as it is being mounted. This is a very dangerous game.

Despite the superficial attraction of a "democratic," opt-out option for minorities, once borders are placed up for discussion the secession process becomes inherently unstable and volatile. If borders of the Yugoslav successor states had been recognized and respected by all parties, the descent into the maelstrom might not have been prevented, but it would not have been as certain as it was once "Yugoslavia" (Serbia) set about redrawing the boundaries of Croatia. "Ethnic cleansing," after all, is an attempt to sanctify redrawing of boundaries on ethnically exclusivist lines by forcibly redrawing human geography.

Clearly, no one in the Canadian debate wants to see ethnic cleansing. The problem is that redrawing boundaries to accommodate some concept of minority ethnic self-determination opens the door to a process that cannot easily be controlled. If, for instance, the anglophones of the Eastern Townships seek to withdraw those parts of Quebec where they form local majorities, what is to prevent the Acadians of northern New Brunswick from choosing inclusion within Quebec? And what then of the minorities within the minorities – anglophones within Acadia, or francophones within the Eastern Townships? Are we not soon talking of population transfers? How long can such a process remain voluntary, and how soon will it begin to take on compulsory features? These questions are of course entirely speculative, but what is disturbing is the underlying logic that seems to push events away from redrawing boundaries to something that looks very much like ethnic cleansing, even if such an outcome were never sought by any of the parties.

RECONCILIATION

How can Aboriginal self-government be rescued from these repulsive scenarios? If Quebec does intend to move toward sovereignty, there must be negotiations that precede rather than follow the declaration of sovereignty. These negotiations must begin with recognition of Quebec's right to national self-determination, but they must also squarely face the necessity of establishing a joint protocol, agreed to by both Quebec and Canada, establishing recognition of the same constitutional rights of Aboriginal self-government and self-determination on both territories. Aboriginal rights would have to include shared and co-managed resources on Aboriginal lands, including northern Quebec. This agreement would have to go hand in hand with a clear undertaking that current borders are not negotiable (northern Quebec will not be annexed to Canada, nor Labrador to Quebec). Opening up the borders question invites a spiral into a Yugoslav-style disaster.

Borders must be rendered irrelevant to the question of Aboriginal self-government. A joint constitutional protocol would set Quebec sovereignty aside from the Aboriginal question. Negotiating such a protocol broadly acceptable to Quebec and Canada as well as to all the key Aboriginal parties would be a complex and difficult process, especially in the volatile context of the secession of Quebec and the inevitable redrawing of relations within

Canada among regions and provinces in the wake of Quebec's departure.[13] Yet however difficult it might be, anything short of this approach risks catastrophe. It may be the only way to avoid a fatal nexus of conflicting rights claims.

The language of the right to national self-determination obviously speaks to deeply held feelings of justice, identity, and yearnings for community. These feelings can be ignored only at considerable peril. Yet however expressive of legitimate sentiments, this same language, if unchecked and not moderated by the spirit of compromise and conciliation, will form part of the problem rather than part of the solution. The fatal weakness of the language of national self-determination lies ultimately in the problem of community membership – who is included and who is excluded. The expression of a democratic will, via a referendum, is certainly essential to building legitimacy for national self-determination, but so long as the problem of majorities and minorities persists, and especially when these categories overlap and cross-cut those of "nations" and "peoples," the mandate of "*the* people" remains ambiguous and indeterminate.

There is a way out of this dilemma. All parties have to recognize that the right to national self-determination contains both moral claims based on notions of justice and democratic legitimacy as well as power-political claims based on resources, capacities, will, and political calculation. On the latter terrain, compromise is not only possible, but imperative.

NOTES

1   For a more exhaustive treatment of the problem that deals extensively with the Quebec question, among others, see Allen Buchanan, *Secession: The Morality of Political Divorce from Fort Sumter to Lithuania and Quebec* (Boulder, Col.: Westview Press, 1991). I am in general agreement with Buchanan's arguments, but their scope is much wider than the narrower band of issues addressed here. See also David R. Cameron, *Nationalism, Self-determination and the Quebec Question* (Toronto: Macmillan, 1974).

2   The paradoxical transformation of Quebec society has been described in William Coleman's *The Independence Movement in Quebec 1945–1980* (Toronto: University of Toronto Press, 1984). Charles Taylor has written with great insight and sensitivity about the apparent paradox of modernization leading to an enhanced desire for national identity: see his *Reconciling the Solitudes: Essays on Canadian Federalism and Nationalism*, ed. Guy Laforest

(Montreal: McGill-Queen's University Press, 1993), and *The Malaise of Modernity* (Concord, Ont.: Anansi 1991).

3 This qualification is obviously contentious, and might be taken to exclude the claims of Aboriginal peoples in Canada, to which more extensive reference is made below. However, Aboriginal claims are qualitatively different in that they appear to focus on forms of self-government that fall short of complete independence in the sense of nation-statehood. In this section I am examining claims for national self-determination that seek sovereign nation-statehood as the preferred solution. In this sense, Jewish claims in the diaspora could not focus on full national self-determination until they became Zionist claims to self-determination on a territorial state.

4 Even in the case of the United States in the Civil War, the cause of the Union, however powerful as a mobilizing symbol, was ultimately seen as instrumental, means to the end of advancing the values for which the Union stood, and to which the values of the slave-holding South were antithetical. When national unity or geopolitical integrity ('mappism,' in Abraham Rotstein's telling phrase) is allowed through rhetorical excess to appear as an end in itself, the values that it ought to serve are themselves brought into question. Hence the ambiguity surrounding the publicity campaign at the time of the Charlottetown referendum deploying the slogan "My Canada includes Quebec." In one sense, this suggests a liberal, tolerant sense of an inclusionary Canada (undoubtedly the inspiration of the campaign). Yet Quebec sovereigntists could, and did, take it in a less generous spirit. The inherent ambiguity can be understood by a cultural transposition: imagine an ad on Belgrade TV on the theme "Slobodan Milosevic says 'My Yugoslavia includes Bosnia.'" Of course there was no intention to treat Quebecers like Bosnian Muslims, but "My Canada includes Quebec" is, like all national unity slogans, open-ended. The real question is the nature, and values, of "my" Canada.

5 Canadian Press, 17 Oct. 1994.

6 Charles Taylor, *Multiculturalism and the "Politics of Recognition"* (Princeton, NJ: Princeton University Press, 1992).

7 This was preceded by a wide-ranging agreement on a self-governing territory for the Inuit (Nunavut), on land in Northwest Territories previously controlled by the federal government.

8 Quoted in Rhéal Séguin, Ann Gibbon, and Graham Fraser, "Quebec Shelves Great Whale Project," *Globe and Mail*, 19 Nov. 1994.

9 Mary Ellen Turpel, "Does the Road to Quebec Sovereignty Run through Aboriginal Territory?" in Daniel Drache and Roberto Perin, eds., *Negotiating with a Sovereign Quebec* (Toronto: James Lorimer & Co., 1992) 93–106.

10 Ibid., 101. Though I am quoting Turpel, her argument has often been echoed by leading Aboriginal spokespersons in public discussion.

11 A political cartoon illustrates this truth: figures representing the Quebec government and Hydro Québec, surveying the land for James Bay II, are completely flattened from behind by a steamroller driven by "Chief Billy Two-Fax-Machines."

12 David J. Bercuson and Barry Cooper's bestselling *Deconfederation: Canada without Quebec* (Toronto: Key Porter, 1991) couples recognition of Quebec's sovereignty with large-scale dismembering of its territory. A less bloody-minded discussion is Scott Reid, *Canada Remapped: How the Partition of Quebec Will Reshape the Nation* (Vancouver: Pulp Press, 1992.) Reid assumes that some form of partition must accompany sovereignty but thinks that this could be effected peacefully, as apparently do Patrick Monahan and Lynda Covello, *An Agenda for Constitutional Reform: Final Report of the York University Constitutional Reform Project* (North York, Ont.: York Centre for Public Law and Public Policy, 1992), 100–4. I think that the idea of a peaceful partition involves a serious delusion.

13 It would also greatly complicate the conditions for a relatively quick negotiation of separation. These conditions, drawn up on the basis of actual experiences elsewhere, are summarized ably by Robert Young, "How Do Peaceful Secessions Happen?" *Canadian Journal of Political Science*, 27 no. 4 (Dec. 1994), 1–20. Despite the serious complication, it is difficult to see how any peaceful transition could come about without such a joint agreement on equivalent Aboriginal rights.

Contributors

HOWARD ADELMAN is Professor of Philosophy at York University. During the last year he coedited two books, *Immigration and Refugee Policy: Australia and Canada Compared* and *African Refugees*. He is working on a study of Canadian Jewish identity.

JANET AJZENSTAT is Assistant Professor of Political Science at McMaster University. She is the author of *The Political Thought of Lord Durham* and the editor of *Canadian Constitutionalism 1791–1991*. She is currently at work on a book about Canada's ideological origins.

JOSEPH H. CARENS is Professor of Political Science at the University of Toronto. He has written *Equality, Moral Incentives and the Market* and edited *Democracy and Possessive Individualism*. He is preparing a volume on immigration and political community.

WAYNE NORMAN is Associate Professor of Philosophy at the University of Ottawa. He is the author of *Taking Freedom Too Seriously?*, has written articles for *Ethics*, *Political Studies*, and numerous other journals, and is working on a study of the political philosophy of nationalism and citizenship.

ROBERT VIPOND is Associate Professor and Acting Chair of the Department of Political Science at the University of Toronto. His writings include *Liberty and Community: Canadian Federalism and the Failure of the Constitution*, several articles on Canadian constitutional politics, and a book in preparation on Canadian rights talk in the 1960s and 1970s.

REG WHITAKER is Professor of Political Science at York University. His most recent books are *Cold War Canada: The Making of a National Insecurity State 1945-57* and *A Sovereign Idea: Essays on Canada as a Democratic Community*; he is working on a study of the surveillance state.

Index